THE AUTHOR

George Watson was born in Brisbane, Australia, in 1927. He graduated in English from Trinity College, Oxford, in 1950, and has been a fellow of St John's College, Cambridge, and a university lecturer in English there since 1959. A contributor to *Encounter, Critical Quarterly* and the *Financial Times*, he has also lectured at a number of universities in Europe, America, Asia and Australia.

George Watson is the author of *Coleridge the Poet* (1966), *The Study of Literature* (1969), *The Literary Thesis* (1970), *The English Ideology* (1973), *Politics and Literature* (1977), *The Discipline of English* (1978), *The Story of the Novel* (1979), *The Idea of Liberalism* (1985) and *Writing a Thesis* (1986), as well as *The Literary Critics* (1962), updated for this edition. He has twice stood for Parliament as a Liberal, has been editor of the Unservile State Group since its foundation in 1953, and was the editor of *The New Cambridge Bibliography of English Literature* (1969-73).

THE
LITERARY
CRITICS

*A Study of English
Descriptive Criticism*

George Watson

THE HOGARTH PRESS

LONDON

To Renford Bambrough

Published in 1986 by
The Hogarth Press
Chatto & Windus Ltd
40 William IV Street, London WC2N 4DF

First published in Great Britain by Penguin Books Ltd 1962
Hogarth edition offset from Chatto 1964 edition, with revisions
Enlarged edition first published in Great Britain 1986
Copyright © George Watson 1962, 1986

British Library Cataloguing in Publication Data

Watson, George, 1927 –
The literary critics: a study of English
descriptive criticism. – Enl. ed.
1. English literature – History and
criticism
I. Title
801'. 95' 0942   PR63

ISBN 0 7012 0725 6

Printed in Great Britain by
Cox & Wyman Ltd
Reading, Berkshire

PREFACE TO THE ENLARGED EDITION

SOME years ago I took to lecturing at Cambridge on the history of descriptive criticism in England and the United States from its beginnings three centuries ago, and the first edition of this book was the result. It was an attempt to show by what leaps and starts the art of analysing English literary works evolved from its early experiments into the techniques of our own age: leaps and starts, since I never thought steady and gradual evolution a likely hypothesis, and saw the story (as I still do) as a chronicle of great minds and subversive utterances.

My chronicle was, and remains, argumentative. It identifies revolutionary figures and explains the intellectual revolutions they caused or tried to cause – ignoring, with regret, a good deal in the process that is merely respectable, and presenting great critics as pioneers of an attitude or a method. What kinds of questions have the major English critics posed; and how far, and with what tools, have they succeeded in confronting them? The emphasis has lain squarely on issues like these.

When *The Literary Critics* first appeared, I felt narrowly entitled to call it the only British history of literary criticism composed in this century, since George Saintsbury's history had begun to appear in the last year of the nineteenth; its only successor, by J. W. H. Atkins, lying becalmed and unfinished at a point around 1800, with most of the story still untold. Oddly enough, that claim to uniqueness would still be justified. Two American histories, it is true, appeared (or began to appear) in the 1950s, by W. K. Wimsatt and René Wellek; but the gap remains. Hence the new and enlarged edition of this book. The first ten chapters remain much as they were, from Dryden down to the mid-twentieth century. But, since I first wrote, the four principal actors in my tenth chapter have all died: T. S. Eliot in 1965, F. R. Leavis in 1978, I. A. Richards in 1979 and Sir William Empson in 1984 – Empson's last book, a collection of well-established essays on Marvell, Dryden, Fielding, Eliot and Joyce, appearing posthumously in 1984 as *Using Biography*. Meanwhile, the Anglo-American critical tradition, which has always excelled at the analysis of the particular, has met and (after some famous skirmishing and polemics that reached even the tabloid press) repelled what was meant to be a destructive onslaught by French critical theory. By the late 1980s, the Twenty Years' War of Theory *versus* Practice looks ended, with the theorists dispirited and practitioners in possession of the field. The very title *Using Biography* proclaims that the Death of the Author announced in Paris in the 1960s was premature, and that biography is there for critics to use. To record and celebrate that victory I have written an entirely new chapter for this edition on 'Theory and Practice since 1960'.

St John's College, Cambridge   G.W.
May 1986

NOTE ON THE NEW EDITION

THIS history of English criticism appeared for the first time as a Pelican in May 1962, and the present hardback edition has given me the opportunity of making a number of additions, corrections, and revisions, both to the text and to the bibliography. Reflection has done much; I should like too to record my deep gratitude to the friends, reviewers, and correspondents who have helped me to make this a better book.

G. W.

March 1963

PREFACE

THIS book, which is a brief history of descriptive criticism in England (and latterly in the United States) from its beginnings some three hundred years ago, is an attempt to show by what stages the art of analysing English literary works has evolved from the early experiments of the seventeenth century into the techniques of the twentieth. In such an argumentative survey, which tries to identify revolutionary figures and to explain the significance of the revolutions they caused, a vast amount of respectable work is bound to be neglected, and major critics themselves are likely to appear in an unfamiliar light as pioneers of a method or of an influential attitude to the descriptive problem. What *kinds* of questions have the major English critics posed in analysis; and how far, and with what tools, have they succeeded in answering them? The emphasis, in this history, lies squarely on issues like these.

Much of this book began as lectures on the history of criticism delivered in Cambridge during the years 1959 and 1960, and my chief debt is to an audience who, itself the product of the evolution I have tried to describe here, encouraged me by a critical interest in what I had to say. The subject is not much explored. But I hope that, for their sake, I have found some right answers; and that, where I have not, I have at least posed questions in a more precise form than other historians of criticism have done.

St John's College, Cambridge
June 1961

CONTENTS

Chapter 1

FIRST PRINCIPLES

THE THREE KINDS OF CRITICISM

SOME things are most readily defined by their contraries, but the ultimate condition of a literature without criticism is one that modern England has happily never known, and we must leave a stranger to speak. These are the words of the Hungarian poet Miklos Gimes, later hanged by the Kadar Government, describing intellectual life in the Socialist countries before the rising of 1956:

Slowly [under Stalin] we had come to believe . . . that there are two kinds of truth. If there is a truth of a higher order than objective truth, if the criterion of truth is political expediency, then even a lie can be 'true'; . . . and so we arrive at the outlook which infected not only those who thought up the faked political trials, but often infected even the victims: the outlook which poisoned our whole public life, penetrated the remotest corners of our thinking, obscured our vision, paralysed our critical faculties, and finally rendered many of us incapable of simply sensing or apprehending truth.[1]

Criticism, of course, cannot prevent lies from being told. But it does make it its business to see that they do not establish themselves as truth. It presupposes an open society, and it is one of the conditions by which such a society survives. But English criticism, though prone to sudden convulsions and revolutionary situations, has not suffered much from ruthless authoritarianism. The record is rather one of great revolutionary individuals – their achievement is the subject of this history – who have attacked established complacency, dismissed the assumptions of their predecessors, and struck out in new directions.

The second half of the twentieth century marks, in a rather negative sense, a revolutionary phase in the evolution of English criticism, a pause imposed by an access of doubt. The 1950s brought with them a flood of warnings against critical arrogance and a series of demarcation-disputes, following upon half a century of

[1] *Béké és Szabadsaq* (3 October 1956), quoted in translation by Michael Polanyi, 'Beyond Nihilism', *Encounter* (March 1960), p. 42.

unparalleled activity. The very titles of T. S. Eliot's 'The Frontiers of Criticism',[1] Helen Gardner's *The Limits of Literary Criticism* (1956), and John Holloway's 'The New "Establishment" in Criticism' all suggest that caution is in the air. The process of stocktaking, too, is already well under way, and two American histories have appeared to record at length the progress of the English-speaking, even of the Western, critical tradition. My purpose is more modest, and based on principles that are not theirs. It is to trace one kind of activity only among the many confused under the name of 'literary criticism' as it has been practised in the British Isles, and ultimately in the United States as well, since its emergence some three hundred years ago: descriptive criticism, or the art of analysing works of literature that actually exist.

The oddity is that any historian should ever have attempted in one work to do more. But all previous histories – Saintsbury and Atkins in their day, as much as Wellek and Wimsatt in ours – have assumed that what we call literary criticism is, with some embarrassing exceptions, a single activity, and that its history is the story of successive critics offering different answers to the same questions. We may call this the Tidy School of critical history. Allen Tate has defined its main premise in an extreme form: 'The permanent critics . . . are the rotating chairmen of a debate only the rhetoric of which changes from time to time,'[2] Wimsatt and Brooks have insisted on the principle of 'continuity and intelligibility in the history of literary argument'.[3] I must say at once that the kind of order they see is not visible to me. Where they see a tidy evolution of doctrine, I see a record of chaos marked by sudden revolution. Where they see a continuing debate down the centuries around the same questions, I see a pattern of refusal, on the part of the major critics, to accept the assumptions of existing debate. The great critics do not contribute: they interrupt. Coleridge does not try to answer questions posed by Dryden and Johnson: he poses questions of his own, questions Dryden and

---

[1] See Select Bibliography, p. 206, for a list of critical studies and histories cited in this chapter.

[2] 'Longinus and the New Criticism' (1948), reprinted in his *The Man of Letters in the Modern World* (New York, 1955), p. 192.

[3] W. K. Wimsatt and Cleanth Brooks, *Literary Criticism: a Short History* (New York, 1957), p. vii.

Johnson had not thought of and would not have understood. Arnold, again, is not finishing Coleridge's work: there is scarcely a moment in his essays where we are made aware that he has read Coleridge's criticism at all.

More than that, the English critics – like European critics in general – are not all engaged on work of a logically comparable kind. It was Dryden[1] who first used the word 'criticism', in print at least, in the now familiar sense of 'any formal discussion of literature', and so helped to confuse in a single term three kinds of discussion that have nothing in common except a reasoned concern for poetry:

Legislative criticism, including books of rhetoric. Such criticism claims to teach the poet how to write, or how to write better. It was the standard – very nearly the only – kind of criticism practised by the Elizabethans, and for half a century after: Sidney apart, nearly all Elizabethan critics directed their remarks to poets rather than to readers of poetry. Their writings, for the most part depressingly uninspired, are the critical equivalent of the recipe-book, and they are based on the master-chef's assumption that any pupil of good intelligence can learn the business if only he is shown how. The imperative, of course, is the characteristic (though not the only) mood of the legislative critic:

Frame your stile to perspicuity, and to be sensible.
> George Gascoigne, 'Certayne Notes of Instruction concerning the Making of Verse', in his *Posies* (1575).

First, ye sall keip just cullouris.
> King James VI of Scotland, 'Ane Schort Treatise conteining some Reulis and Cautelis in Scottis Poesie,' in his *The Essays of a Prentise* (1584).

Our proportion poeticall resteth in five points: staff, measure, concord, scituation, and figure.
> George Puttenham (?), *The Arte of English Poesie* (1589), II, i.

Iambick and trochaick feete, which are opposed by nature, are by all rimers confounded.
> Thomas Campion, *Observations in the Art of English Poesie* (1602).

[1] In the preface to *The State of Innocence* (1677): 'Criticism, as it was first instituted by Aristotle, was meant a standard of judging well.' But the term 'critic', in a literary application, is at least as old as Bacon's *Advancement of Learning* (1605), I, vii, 21.

We should not so soone yeeld our consents captive to the authoritie of antiquitie, unlesse we saw more reason; all our understandings are not built by the square of Greece and Italie. We are the children of nature as well as they.

Samuel Daniel, 'A Defence of Ryme', a reply to Campion, in his *Panegyrike to the King*, etc. (1603).[1]

These quotations from five Elizabethan critics are all 'legislative', though in ascending order of sophistication: only the first is imperative in syntax, and the last, torn from its context, looks almost modern in its apparent concern for the taste of the reader – until we remember that Daniel's 'we' refers, not to all Englishmen, but to his fellow-poets.

There is no need here to examine the pretensions of legislative criticism. It is dead. In England, indeed in Western Europe, it dominated the sixteenth century and died in the course of the seventeenth, with Dryden representing the point of change. We shall never again see the day when flocks of young poets sought instruction in their craft from rhetoricians. In the whole English-speaking world, legislative criticism survives, outside the schoolroom, only in the post-war trickle of hand-books of composition and 'creative writing' assembled by American academic critics for American college students.[2] For the rest, critics are not even the unacknowledged legislators of poets. For three hundred years they have sensibly sought their public not among poets but among readers of poetry.

Theoretical criticism, or literary aesthetics. The form first arose in England in the Sidney circle, in the 1570s, under the influence of Spanish and Italian critics such as Vives and J. C. Scaliger. Perhaps the first work in the form by an Englishman was the very derivative treatise by the ex-Jesuit Richard Wills, *De re poetica* (1573). Sidney's own *Apologie for Poetrie* was written soon after, though it did not appear till 1595, nine years after his heroic death on a Dutch battlefield. To tell the truth, it is not much less derivative

---

[1] *Elizabethan Critical Essays*, edited by G. Gregory Smith, 2 vols. (Oxford, 1904), I, 53, 212; II, 68, 330-1, 366-7.

[2] e.g. Cleanth Brooks and Robert Penn Warren, *Modern Rhetoric* (New York, 1949).

than Wills's Latin essay, though Sidney's superior ability in absorbing his continental sources, his decision to write in English at all, and his own distinction as a poet have saved the *Apologie* for some sort of immortality. Its intrinsic interest is small. The seventeenth-century critics, such as Dryden, showed a continuing but occasional interest in aesthetics. But by this time most literary forms other than the drama had already won their respectability, and there is certainly no suggestion in Hobbes or Dryden that, as Sidney had once complained, poetry had 'fallen to be the laughing-stocke of children'.[1] A new source of theoretical curiosity had to be found. From Hobbes onwards, interest shifts away from such Platonic issues as the nature of poetic truth towards such psychological questions as the nature of the creative act. By the eighteenth century, aesthetics is a mania among the English in an age when, as Boswell shows, the theory of beauty formed part of the small talk of polite London drawing-rooms. From Addison's essays on the imagination in the *Spectator* of 1712, through the treatises of Lord Kames, Burke's *The Sublime and Beautiful* (1757), and Sir Joshua Reynolds's *Discourses* (1778), the long line comes to an abrupt end in Coleridge's *Biographia Literaria* (1817), largely written in the summer of Waterloo. And there, in England, the story ends. The Victorians, repelled by Coleridge's obscurity, and impressed by the rising prestige of historical studies, readily abandoned theoretical criticism to the Germans. There is no Victorian literary aesthetic before Pater and Wilde, and no formal aesthetic of any kind after Coleridge until the work of I. A. Richards in the 1920s, and R. G. Collingwood's *The Principles of Art* (1938). In spite of some isolated attempts on the part of British philosophers to interest themselves in the Beautiful,[2] critics and philosophers have drifted further and further apart since the age of Coleridge.

Descriptive criticism, or the analysis of existing literary works. This is the youngest of the three forms, by far the most voluminous, and the only one which today possesses any life and vigour of

[1] *Elizabethan Critical Essays*, op. cit., I, 151.
[2] For example, contributions by Stuart Hampshire, Margaret Macdonald, J. A. Passmore, Gilbert Ryle, and others to *Essays in Aesthetics and Language*, edited by William Elton (Oxford, 1954).

its own. In England it is some three hundred years old, if we confine our attention – as we must – to what survives in print; though it is worth remembering that what we see is the very tiny tip of an impossibly vast iceberg. Verbal (not to say unspoken) comment on poetry must be as old as poetry itself, and in any age the proportion of comment that sees print must fortunately be very small. 'To breathe is to judge' – Dryden's discovery in the 1660s was not that plays and poems are worth discussing, but that they are worth discussing in print. For the rest, we can only guess at the table-talk of English poets before the Restoration about themselves and their fellow-poets, with the unique exception of Ben Jonson, whose comments on his contemporaries – spiteful, bookish, and obviously authentic – luckily survive in a record made by his host, the Scottish poet William Drummond, of Jonson's vist to Hawthornden in 1618-19. Descriptive criticism in English, which is the subject of this history, begins as talk and survives as talk that someone has thought worth writing down. It is the perfect symbol of the way our critical tradition began that the earliest surviving examples occur in Dryden's essay *Of Dramatick Poesie* (1668): for all its stilted contrivance, it is in the form of a dialogue.

I shall try to show that, as anyone might reasonably expect, descriptive criticism begins introspectively, often as self-justification, with poets discussing their own works, as Dryden in his prefaces defended his plays from his detractors. It shelters nervously, at first, behind a respectable façade of legislative or theoretical criticism, and in later ages, as in Coleridge and Richards, it sometimes chooses to revert to the status of illustrating general propositions. But the break is absolute in logical terms. For whereas the legislative critic had said 'This is how a play should be written', and the theoretical critic, like Aristotle in the *Poetics*, 'This is the nature of tragedy in general,' Dryden simply says: 'This is how I have tried to write my play, and why.' Descriptive criticism is particular in a unique sense and falsifiable to a unique degree. It is about one thing, a given text to which critic and reader may appeal equally for confirmation.

Whether the achievement of such criticism over three hundred years has been important or not is something that must be allowed to emerge. But a few classic objections to our critical tradition may be answered at once. Some extremists have argued that the very existence of the critic as middleman between poet and reader is an impertinence; or, alternatively, that the critic is a symptom of a decadent, over-sophisticated civilization. Some literary cultures (e.g. the Indonesian), it is said, are self-explaining, and the profession of critic is unknown among them. But it should be obvious at once that a poetry that does not prompt or demand comment is in its nature trivial. As for the claim that 'there is too much criticism nowadays', it seems to be based on a confusion of language. It can be no more true to say that we have too much criticism than to say we have too many novels. Of course we have more of either than any individual can read, and more than is worth reading. But good criticism, like good novels, is in strikingly short supply. It is, after all, immensely difficult. Henry James once noticed how rare the critical talent was, 'that quantity of opinion, very small at all times, but at all times infinitely precious, that is capable of giving some intelligible account of itself'.[1] The gaps, indeed, are startling: there has been no major critical assessment of a novelist as significant as Defoe since Leslie Stephen's essay of 1874, there is still none of many a significant eighteenth-century poet. Shakespeare's imagery remained uninvestigated for more than three hundred years after his death, and to this day practically the whole of English medieval poetry awaits its Samuel Johnson.

Again, English criticism has been called derivative and unoriginal. Source-studies have made us conscious of Dryden's debt to Hobbes and Corneille, Coleridge's to the Germans, Arnold's to Sainte-Beuve, Eliot's to Rémy de Gourmont, and so on. There are moments when one feels as if every major English critic has some continental skeleton in his cupboard. But we should remember that original *ideas*, in the strict sense, are not the stock-in-trade of the descriptive critic. Samuel Johnson is a classic case of a great critic of this sort, for it is not clear that he ever had an original abstract intuition about literature in his life. Coleridge is a far greater *critic* than any of the Germans whose ideas he allegedly borrowed. From this point of view – a severely practical one –

[1] From 'The Lesson of Balzac' (1905), reprinted in *The House of Fiction*, edited by Leon Edel (1957), p. 60.

anyone can have an idea: it is essentially the business of the descriptive critic to perceive connexions in terms of actual texts.

Finally, criticism is often condemned as being secondary and parasitic, inferior to what is usually called 'creation'. I do not know what 'creative' means when it is used to include Johnson's *Vanity of Human Wishes* and to exclude his life of Milton. It is not obvious that these two works are of a different logical order – both, after all, are reasoned statements of experience – and it is premature to assume that criticism is of a lower order than poetry until we have shown it to be of a different one. Certainly the careers of many of our major poets since Dryden do not suggest that they conceived of criticism as an inferior activity. Johnson, Coleridge, and Arnold all abandoned poetry for criticism in early middle age; Dryden and T. S. Eliot have enjoyed long careers as critic-poets, the one concern complementing the other, and Eliot's early essays, collected in *The Sacred Wood* (1920), identify the very qualities in Renaissance English which he emulated in his own early poems. The very poetry of such poets as these is a critical activity, in that it takes its rise from a will to determine, and perhaps to alter, the nature of a given literary inheritance. Again and again, great criticism happens by a similar progress of events: a highly self-conscious, deliberate poet with revolutionary objectives conceives a certain dissatisfaction with his career in early middle age, and attempts in criticism to define more closely what he is about. This recurrent metamorphosis of poet-into-critic, which Eliot has traced in his *The Use of Poetry and the Use of Criticism* (1933), was established in England by Dryden, for whom poets, as he remarked in the preface to *All for Love* (1678), 'make the most proper, though . . . not the only critics'. At the moment where 'Kunst wird Kritik', in Thomas Mann's phrase, where art turns into criticism out of a passion for establishing principles, it is not criticism that the poet feels to be secondary and second-rate. Perhaps, as Baudelaire[1] thought, the crisis is an inevitable one in the career of the conscientious artist. At all events it will hardly do to belittle how

---

[1] '*Tous les grands poètes deviennent naturellement, fatalement, critiques.*' Baudelaire goes on to speak of '*une crise . . . où [les poètes] veulent raisonner leur art*'. Cf. his review 'Richard Wagner et Tannhäuser à Paris' (1861), posthumously collected in his *L'art romantique* (Paris, 1869).

much such crises of critical doubt and reappraisal have done for the awareness of Western man.

DESCRIPTION: ITS THEMES AND LANGUAGES

This history attempts to trace the development of techniques for describing literary works since, three centuries ago, Englishmen began to take such description seriously enough to publish examples. Nobody can doubt that the story is one of progress in a very simple sense. The average schoolboy of today is probably capable of analysing more closely and more accurately than Dryden or any of Dryden's contemporaries, and the ordinary reviewer often enjoys a similar unearned advantage over the greatest of English critics before the twentieth century. What matters is to identify the nature of these advances and to attribute them, where possible, to individuals.

The question might be approached from two points of view, substantive or linguistic. What kinds of question do the major critics attempt to answer in their descriptive criticism? Or, alternatively, in what kinds of descriptive terms does the language of each critic excel? And these, on investigation, prove to be in no sense merely different aspects of the same issue. It may seem natural to suppose that the critic who excels, for example, in the variety and precision of his metrical terms is attempting to answer questions about metre, and so on. No doubt it might ideally be so, and this history would have proved less complicated, and English criticism better, if it had been so. But it is not. On the contrary, criticism has been too idiosyncratic an affair, too subtly interwoven with the careers of critics who are also poets, to allow for any such direct relationship between the special language of criticism and its real subject. Besides, critics commonly inherit their language rather than create it, and though the terminological innovations of Dryden, Arnold, or Leavis tell us something significant about their purposes, we cannot expect even the most original of critics to do more than adapt and amplify a language others have made. Dryden's language, for example, is quite unusually rich in terms for describing the parts of the play, and some of them may be his own invention: terms like 'discovery' and 'unravelling' (for *dénouement*), the 'continuity of scenes' (for Corneille's *liaison de scènes*), and so on. But we do not turn to Dryden for technical accounts of the structure of plays, and it is doubtful if anyone ever did; and this because we recognize that, as I shall try to show, such analysis in Dryden is always patchy and partial, more concerned with self-recommendation or the detection of tricks useful to the working dramatist than with the total anatomy of drama. The question posed by his essay *Of Dramatick Poesie* (1668) is not the nature of dramatic excellence in the abstract, but the prospects for a successful rhyming drama on the French model in the immediate circumstances of Restoration England. In a similar way, Arnold's essays excel in the language and tactics of ninetenth-century biography after the manner of Sainte-Beuve; but I shall indicate, in a later chapter, in what sense Arnold's biographical interests are spurious, and in what other directions his real interests lie. Other critics, such as Coleridge, are bolder and less concessive to popular taste in their procedures. But it will never do to confuse the terminology of criticism with its ultimate purposes.

The record has, in any case, been a conservative one, and no one-man revolutions in critical language have met with much success. Most of Dryden's adaptations from the French failed to take on, as Johnson noticed a century later, and Coleridge never found acceptance for terms like 'coadunative' and 'esemplastic', or for his special definitions of 'imagination' and 'fancy'. Certain enrichments of the language as a whole, such as the invasion of Freudian and Marxist terms in the 1930s, have affected the language of criticism, but the successful invention of standard terms, like Eliot's 'dissociation of sensibility', is highly exceptional. The fact is that critical terminology has evolved slowly. And it has moved in an unexpected direction. We should have expected it to acquire an increasing number of terms especially suited to literary description as descriptive criticism itself grew more precise and more fashionable. In fact, just the reverse has happened. English critical terminology has been steadily impoverished since the sixteenth century, when it stood at its highest point in richness and variety. Puttenham uses far more critical terminology than Dryden, Dryden more than Johnson, and Johnson more than Arnold or Eliot. This may be something to regret, and there will be professional voices raised to demand a new language of rhetoric to replace the disused terminology of the Elizabethans. Mine will not be one of them. For the fact remains that such special language has been used in English rather for legislative criticism (critic-to-poet) than for analysis (critic-to-reader), and that modern analysis, para-doxically or not, has thrived without it. But this is only part of the answer. To understand how descriptive criticism in English has achieved so much without acquiring or extending a special lan-guage of description, we must turn to our first, substantive ques-tion: what kinds of question have been posed by critics over the past three hundred years?

On a broadly historical view – that is to say, omitting false starts (like Fielding on the novel) and mere discipleship – several major phases emerge, and we shall not falsify the story much if, for the sake of simplicity, we give them the names of Dryden, Cole-ridge, and Arnold. With Dryden in the 1660s description was practised for the first time in English as a diplomatic compound of formal analysis and self-justification, the critic seeking in his sub-ject – usually a poem or play of his own – the structural origins of its success. This formal school of criticism, which the historians have usually dubbed 'neoclassicism', sets the scene for the great shift of interest on the part of the critic from poet to reader, as in Addison; so that as it draws towards its end, in the final triumph of Johnson's *Lives* (1779-81), it has assimilated both elements: a confident knowledge that the old laws of Renaissance criticism can be usefully turned upon modern vernacular literature, and an awareness that there are thousands of English readers eager to see it done. The second stage, called 'romantic' criticism, with Coler-ridge, is marked by the discovery that historical information is not a mere accessory to analysis, as in Johnson's *Lives*, but an essential insight to enable the reader to see poems as documents in time, or the products of a creative act. As for the third stage, I have called it Arnold, in spite of the grave ambiguities in Arnold's tactics as a critic, because I believe that the reactionary anti-history of much of English criticism in the early twentieth century, in Eliot, Richards, and the early Empson, takes its rise from him.

The subjects of English criticism in terms of literary *genre* evolve less certainly down the centuries and are affected by many con-flicting forces. English criticism has often proved itself ill-adjusted to the real literary achievements of its time. In some periods, for example that of the Metaphysical poets, or the first century of the English novel, analysis has simply failed to exist, and several major English critics of later date, including Coleridge and Arnold, have almost ostentatiously abstained from confronting the poetry of their own day. Other critics, such as Dryden and T. S. Eliot, have viewed the contemporary scene only through the distorting glass of their own literary ambitions; so that, if you were to read Dryden's criticism in the 1660s and 1670s as a chronicle of the period, you would imagine the Restoration to be essentially an age of the theatre, while Eliot's essays between the wars tells us practically nothing about Joyce, or D. H. Lawrence, or Auden, or Isherwood. This is not disparagement: critics have no obvious moral duty to talk about the contemporary scene, and the tactic adopted by Dryden and Eliot of using criticism as a preparative to publication – the prefatorial mode of criticism – or Coleridge's passion for ultimate principles, or Arnold's moralism, all have their own justification. The only danger is that they should be mistaken for some other thing, and that we should, for instance, confuse the history of English criticism with the history of English taste. It is worth remembering that the prefatorial critics analyse not so much the poems they have written as the poems they hope to write – hence Dryden's otherwise inexplicable obsession with heroic tragedy, Eliot's with poetic drama, and Arnold's (in the 1853 preface) with the epic. This productive, and perhaps inevit-able, distortion of interest through unfulfilled literary ambition has proved fairly general, though we may distinguish as notable exceptions the cases of Samuel Johnson and Henry James. The Johnson of the *Lives*, at least, is writing of the age he knows, and he inevitably finds himself discussing the current poetic forms of that age – the verse-satire, the elegy, the classical translation, the ode – largely to the exclusion of drama and the epic. We should not much respect his judgement of either. And James, of course, almost exclusively a novelist, writes almost exclusively about the novel. But such efficient specialization is rare. Some may regret it: its rarity makes English the poorer in classic analysis. But English criticism has not usually triumphed by caution, and nobody who loved the critical spirit can regret that English poets have dared to explore areas where their formal qualifications were uncertain.

In any case it is not, on the whole, so much the vogue of one or another literary form, such as that of the novel in the nineteenth century, that has provoked analysis. It has rather been the scope of current analytical techniques. Some techniques are good only for some kinds of literature. The Augustan technique, for example, of identifying the formal 'parts of the poem' in the established terms of classical and Renaissance criticism is useful only for classical forms of literature, notably the epic and the tragedy, and chaos results when someone tries to apply it to *Tom Jones*. Between the wars, both in England and in America, we have seen a similar kind of abstention in the neglect of the novel by the New Critics, with their general preference for verbal analysis. It did not matter in the thirties that the novel was a more important form, both quantitatively and qualitatively, than the short poem. The short poem was 'analysable' by that age in a sense that the novel was not, and it was duly analysed. It was not a matter of private incapacity – Empson, for example, has latterly shown himself a masterly critic of the novel[1] – but of the nature of the tools to hand. Broadly, then, it has seemed as if the drama and the classical forms of poetry have suited the Augustan mode in criticism best, while the nineteenth century has excelled in the analysis of prose forms, including the novel, and the early twentieth century in short poems. But this strange evolution has been governed not by one factor but by several, in varying degrees; and some lapses – such as the failure of early Stuart England to analyse its own poetry at all, in spite of the wealth of rhetorical terms left to it by the Elizabethan critics – remain forever unexplained.

But, as I have tried to show, the language of descriptive criticism (if by 'language' we mean the special terms, or jargon, that distinguish each school) does little or nothing to identify the issues of the great critical schools. Jargon is, in any case, a diminishing element in English criticism, so that what is merely misleading in

[1] In his last phase, following his abandonment of verbal analysis; cf. his article '*Tom Jones*' (*Kenyon Review*, xx, 1958). It is, of course, possible to expose a brief extract from a novel or epic to verbal analysis: the technique is only unconvincing to the extent that we remain uncertain how far the extract is representative of the whole; cf. Ian Watt, 'The First Paragraph of [Henry James's] *The Ambassadors*', *Essays in Criticism*, x (1960).

the writings of the neoclassical critics largely disappears in critical analysis since Coleridge. But there is another sense of 'language' wider and less easily defined than this – so wide, indeed, that to say that the issues of criticism are defined by language in this second sense is almost a tautology. If by 'language' we mean something like 'the total linguistic range' of any given critic (as we speak of 'the language of Shakespeare', or 'the language of the Authorized Version'), then it is self-evidently true that what a critic states or implies is contained within such a linguistic pattern. We shall notice such characteristic patterns in the course of this history – the special quality of Arnold's urbanity, or Eliot's technique of the parenthetical insult – and such patterns are characteristic in the fullest sense. That is, we cannot remotely imagine similar devices in the mouth of any previous critic: try to conceive of Eliot's notorious 'not that Montaigne had any philosophy whatever'[1] in the mouth of Dryden, or Addison, or Arnold. Certainly, in this wider sense of 'language', we may sensibly claim that the language of a critic ultimately holds the key to his achievement. And, again in this wider sense, we may sensibly attempt to generalize about the language of description in terms of period, certain (for example) that an extract from an Addisonian analysis could only have occurred in eighteenth-century England, however uncertain we may remain about our reasons for thinking so.

A series of extracts should establish the point at once and offer ground from which to advance the argument a further stage. They are in chronological order.

Dryden: I will observe yet one thing further of this admirable plot: the business of it rises in every act. The second is greater than the first; the third, than the second; and so forward to the fifth. There too you see, till the very last scene, new difficulties arising to obstruct the action of the play; and when the audience is brought into despair that the business can naturally be affected, then, and not before, the discovery is made . . .

Of Dramatick Poesie (1668)

Addison: I look upon the disposition and contrivance of the fable to be the principal beauty of the Ninth Book, which has more *story* in it, and is fuller of incidents, than any other in the whole poem. Satan's

[1] cf. p. 186, below.

traversing the globe, and still keeping within the shadow of the night, as fearing to be discovered by the angel of the sun, who had before detected him, is one of those beautiful imaginations with which he introduces this his second series of adventures . . .

Spectator, no. 351 (12 April 1712)

Johnson: He borrows too many of his sentiments and illustrations from the old mythology, for which it is vain to plead the example of ancient poets: the deities which they introduced so frequently were considered as realities, so far as to be received by the imagination, whatever sober reason might even then determine. But of these images time has tarnished the splendor. A fiction, not only detected but despised, can never afford a solid basis to any position, though sometimes it may furnish a transient illusion or slight illustration. No modern monarch can be much exalted by hearing that, as Hercules had had his club, he has his navy . . .

Life of Waller, from *Lives* (1779-81)

Coleridge: A unity of feeling pervades the whole of his plays. In *Romeo and Juliet* all is youth and spring – it is youth with its follies, its virtues, its precipitancies; it is spring with its odours, flowers, and transiency: the same feeling commences, goes through, and ends the play. The old men, the Capulets and Montagues, are not common old men; they have an eagerness, a hastiness, a precipitancy – the effect of spring . . .

Lecture 1 (October 1813)

Arnold: His expression may often be called bald, as, for instance, in the poem of 'Resolution and Independence'; but it is bald as the bare mountain tops are bald, with a baldness which is full of grandeur. Wherever we meet with the successful balance, in Wordsworth, of profound truth of subject with profound truth of execution, he is unique. His best poems are those which most perfectly exhibit this balance. I have a warm admiration for 'Laodameia' and for the great 'Ode'; but . . . I find 'Laodameia' not wholly free from something artificial, and the great 'Ode' not wholly free from something declamatory . . .

'Wordsworth' (1879), in *Essays in Criticism: Second Series* (1888)

Eliot: The wit of the Caroline poets is not the wit of Shakespeare, and it is not the wit of Dryden, the great master of contempt, or of Pope, the great master of hatred, or of Swift, the great master of disgust. What is meant is some quality which is common to the songs in

Comus and Cowley's Anacreontics and Marvell's Horatian Ode. It is more than a technical accomplishment, or the vocabulary and syntax of an epoch; it is . . . a tough reasonableness beneath the slight lyric grace. You cannot find it in Shelley or Keats or Wordsworth . . .

> 'Andrew Marvell' (1921), in *Selected Essays* (1932)

Empson (on Donne's 'A Valediction: Of Weeping', st. 2, 'On a round ball . . .'): The first four lines are defining the new theme, and their grammar is straightforward. Then the *teare* may be active or passive, like the *workeman* or like the *ball*; on the face of it, it is like the *ball*, but *so doth* may treat it as like the *workeman*. For *doth* may be a separate verb as well as an auxiliary of *grow*; while, in any case, *grow* may either mean 'turn into' or 'grow larger' . . .

> *Seven Types of Ambiguity* (1930, 1953), Ch. iv: 'In the fourth type the alternative meanings combine to make clear a complicated state of mind in the author.'

Anyone can see that each of these seven examples of description is intensely characteristic of its own age: an informed reader of English criticism could date all of them without effort, and in most cases he could guess the author too. But suppose we were asked to explain why we are so certain, and suppose that, in answering, we confined ourselves to the critical substance of each extract. Several conclusions spring to mind at once.

1. The evolution of critical description, as represented here, is almost circular in its concern for what we nowadays call 'close reading'. It has not, as one might first have guessed, evolved in one direction, ever closer to the text: Dryden, after all, is much 'closer to the text' of *The Silent Woman* than Addison is to *Paradise Lost*, or Johnson to any single poem of Waller, or Coleridge to *Romeo and Juliet*, or Arnold to what he thinks are Wordsworth's best poems, or Eliot to the Horatian Ode. Only Empson, in a passage which is a fair run-of-the-mill example of twentieth-century 'verbal analysis', shows himself closer to his text than Dryden was to his, and it is a closeness of a sort Dryden never attempted. For Dryden's analysis, of course, was not verbal but structural – and so was Rymer's, and so, at times, was Addison's and Johnson's. But Empson's attempt – which would look schoolmasterly if it were not so novel – to explain in detail the meaning of an English poem is more minute and, in principle, more exact than anything

before 1930. And if we look harder at this nearly circular evolution from Dryden to Empson, we can see that the details confirm our first impression of the general pattern. The first three extracts (Dryden, Addison, Johnson) take us further and further from the texts. Addison is admittedly commenting on a specific passage in *Paradise Lost* (IX, 58ff.), but his comment could not be dignified with the term 'analysis', as Dryden's fairly could – it is rather concerned, like a chairman's remarks, with careless recommendation ('beautiful imaginations'). And Johnson has no text: in the whole Life of Waller he expends only a few sentences on specific poems, and then his comments are only snap judgements ('elegant and happy', 'empty and trifling'), whereas thousands of words are spent in generalizing about Waller's talent, its characteristic virtues and faults. The next three extracts (Coleridge, Arnold, Eliot) represent a hesitating return to the particular on fresh, historical principles: Coleridge attributes a psychological condition to Shakespeare in one of his plays, Arnold plays amateurishly with an inference concerning a Wordsworthian 'balance', Eliot makes a bold historical generalization, while faintly disparaging the historical method (wit is more than 'the vocabulary and syntax *of an epoch*' – but, presumably, it is that too). With Empson, of course, we have come more than full circle, but Empsonian minuteness is possible only because of nineteenth-century research: it devours every kind of historical information in its progress, especially the lexicographical.

2. The terminology of criticism diminishes steeply, and if only we had an extended example of Elizabethan analysis – but, as we have seen, there is no such thing – we should think the decline even steeper. Dryden's interests in design and structure make a special language indispensable, and the passage quoted is characteristically rich in it: *plot*, *business* (i.e. dramatic action), *act*, *scene*, *discovery* (i.e. *dénouement*). Addison begins in a similarly business-like style ('the disposition and contrivance of the fable', i.e. the structure of Milton's plot); but he makes us feel at once that, unlike Dryden, he is writing for amateurs rather than for professionals by explaining his terms in extravagantly – even misleadingly – simple language. Book IX 'has more *story* in it, and is fuller of incidents', which does not, as he seems to suppose, in itself

prove its structural superiority. Johnson's terms, such as they are, can hardly be called proper to criticism at all, in the simple sense that Dryden's were: words like 'imagination' and 'reason' would call for explanation on the part of a conscientious editor only in terms of eighteenth-century philosophy and psychology – they are part of the general current of eighteenth-century ideas. Coleridge, in this instance, has no critical terminology, and where he has it is usually self-invented and self-defined – an obvious symptom of the decline of jargon; and much the same is true of Arnold and Eliot. And this decline has proved general. Rhetoric is dead – how many people, off-hand, could tell you what 'paralipsis' means, or 'litotes', or 'catachresis'? Words for 'the parts of the poem' have largely disappeared, except for a few indispensables like 'act' and 'scene'. Metrical terms still exist (*sonnet, foot, iambic*, etc.), but under a cloud of unbelief, and phoneticians will tell you that most of them do not correspond to the facts of the language. A few terms in a new rhetoric (*ambiguity, tension, irony*, etc.) do not compensate numerically for a loss which for two hundred years has liberated English criticism by rendering it less exact and more available.

3. The readership of criticism changes, after Dryden, from poets to readers of poetry, from professionals to amateurs, from producers to consumers; one cause, no doubt, if it is not also the result, of the simplification of the language of criticism I have just noticed. Dryden's remarks on *The Silent Woman* could only be intended for fellow-dramatists – it would be an unimaginably analytical spectator who would want to know about such technical devices as the accelerating tempo by which Jonson's comedy works. But with Addison, the revolution is already complete, and though we cannot feel certain that an Augustan epic-poet like Blackmore might not have learned something from the *Spectator* papers on *Paradise Lost*, we may feel utterly certain that they were not written for him: the discussion is altogether untechnical in its emphasis, and the critic's function, like a tourist-guide's, is to point out the principal beauties. Johnson is doing the same thing better, Coleridge and Arnold a similar thing differently. But with Arnold we already sense a new limitation imposed by intellectual snobbery upon the audience of criticism. It is there in Arnold's arch,

deprecatory tone, based upon a rhetoric which is more complex and more oblique than Johnson's outspoken rigour ('I find "Laodemeia" *not wholly free* from something artificial . . .'). And it is there in Eliot's assumption that his readers are scholars, and not only of English literature; and in Empson's assumption that his readers are grammarians.

4. The evaluative concern of criticism is a steadily increasing one. This is the more difficult to prove because of the complicated interrelationship in critical language – as in most other language – between description and evauzation. No doubt we can all think of very simple critical statements – e.g. '*Paradise Lost* is an epic' – which are entirely descriptive and which make no judgement. But criticism that counts does not work on this simple level. If we were to attempt, in the coldest of cold blood, to describe what *Paradise Lost* is like above and beyond half a dozen simple statements – it is an epic, it is long, it is in blank verse – we should soon find that the language of criticism did not permit us to describe it without judging it. Even Dryden, with his wealth of technical terms, is unable to show us what *The Silent Woman* is without making it sound like a good play, and even if the one frankly evaluative term in the entire extract, 'admirable', were deleted, we should still be certain that Dryden was recommending the play as well as analysing it. And this for two reasons: first, because he has chosen to describe one of the virtues of Jonson's plot, where he could as easily have chosen one of its defects; and second, because his total description is cast in the language of the exemplary case, as only a close examination of its vocabulary and syntax could reveal. Imagine if, in the last sentence, you were to substitute for the commendatory phrase 'then, and not before' another phrase which might fit as well the objective facts of the play, 'then, at long last'. It is by such scarcely visible touches that the language of critical description ceases to be pure. Readers who think that Dryden is over-rating *The Silent Woman* cannot usefully charge him with inaccurate description. (The inaccuracies are there, no doubt, but they are not crucial.) The best they can say is that Dryden has subtly weighted the evidence, by verbal tricks, for the sake of a favourable judgement.

And here, perhaps, we may identify one of the reasons why the evaluative content of English criticism has risen from age to age. Technical language, as we have seen in Dryden, may be used to some subjective purpose; but *only* a technical language, or a language artificially maintained by a continuing discipline (like the languages of some natural sciences), could in principle be judgement-free. And yet English critics since Addison have abandoned all prospects of such a technical language in favour of a wider public. And a critical language poor in technical terms is doubly likely to be value-charged. With Addison, recommendation is the explicit purpose of criticism; with Johnson, recommendation and condemnation are elevated into an inquiry of principle. Johnson does not merely blame Waller for his classical references: he uses Waller's mistake of including too many in his poems as a directive to the reader to condemn such excesses wherever they are found ('A fiction . . . can *never* afford a solid basis to any position . . .'). By the nineteenth century, the question whether the language of criticism is descriptive or evaluative, or in what proportion it is one or the other, no longer makes sense, for the historical method of the romantics so humanized the concept of the poet (Wordsworth's 'man speaking to men') that we can not longer unpick the elements. In such criticism, all description passes judgement, and all judgement affects to describe. If Coleridge thinks that the 'feeling' of *Romeo and Juliet* is 'all youth and spring', we do not pause to ask ourselves whether this is an objective fact about the play or a subjective experience of Coleridge's. It is both – or, at least, it offers itself as both. And much the same, of course, is true of Arnold, Eliot, and Empson, for it is an assumption that what they distinguish for our attention is both there and worth looking at. If Empson were to fail, for once, to discover his ambiguity, we should hardly know where to turn; but he chooses his own examples, justifiably enough, and that is why the effects he admires are there.

So much and a good deal more we might say, faced with seven representative examples of descriptive criticism over three hundred years: that over the centuries English criticism has tended to move away from the text and then back towards it; that it is rapidly and early stripped of all but a few of the technical terms that it inherited from the European tradition; that it began as a dialogue between poets and ends as a demonstration before readers; and that the task of distinguishing the better from the worse has grown more insistent with the generations. It has, in fact, tended to win popularity at the expense of precision, and self-importance at the expense of both.

Chapter 2

JOHN DRYDEN

THE PRECURSORS

THE first Englishman to attempt extended descriptive criticism
was John Dryden, and this history must begin with him. But we
ought to be clear from the start how feeble the Elizabethan and
early Stuart inheritance was, and how revolutionary in their age,
in their bulk and seriousness of purpose, were Dryden's analyses
of Ben Jonson and Shakespeare, and of his own plays.

All English criticism before 1660 was essentially legislative or
theoretical, its theoretical content rising steeply in the seventeenth
century, notably in Hobbes's occasional interest in the psychology
of the creative act. Descriptive criticism before the Restoration is
limited to occasional phrases and sentences in essays directed to
some other end: the reform of letters, or the continuation of the
Platonic argument about poetic truth. These snatches of description, written in an age when description had no purpose and no
dignity of its own, read to us now like extracts from a schoolboy's
essay. They are mainly simple evaluative statements, for though
the Elizabethan critic inherited the common European stock of
genre-words (*tragedy, pastoral*, etc.), rhetorical terms for describing
figures-of-speech, and a system of metrical description – an immense battery of technical terms, far greater than anything wielded
by the twentieth-century critic – he paradoxically inherited no
tradition of using them for literary analysis. For him, they simply
defined exemplary (or cautionary) cases. We are left with the
embarrassing spectacle of a critic as intelligent as Sidney solemnly
telling us that 'Chaucer, undoubtedly, did excellently in hys
Troylus and Cresseid', or that Spenser's *Shepheardes Calendar* (1579)
'hath much poetrie in his eglogues: indeede worthy the reading,
if I be not deceived'.[1] George Puttenham (or whoever wrote the
1589 *Arte of English Poesie*) is a legislative critic who, in his vigorous honesty, still impresses us as a good master for a young poet.

[1] *Elizabethan Critical Essays*, op. cit., 1, 196.

But a descriptive problem leaves him looking merely flatulent:

> Henry Earle of Surrey and Sir Thomas Wyat, betweene whom I finde very litle difference, I repute them (as before) for the two chief lanternes of light to all others that have since employed their pennes upon English poesie: their conceits were loftie, their stiles stately, their conveyance cleanly, their terms proper, their meetre sweete and well proportioned, in all imitating very naturally and studiously their Master Francis Petrarcha.[1]

There is not much 'cleanly conveyance' here: Puttenham has managed to say nothing except that Wyatt and Surrey are good Petrarchan poets. Perhaps the best thing that can be said for Elizabethan critics, considered in this purely eccentric sense as the pioneers of descriptive criticism, is their clear if rudimentary sense of literary history. There is Sidney's magnificent appeal to the Puritan detractors of poetry, such as Stephen Gosson, to maintain some decent reverence for the past of European poetry, from Homer to Chaucer: 'they goe very neer to ungratfulnes, to seek to deface that which, in the noblest nations and languages that are knowne, hath been the first light-giver to ignorance.'[2] The first of Puttenham's three books (the second and third are legislative and technical), entitled *Of Poets and Poesie*, recounts in historical order the progress of poetry from its mythical and priestly sources through classical and medieval times. But, like Sidney, Puttenham can only use the historical method, and then fleetingly, for an argumentative purpose, to prove that in most societies 'good poets and poesie were highly esteemed and much favoured of the greatest princes'.[3] The Campion-Daniel debate, too, on rhyme (1602-3) calls glibly on ancient and medieval practices to score points in a debate of interest only to fellow-poets.

It would be a fair summary to conclude that there was no Elizabethan tradition in descriptive criticism. There is no surviving Elizabethan analysis of an Elizabethan play, and no contemporary analysis, in the age that followed, of a Metaphysical poem. The nearest approach to Dryden's achievement, perhaps, in the

---

[1] *Arte*, I, xxxi; edited by G. D. Willcock and Alice Walker (Cambridge, 1936), p. 62.

[2] *Elizabethan Critical Essays*, op. cit., I, 151.

[3] *Arte*, I, viii; ed. cit., p. 16.

years before the Restoration, is to be found in the critical preface
of Sir William Davenant (1606-68), 'A Discourse upon *Gondibert*,' published in Paris in 1650 for the exiled Royalist poet before
he had written his epic – it was, in fact, never finished – and oddly
including an 'Answer' by Thomas Hobbes, who was then completing his *Leviathan* (1651) after a ten-year absence from the
England of the Civil War. Davenant's idea of writing serious and
extended criticism in prefatorial form looks strikingly like a premonition of the stratagem Dryden was to adopt a dozen years later
– especially as Davenant uses the preface, like Dryden after him,
for critical self-justification, to defend his poem as an edifying
Christian epic. Hobbes's Answer is boldly theoretical, dividing all
European poetry into three categories designed for court, city, and
country, and each category into the dramatic and the narrative.
It is just possible that Dryden took some courage from this early
assertion, by two exiled Englishmen, of the usefulness of criticism
in defending in advance a poet's reputation. But the *Gondibert*
debate of 1650 is not a very impressive example of descriptive
criticism, and for a very simple reason: it is about a poem that does
not exist, so that the argument is only speciously particular where
it is particular at all. In Hobbes's reply, indeed, all pretence at the
particular is cast aside: you cannot analyse a poem that is not there.
The vacuum may be regarded as fully significant. Dryden inherited from earlier English critics a mass of critical terminology
and a few simple notions of poetry as a historical sequence stretching from Homer. But he could have found all this, and more, in
his continental sources. As for a native tradition in critical analysis,
he was forced to start from scratch.

THE EARLY DRYDEN

Whatever we may make of the elusive achievement of Dryden
(1631-1700) as a critic, we can hardly expect our estimate to be
one he would have understood himself. For that matter, we can
hardly imagine him understanding Johnson's claim, in his Life of
Dryden, that he was 'the father of English criticism'. No critic
achieves so much with so little sense of his own dignity. He wrote
only one work of formal criticism in a crowded literary career of
over forty years, the essay *Of Dramatick Poesie* (1668), and all the

remaining works of his in which criticism predominates are pre-faces, most of them to his own plays and poems. There is no reason to suppose that he thought the function of the critic an important one: we cannot imagine him writing, like Arnold, an essay called 'The Function of Criticism at the Present Time'. And the works of other poets occupy a very modest proportion of his critical interests. And yet he is clearly the founder of descriptive criticism in English. The modern preoccupation with literary analysis emerges, patchily but unmistakably, in his prejudiced and partisan interest in his own plays and poems.

The truth is that Dryden is a descriptive critic almost without knowing it. Most of his criticism offers itself, in traditional terms, as legislative or theoretical. He never attempted to write anything we can call radically descriptive. The first such work in English is not by Dryden at all: it is Thomas Rymer's *The Tragedies of the Last Age* (1678), an attack upon Elizabethan and Jacobean drama by a learned lawyer, and we know that Dryden read and wel-comed it as soon as it appeared without attempting to emulate it: he had already conceived, and failed to write, such a work him-self.[1] On the other hand, he wrote some twenty-five critical prefaces to his own works (1664-1700), three classical lives (Plutarch, Polybius, and Lucian), the dialogue *Of Dramatick Poesie*, and a handful of prefaces to the works of his contempor-aries. It is in the prefaces to his own works that the silent trans-formation of English criticism occurs.

Dryden's first critical essay, the dedicatory letter to his first-published play *The Rival Ladies* (1664), illustrates the transition. The young poet is defending the second play he wrote, a rhymed heroic play in the new French mode, against the sort of attacks that new fashions usually provoke. He defends himself in two ways: first, by an appeal to a noble and powerful patron, Roger Earl of Orrery, the first author of such plays in English; and second, by an appeal to critical principle in favour of rhyme on the stage. It is only the second part of his preface that concerns us here

---

[1] Cf. *Of Dramatick Poesie* (1668), 'To the Reader': 'I promise to myself a better success of the Second Part, wherein the vertues and faults of the English poets, who have written either in this [the dramatic], the epique, or the lyrique way, will be more fully treated of.'

– though the flattery of the first part is less irrelevant than is usual
in the compliments of Restoration poets, since Orrery really was
a dramatist as well as a public figure. The second part is an example of descriptive criticism in its most impure form. Dryden is
talking about an actual literary work, but it is his own, and though
the poet must always be considered an important witness in such
a matter, he is also a suspiciously interested one. In any case, the
discussion is entirely general: no speech or scene of *The Rival
Ladies* is specifically defended, and no aspect of it, apart from
rhyme, is really discussed. And much of the defence of rhyme
consists of mere appeals to authority. The critical residue, in fact,
is extremely small; it is confined to the penultimate paragraph,
when we are unexpectedly admitted to the studio and allowed to
watch the poet at work:

> But that benefit which I consider most in it [rhyme], *because I have
> not seldome found it*, is that it bounds and circumscribes the fancy. For
> imagination in a poet is a faculty so wild and lawless that, like a high-
> ranging spaniel, it must have cloggs tied to it least it outrun the
> judgment. The great easiness of blanck verse renders the poet too
> luxuriant . . .

The veil is lifted only for a second, But there, for a moment, is a
young poet discussing one of his own problems as a poet. The
question whether rhyme or blank verse best suits the stage is a
genuinely practical question that the Restoration poet had to face,
and the problem of intellectual discipline is one that young poets
face in any period. We are within shouting distance of descriptive
criticism, near enough to be disappointed that it does not happen.
For the advance, from this point, is logical and natural: a poet
who is prepared, however briefly, however insincerely, to discuss
the psychological processes by which his poems are composed, has
reached a point from which he can explain the faults and virtues
of his own work; and, interested at all such discussions must be,
they are in turn the starting-point for criticism of the works of
others. It is this path that the greatest of critics have trodden:
Coleridge, passing from the authorship of 'The Ancient Mariner'
to his notes towards the 1800 preface which seeks to explain and
justify such poetry, and so to the Shakespearean lectures and the
Biographia Literaria; Matthew Arnold, from his own poetry

through the 1853 preface and on to the *Essays in Criticism*; or Baudelaire, or T. S. Eliot. Dryden, in his early thirties, stands at the point where art turns to criticism.

The essay *Of Dramatick Poesie* (1668), Dryden's only formal work of criticism – and the only one he ever troubled to revise – can only have been written by a kind of accident. There was no money in criticism in the seventeenth century, and no reputation either, and an ambitious young dramatist like Dryden in the early years of the Restoration would never have allowed precious time on criticism which he could have profitably employed in writing for the stage. But the Great Plague interrupted Dryden's career as a playwright when it was only two years old.

The story, in brief, is this: in June 1665, at the beginning of the Plague, the London theatres closed, and Dryden retired to the country-house of his father-in-law, the first Earl of Berkshire, at Charlton Park near Malmesbury, where he stayed for eighteen months. It seems natural to suppose that the Essay was the first task he set his mind to. It celebrates the naval victory over the Dutch off Lowestoft on 3 June 1665, whereas the poem *Annus Mirabilis* (1667), though published some six months before the Essay, describes the Great Fire of September 1666 as well. And the preface to that poem, addressed to his brother-in-law Sir Robert Howard, discusses the problem of the language of poetry in a way that seems to presuppose much of the debate of the Essay, and contains a brief pyschological analysis of the creative act (Invention, Fancy, Elocution) – an outgrowth of Hobbes's aesthetics to which, oddly enough, he scarcely returned. There remains a puzzle: the Essay lay unpublished for some two years, and did not appear until August 1667, with '1668' on its title-page. I can only suppose that Dryden guessed how angry Howard would be at this portrait of Crites, and paused to allow the *Annus Mirabilis*, with its complimentary preface, to go on before and smooth the way.

The Essay is a manifesto, a work of legislative criticism, though secreting within itself the first critical analysis of a literary work in English, the examen of Ben Jonson's *Silent Woman*. It is important, however, that we should appreciate its real nature for what it is before we admire it for virtues which must have seemed to

Dryden incidental. His object in the Essay is not, in principle, very different from his object in the prefaces to his plays. It is self-justification. In the preface to *The Rival Ladies* he had defended his first attempt at the heroic play by an appeal to Orrery's example; as he later defended the same form at greater length in the essay 'Of Heroique Playes' prefixed to *The Conquest of Granada* (1672), or his use of blank verse in *All for Love* (1678) in his preface to that tragedy. In the same way, *Of Dramatick Poesie* is a formal and general defence – this time in advance of events – of the kind of play he hoped to write: a recognizably English version of the heroic play, that alien import into Restoration England, which rejects Elizabethan blank verse in favour of rhyme but which remains Elizabethan in its variety of plot and temperament. It is about a play he never quite managed to write, as T. S. Eliot has never quite managed to write the play foreshadowed in his essay 'Poetry and the Drama' – *All for Love*, the most vigorous and 'English' of Dryden's tragedies, is not in rhyme, and his heroic plays remain stubbornly unacclimatized, redolent of the French inspiration he so often disclaimed. Eliot has written enthusiastically of the 'almost ideal balance between the critic and the creative poet'[1] that Dryden achieved; and it is the essence of such a balance that the critic should excel at those points where the poet has failed, and feel no special need to exert himself where the poet has succeeded. Dryden's later 'Discourse concerning the Original and Progress of Satire',[2] considering it is the work of a great satirist in full maturity, is one of the most disappointing essays in the whole canon of Dryden's criticism, while more than two-thirds of his criticism is concerned with the drama, a record of his frustrated ambitions.

Dryden was evidently embarrassed by his legislative intention, and took some trouble to disguise it. The real purpose of the Essay, according to the introductory note 'To the Reader', was historical, 'to vindicate the honour of our English writers [i.e. the Elizabethan and Jacobean dramatists] from the censure of those who unjustly prefer the French before them', and Dryden goes on

---

[1] 'Dryden the Critic, Defender of Sanity', *Listener*, v (1931), p. 724. This article has not been reprinted.

[2] Prefixed to *The Satires of Juvenalis Translated into English Verse* (1693).

to confuse the issue still further by denying any intention of influencing the course of Restoration drama: 'This I intimate, least any should think me so exceeding vain as to teach others an art which they understand much better than myself.' All the same, the issues raised in the Essay are argued out as if they concerned all English dramatists of the age; and so, of course, they did. And the Horatian tag on the title-page gives the game away completely: 'I shall play the part of a whetstone, which sharpens steel, though itself incapable of cutting.'

The Essay is in the form of a dialogue among four characters. Eliot has compared it to the dialogues of Plato, and its opening to 'the beautiful introduction to the *Theaetetus*'.[1] But the comparison is only illuminating in a negative sense. Dryden cannot possibly be trying to write anything like a Platonic dialogue. He was a professional dramatist, and knew how dialogue was written, but there is nothing here remotely like the cut-and-thrust of a Socratic inquisition, indeed nothing much like any sort of conversation. Nothing, that is, except in the opening pages, where alone conversation among the four characters is allowed to be general, and where a loose definition of a play – '*a genere et fine*, and so not altogether perfect' – is casually accepted without real argument. The rest of the Essay consists of six set speeches, in three pairs: Crites defends the Ancients, Eugenius the Moderns; Lisideius defends the French drama, Neander (Dryden himself) the English; Crites defends blank verse, Neander rhyme. No scheme could be more inflexible, more obviously pre-designed, less 'Platonic'. Argument, under such a plan, obstinately refuses to advance more than a single step. No issue is ever talked out, since the form only allows of assertion and reply: A makes his case, and B answers back. The second speaker in each of the three exchanges is implausibly required to memorize a list of questions raised by the first speaker, and then to reply to them in something like due order. And it cannot be pleaded, in excuse for Dryden, that the dialogue form was in a primitive state in his day; Plato apart, Sir Thomas More, Francis Bacon, Sir Walter Ralegh, Hobbes, and Izaak Walton had all written dialogues which are more convincing as conversation-pieces than this. Evidently the extreme inflexibility of dialogue in

[1] 'Dryden the Critic', op. cit.

the Essay is deliberate – it is more likely to be modelled on the stiff, formal, expository pattern of Cicero's *De oratore* than on anything Platonic, or at least early Platonic – and it is worth asking what Dryden's reason can have been for choosing such a model.

The most probable answer is Dryden's extreme tactical caution as a critic. We have already considered the note prefixed to the Essay, in which he denies any legislative purpose; and his delay in publishing the Essay at all is probably suggestive of caution. Dryden's whole career as a critic is permeated by what we might tactfully call this sense of occasion: Pyrrhonism, or philosophical scepticism, liberated him from the tyranny of truth.

> Dim as the borrow'd beams of moon and stars
> To lonely, weary, wandring travellers,
> Is reason to the soul.[1]

Since no human proposition can ever certainly be true, the poet, in Dryden's view, does not prostitute himself in becoming the paid pen of the Court, and the critic is only showing proper professional caution in refusing to commit himself to ideals he may later find it inconvenient to live up to. Dryden is remarkable as a critic not only for the casual ease with which he contradicts himself,[2] but for the care he takes in advance to ensure that there will not be much in future to contradict. And for this kind of caution, the carefully contrived order of the essay *Of Dramatick Poesie* is admirably suited. Dryden does not *want* the argument to advance more than one step at a time. An inference is left – but it is only an inference – that truth, in each of the three exchanges, had the last word, and that Dryden is arguing for the Moderns, the English, and rhyming plays against the Ancients, the French, and blank verse. In the second and third controversies, especially, Dryden seems to be speaking in his own person, in the character of Neander, the 'New Man'. But, in reality, he commits himself to nothing. The dialogue form allows him to fly a number of kites, and his self-justification is tactfully semi-anonymous. He is so con-

---

[1] *Religio Laici* (1682), ll. 1-3.
[2] For example, his barefaced reversal of attitude in favour of blank verse in *All for Love* (1678), where he merely notes in the preface: 'Not that I condemn my former way [rhyme], but that this is more proper to my present purpose.'

fident, indeed, that he indulges in his last paragraph in a mild Chaucerian joke at his own expense: he goes on talking after the barge has drawn up at Somerset Stairs, and has to be cut short by his friends.

Where, for all this careful rhetorical contrivance, can Dryden's convictions be said to lie in the essay *Of Dramatick Poesie*? It is surely clear that they are to be found, if anywhere, in the second and third exchanges, when Neander has the last word, and scarcely at all in the introductory conversation, or in the controversy over Ancient and Moderns – a perennial issue of Renaissance criticism which never seems to have interested him much. The introductory passages of the Essay, culminating in Lisideius's bad definition of a play, are superbly contrived, but their excellence is stylistic, not critical; it is notable, for example, that though the definition is not a good one, and though Crites shows that it is not, no attempt is made to arrive at any better: 'A just and lively image of humane nature, representing its passions and humours, and the changes of fortune to which it is subject, for the delight and instruction of mankind'. This is an umbrella indeed, and Aristotle had offered a better account two thousand years before – but Dryden's indifference to theory is so deep-rooted that he will not pause to improve his definition. The contrivance of the opening paragraphs is of the same sort. Dryden is only slightly embarrassed by the inconvenient fact that the naval battle which is the alleged occasion of the dialogue is not against the French, but against the Dutch, and that in any case it is likely to provoke not bad plays but bad poems. And yet the improbable metaphor is put to good use: the battle is an occasion for general patriotism, a mood later matched by Neander in his abuse of the French dramatists; and Crites arbitrarily limits the dispute to 'dramatic poesy' – by which time we have forgotten how the Dutch got into the story at all. So, by a double somersault, the young dramatist has successfully invoked a great public event, the defeat of the Dutch, and contrived to turn the discussion to his own dramatic art. The effect of this opening is only partly dissipated by the diffuse and derivative exchange that follows on ancient and modern observance of the three unities. Dryden leans so heavily here upon the third of Corneille's three *Discours* of 1660 ('Discours des trois unités'), that he takes trouble to discount any sort of French influence in Neander's first long speech: 'Corneille himself, their arch-poet, what has he produc'd except *The Lier*,[1] and you know how it was cry'd up in France; but when it came upon the English stage, though well translated, . . . the most favourable to it would not put it in competition with many of Fletcher's or Ben Johnson's.' He goes on to defend the Elizabethan drama on contradictory grounds: 'First, that we have many playes of ours as regular as any of theirs [the French] . . . and secondly, that in most of the irregular playes of Shakespeare or Fletcher . . . there is a more masculine fancy and greater spirit in all the writing than there is in any of the French.' Like many another Renaissance critic, Dryden, when he tries to theorize about poetry, is never so happy as when he eats his cake and has it too: he praises Elizabethan drama for its regularity and for its irregularity alike. But there are better things to follow.

'I will take the pattern of a perfect play from Ben Johnson, who was a careful and learned observer of the dramatique lawes, and from all his comedies I shall select *The Silent Woman*; of which I will make a short examen, according to those rules which the French observe.' This passage ushers in three general estimates of Shakespeare, Beaumont and Fletcher, and Ben Jonson, and there follows immediately the first extended analysis of any English poem or play: it is the earliest substantial example of descriptive criticism in the language.

Certain significant facts emerge at once. First, the analysis of *The Silent Woman* is conducted within the framework of a legislative treatise. It is not, like a modern critique, gratuitous, in the sense that it is not based on our own assumption that literary works of excellence deserve analysis in their own right. *The Silent Woman* is not just a good play to Dryden: it is 'the pattern of a perfect play', it has secrets to yield up to the modern practitioner of the drama. Second, Dryden himself is aware that there is no English precedent for what he is doing, no native tradition in literary analysis. The very word he uses is scarcely an English one – *examen* – but a Latinism still new to English and probably re-borrowed, for this purpose, from the French of Corneille.

In 1660 Corneille, in reply to attacks made upon him by the

---

[1] I.e. *Le Menteur* (Paris, 1643), one of his comedies.

French Academy, had collected his plays into three volumes, heading each volume with a '*discours*' or theoretical essay and an '*examen*' of the group of plays included there. The example was a spur to self-criticism. Other European dramatists – Ben Jonson, for instance, and the Frenchman Jean Mairet – had provided some of their plays with critical prefaces. But none had attempted the wholesale self-vindication of Corneille's *Théâtre* of 1660. Dryden owes Corneille a double debt as a critic: he borrows heavily from Corneille's theoretical views, especially from his liberal view of the three unities in the third *Discours*: and he takes confidence from Corneille's *examens* to embark on a pioneer attempt at literary analysis of an English poem. There was simply no English source from which he could borrow an example of critical analysis.

The examen of *The Silent Woman* suffers from much of the crudeness and imprecision we associate with pioneer work. It would not be acceptable as pass-work in any modern school of English. The patriotic, anti-French bias we may excuse as a peccadillo; but Dryden offends badly in referring the play to a set of criteria – the three unities – which, on his own admission, it is a venial fault to ignore. And he is not very accurate: he even distorts the facts about Jonson's play in order to make his point – a point that, on his own admission, was not worth making in the first place: 'it lies all within the compass of two houses,' he claims, whereas in fact three houses and a lane (II, vi) are mentioned in the text. And his claim that 'the action of the play is intirely one: the aim or end of which is the setling Morose's estate on Dauphine' can only be maintained by juggling with the evidence – there are farcical scenes in the play that scarcely relate to the main plot. Dryden is a radically inaccurate critic when the facts do not suit the story he is determined to tell. And finally, he seems at first obtusely unhistorical in his failure to understand the nature of a Jonsonian humour, and we wonder what kind of a reader of Elizabethan plays could talk like this:

. . . Morose, or an old man, to whom all noise but his own talking is offensive. Some who would be thought criticks say this humour of his is forc'd: but to remove that objection, we may consider him first to be naturally of a delicate hearing . . .; and secondly, we may attribute much of it to the peevishness of his age . . . Besides this, I am assur'd from diverse persons that Ben Johnson was actually acquainted with such a man . . .

This is criticism on the how-many-children-had-Lady-Macbeth principle with a vengeance, and might lead us to think that Dryden supposes a humour to be a character in the naturalistic tradition; but on the next page he surprises us with a definition of the humour which a modern literary historian, with his card-index beside him, could hardly improve on: '. . . by humour is meant some extravagant habit, passion, or affection, particular . . . to some one person, by the oddness of which he is immediately distinguished from the rest of men . . .' Nobody, after that, can say that Dryden is generally deficient in the historical sense, though of course his history is naïve by our standards: he certainly has a real awareness that an Elizabethan play and a Restoration play are governed by different conventions. But his analysis of the plot of the play, though very much the analysis of a professional who has written plays himself and means to write more, is patchy by twentieth-century standards. He acutely notices that the play moves at an accelerating pace: 'the business of it rises in every act. . . . There too you see, till the very last scene, new difficulties rising to obstruct the action of the play'. and he notes that the 'untying', as he calls the *dénouement*, or the revelation that Morose has been married to a boy, is contrived to fall upon Morose himself as a shattering discovery. But he is much less satisfactory at doing something where we now expect critics effortlessly to succeed: he does not identify the relationship of the minor characters to the major, or of the subplots to the main plot; and contents himself with a vague assertion: 'all which persons have several concernments of their own, yet all are us'd by the poet to the conducting of the main design to perfection'. This is no doubt true – but the exacting modern reader is inclined to ask how.

The chief triumph of the examen lies in its attempt at comparative criticism, in its balancing of the qualities of the English drama against those of the French. It is undeniably the first example of such criticism in English, and among the very earliest in any modern language. Of course it is seriously vitiated by cultural nationalism – Dryden is out to prove that any English play is worth any two by a Frenchman, and he does not much care how he does it. The only reason why the reputation of the English drama has fallen below that of the French, he claims, is the accident of the Puritan revolution:

Be it spoken to the honour of the English, our nation can never want in any age such who are able to dispute the empire of wit with any people in the universe. And though the fury of a civil war, and power for twenty years together abandon'd to a barbarous race of men, enemies of all good learning, had buried the muses under the ruines of monarchy; yet, with the restoration of our happiness, we see reviv'd poesie lifting up its head. . . .

These partisan words were published within a few weeks of the appearance of Milton's *Paradise Lost*. And Dryden is unobjective enough to pretend that the feeble English dramatic output since the Restoration – a few plays of Orrery, Killigrew, and himself – 'yield not to those of any forreign nation'. But, though he is unfair to the French drama, he has seized upon the quality that distinguishes it from the Elizabethan – the difference between Shakespeare and Racine. It is the doctrinaire inflexibility of the French, their deadening lack of variety.

If they content themselves, as Corneille did, with some flat design, which, like an ill riddle, is found out ere it be half propos'd, such plots we can make every way regular as easily as they; but whene're they endeavour to rise up to any quick turns and counterturns of plot . . . you see they write as irregularly as we, though they cover it more speciously. . . . If you consider the plots, our own are fuller of variety; if the writing, ours are more quick and fuller of spirit . . .

And then, as usual, he goes too far in his attempt to decry the French, and denies that French plays have had any influence on English dramatists: 'We have borrowyd nothing from them; our plots are weav'd in English loomes. . . .' But, deeply biased as the passage is, a new dimension has been added to criticism, that of comparative analysis.

RYMER AND DENNIS

Dryden's twenty-year obsession with the theatre, hopelessly pursued through more than a score of play-prefaces, culminates in the two essays that accompany *The Conquest of Granada* (1672) in

defence of heroic drama, wavers confusedly after the advent of
Rymer in 1677, and ends in embittered disillusion with London
audiences in the preface to *The Spanish Friar* (1681). It is a record
of advance in critical technique and of failure in all else: in dogmatic consistency, in persuasive force, in self-advancement as a
dramatist. We shall probably never know why Dryden took
Rymer seriously as a critic. To answer that question, we should
need more certain information of Dryden's character than we can
derive from his essays. That character was pragmatic, evidently;
evasive on points of principle; easily – much too easily – impressed
by the scholarship and assertiveness of lesser men. 'My chief
endeavours are to delight the age in which I live,' he wrote in his
'Defence of *An Essay of Dramatique Poesie*',[1] and a poet who can
admit that in public is perilously sensitive to the state of literary
opinion. The writings of Thomas Rymer (1641-1713) represented a classicizing trend in English critical thought which he
may have felt it imprudent to ignore.

And yet there can be no doubt of the sincerity of Dryden's admiration for this failed dramatist ten years his junior. In a private
letter to the Earl of Dorset, written late in 1677, shortly after
Rymer had sent him a copy of his *Tragedies of the Last Age*,
Dryden calls the book 'very learned, and the best piece of criticism
in the English tongue . . . I think there is no man will dare to
answer him, or can'.[2] Not long after, he tried to answer Rymer
himself, scribbling his first thoughts into end-papers of his copy –
the notes we now call 'Heads of an Answer to Rymer'[3] – defending Shakespeare in the preface to *All for Love* (1678), and ultimately framing a more formal reply in 'The Grounds of Criticism
in Tragedy'.[4] Both prefaces, like the letter to Lord Dorset, are

---

[1] In the second edition only of his tragedy *The Indian Emperor* (1668), an
angry attack upon his brother-in-law Howard, occasioned by Howard's preface
to *The Great Favourite* (1668), itself a reply to Dryden's *Of Dramatick Poesie* of
the previous year.

[2] *The R. B. Adam Library* (New York, 1929), III, 87-8 (with facsimile);
Letters of John Dryden, edited by C. E. Ward (Durham, N.C., 1942), no. 6.

[3] First published in Jacob Tonson's 1711 edition of Beaumont and Fletcher,
and later, in a different order, by Johnson at the end of his Life of Dryden.
Tonson's version, of which Johnson was unaware, is on the whole superior. The
annotated copy of Rymer's book was destroyed by fire in 1786 or 1787.

[4] In the preface to his adaptation of Shakespeare, *Troilus and Cressida* (1679).

oddly respectful of Rymer. In both we await the thunderbolt that never falls.

Why is Dryden so respectful? To the modern reader, it is self-evident that Rymer's attack on the Elizabethan drama in his first book – he continued it years later in his second, *A Short View of Tragedy* (1693) – is not even superficially impressive. And we recall with a start that, where Rymer rushed in, Dryden forever after refused to tread: he had, as we have seen, in the note 'To the Reader' prefixed to his *Of Dramatick Poesie*, promised a 'Second Part' consisting of a full-scale account, whether historical or not we cannot say, of the whole of English poetry for the past hundred years, and if this is what Rymer's book cost us we have a quite unusually good reason for wishing it had not happened. For Rymer is an appalling understudy to a great master. He conforms with alarming precision to the popular image of the critic as a failed writer – his own tragedy, *Edgar*, published later in 1677, was (as Dryden predicted) a total flop, and the feverish pertness of his prose fails to disguise his petulance and malice. It looks like a catastrophic beginning to the course of descriptive criticism in English: and yet, after all, it is a beginning of a kind. Rymer's *Tragedies of the Last Age* is the first critical book in English which is altogether concerned with analysing the works of other Englishmen. And its sequel, *A Short View of Tragedy* (1693), is the first pure example of literary history in English. It is an astonishing Double First which the conscientious historian, however regretfully, is bound to record.

Rymer starts his analysis of Elizabethan tragedy without theoretical fuss. This is a remarkable fact in itself: but we should remember that Rymer had already said his say, in the legislative sense, in his first book, a translation of René Rapin's commentary on Aristotle, the *Reflections on Aristotle's Treatise of Poesie* (1674). By 1677, then, the rules may literally be taken as read, and analysis for once has pride of place, though there is still no doubt of Rymer's ultimate legislative intentions: the Elizabethan tragedies are presented as cautionary examples of how tragedy is not to be written. Still, analysis it is. Disappointed in the company of a London friend, Rymer tells us (for *The Tragedies of the Last Age* is in the form of a Ciceronian or Senecan epistle), he has stayed in the country reading, as an alternative to suicide, 'those master-pieces of wit, so renown'd everywhere, and so edifying to the stage: I mean the choicest and most applauded English tragedies of this last age'. The inept sarcasm of the opening paragraph estab-lishes the characteristic tone of Rymer's criticism: his will to be-little and to abuse is severely limited by an inadequate vocabulary of invective – Dryden could have helped him here – and an in-ability, strongly characteristic of young authors who are uncertain of their talents, to take trouble with his writing. He has read six old tragedies, he goes on, and is determined to discuss them all. But by the time he has dealt with the first three on his list, from the supposed canon of 'Fletcher's' works – *The Bloody Brother*,[1] *A King and No King*, and *The Maid's Tragedy* – he naïvely announces that he finds he already has a volume 'without more scribbling', and ends with a promise to consider the other three plays at some later stage – Shakespeare's *Othello* and *Julius Caesar*, and Ben Jonson's *Catiline* – a few arrogant apologies for his own careless-ness, and a proposal to attack *Paradise Lost* and the 'slender sophis-try' by which Milton justified his rejection of rhyme. This last impertinence, at least, we are spared, but not the attack upon Shakespeare and Jonson, which Rymer reserved for the final chapters of his *Short View* a full sixteen years later: surely the most remarkable example on record of a conservation of critical bile.

Rymer had already identified himself, by his translation of Rapin, as an extreme advocate of the literary laws of the French neoclassical critics and of the cause of the Ancients. In Rymer's view, the theatre must be restored to its original condition as a 'School of Vertue', and tragedy to the status of a 'Poem for Kings', an epic on boards. Plot, as in Aristotle, is 'the soul of tragedy', but a soul as brutish among the English as it was reasonable among the Greeks. He then sketches in the prehistory of the drama – a sketch mightily extended for *A Short View*, and a foretaste of Rymer's real historical sense – and proceeds to attack Beaumont and Fletcher play by play. His analyses are a travesty, but he does analyse, beginning with farcical summaries of the plots ('fables'),

---

[1] *Rollo: or the Bloody Brother* (Oxford, 1638) is now attributed to John Fletcher, Chapman, Jonson, and Massinger in collaboration, the other two plays to Beaumont and Fletcher.

which are abbreviated by his sheer impatience to condemn them. His fingers are forever twitching for the black cap: 'Now, if you call this a fable, give me one of old Aesop's. . . . Never were the Muses profan'd with a more foul, unpleasant and unwholsome truth. . . .'[1] But he knows how to compare *Rollo* with its source in Herodian, and actually quotes parallel passages to show that while the Greek historian, in his account of the mother's speech, 'seems to show a woman of great spirit, labouring to contain her passion till she may utter her mind', Fletcher's tirade 'seems to present a well-breath'd and practis'd scold'.[2] He is the first English critic to quote abundantly in the course of analysis, and though his comments on quotations are merely generalized insults, they are at least particular in their application. He is capable of raising questions of structure, though not of answering them intelligently, and observes that while the theme of incest is the real plot of *A King and No King*, 'the rest is all episode'. He has, in fact, the astonishing faculty throughout of posing the right critical questions without once getting the right answer to any of them, and without even convincing us that he wants a right answer.

Rymer's sequel, *A Short View of Tragedy* (1693), reinforces the impression that his historical sense is his strongest side. It is a history of a literary form, the drama, in eight chapters, beginning with a defence of the Greek chorus, which he believes is about to be revived among the French, followed by a chronological account of tragedy among the Greeks, the Romans, and the early Christians, of the contemptible medieval vogue of allegorical criticism, of the Renaissance of the drama in Italy, France, and England and the refinement of English by Chaucer and Waller, *Gorboduc*, of the early English pre-eminence in comedy. And finally (to show why Elizabethan tragedy will not do), comes the promised damnation of *Othello* at great length, and the dismissal of *Julius Caesar* and *Catiline*.

Rymer's notorious critique of *Othello* follows exactly the lines laid down by his attacks on Beaumont and Fletcher in the earlier volume: its fame derives only from the fact that the target now is a universally respected one. Experience has only taught Rymer

[1] *Critical Works*, edited by C. A. Zimansky (New Haven, 1956), pp. 24-5.
[2] Ibid., p. 38.

greater self-confidence in being silly-clever; the shape of the analysis is unchanged, beginning with an assertion that the source in
Cinthio has been abused, and continuing with a derisive plot-
summary and a quick, damning value-judgement ('This may be a
caution to all maidens of quality how, without their parents' con-
sent, they run away with blackamoors')[1] and a list of Shakespeare's
failures in maintaining the true dignity of tragedy based on an inflexible insistence upon character as a pure generality: Othello does
not behave like a General, except in his suicide, or Desdemona
like a lady.

And yet Dryden was impressed. He was impressed enough,
perhaps, to abandon his own thoughts of writing a general study
of English poetry. He was impressed enough to call Rymer's first
book unanswerable, and then, with positively embarrassing humility, to try to answer it himself on three occasions. His notes on
the subject, the so-called 'Heads of an Answer', are the most
combatively anti-Rymer and anti-Aristotelian of the three. The
plot, or 'fable', argues Dryden in his private jottings, is 'not the
greatest masterpiece of tragedy' – an audacious attack, this, not
only upon Rymer but upon a basic assumption of the whole school
of French Aristotelian criticism. And, in any case, he goes on,
though Greek plays may be better designed 'to cause terror and
pity', there are other ends of tragedy, which the Elizabethans did
achieve. In any case – and here Dryden's sense of history shows
itself the superior of Rymer's, which limited itself to using historical examples arbitrarily to prove a neoclassical case – Aristotle
was writing in ignorance of any tragedies but the Greek, which are
inferior to the English in certain respects, in their 'narrowness of
plot' and lack of variety; so that a Greek play, by English standards, is a 'very easy' thing to do. Besides, the English have outdone
the Greeks in dealing with several subjects such as love and friendship; and the reformation of many, rather than the moving of pity
and terror, is the proper end of tragedy; though perhaps, Dryden
adds with very characteristic caution, it all comes to the same
thing, since 'pity comprehends this concernment for the good,
and terror includes detestation for the bad'. In any case – and here
the argument is simply reversed – the Elizabethan plays can be

[1] *Critical Works*, p. 132.

justified on Rymer's principles too. They have certainly pleased, which for Rymer is the prime end of poetry. And (again a powerful historical sense emerges) 'though nature, as he objects, is the same in all places, and reason too the same, yet the climate, the age, the disposition of the people to whom the poet writes, may be so different that what pleased the Greeks would not satisfy an English audience'. English characters, too, are more credible for their imperfections, and the plays of the Elizabethans are 'more beautifully written' than those of the Greeks.

Dryden's 'Heads' show how independent he could be of neo-classical bigotry. The fact that he never published them proves that his independence was a cautious and qualified one. The two replies he did dare to publish, the prefaces to *All for Love* (1678) and to *Troilus and Cressida* (1679), are more diplomatic than the 'Heads', and fail, for this reason, to equal them in interest. Dryden's concern for Shakespeare's reputation is very clear in both, and his lasting contempt for the French theatre: 'In this nicety of manners does the excellency of French poetry consist: their heroes are the most civil people breathing; but their good breeding seldom extends to a word of sense.'[1] The essential robustness of the Elizabethan drama is not to be exchanged for a cold correctness, whatever Aristotle may appear to say. The more formal essay, 'The Grounds of Criticism in Tragedy', prefixed to *Troilus and Cressida*, is in part a careful formulation of some of the points listed in the 'Heads' a year and more before, a careful and stylish reconstruction of his objections to Rymer's attack. Aristotle's account of tragedy is conceded at once, for the sake of respectability – the published 'Grounds' is a far less radical document than the unpublished 'Heads' – though the sufficiency of Aristotle's doctrine of pity and terror is again questioned. There is some disagreeable boot-licking of Rymer: 'How defective Shakespeare and Fletcher have been in all their plots, Mr Rymer has discover'd in his criticisms: neither can we who follow them be excus'd from the same or greater errors...' Dryden kisses the rod; and, still on his best Aristotelian behaviour, he solemnly tells us that 'Shakespeare generally moves more terror, and Fletcher more compassion'. But a spirit of sneaking rebellion persists, as in the

[1] Preface, *All for Love* (1678).

mock-innocence of Dryden's discovery that only one Greek play,
the *Oedipus* of Sophocles, actually conforms to Rymer's Aristotelian requirements, or that in *Oedipus Coloneus* the hero ceases
to behave like a king: 'Sophocles . . . lets fall on purpose his tragic
stile; his hero speaks not in the arbitrary tone; but remembers, in
the softness of his complaints, that he is an unfortunate, blind old
man.' The sensitive acuteness of the comment leaves us wondering
how Dryden can ever have thought Rymer anything better than
a bigot and a boor.

The best that can be said for Rymer, perhaps, is that he provoked such replies. *A Short View*, with its more detailed attack on
Shakespeare, was answered by John Dennis (1657-1734), like
Rymer a failed dramatist, and the first Englishman to earn a living
as a literary critic. *The Impartial Critick: or Some Observations upon
a Late Book Entitled A Short View of Tragedy* (1693) is a series of
five dialogues in which Rymer's points are met after a clumsy
fashion, tragedy being conceived as a moral fable and Shakespeare
defended as possessing beauties as well as faults, though Rymer's
censures are called 'very sensible and very just'. For Dennis's *The
Genius and Writings of Shakespeare* his public, if he had one, had to
wait till 1712, when they found Shakespeare's genius abruptly
tested on Rymer's principle of Poetic Justice, by which all good
characters must end happily, and all evil characters otherwise.
Dennis is no doubt a very slightly better critic than Rymer, on the
negative ground that he lacks Rymer's passionate perversity. He
is, by the narrowest of margins, the more likely of the two to
reach a sensible conclusion. He is none the less impossibly long-
winded, a colossal bore, interesting at best for his discipleship to
Longinus; at least Rymer's essays have the virtue of brevity. And,
like Dryden and Rymer, Dennis never quite liberates himself
from the illusion that the critic's task is to legislate to poets. The
stated purpose of his *The Grounds of Criticism in Poetry* (1704) is
not, as its title might suggest, to form a tradition in critical reading, but 'to shew both by reason and examples that the use of
religion in poetry was absolutely necessary to raise it to the greatest
exaltation of which so noble an art is capable; and, on the other
side, that poetry was requisite to religion'.[1] His design, accord-

----

[1] *Critical Works*, edited by E. N. Hooker (Baltimore, 1939-43), I. 325.

ingly, is 'to restore poetry to all its greatness, and to all its innocence'.[1]

THE LATER DRYDEN

The failure of Dryden's contemporaries to create, or even follow,
a tradition of critical awareness tempts us to overrate the achievement of Dryden himself. It is, indeed, difficult to credit – almost
forty years (1664-1700) of scarcely interrupted activity as a critic.
From the appearance of the essay *Of Dramatick Poesie* in 1667 he
confined himself to prefaces, usually to his own works, and it is
difficult for us now to realize how extravagant this prefatory habit
must have seemed to his contemporaries. He had practically no
English precedents – only Ben Jonson, among the older dramatists, had made a practice of justifying himself in prefaces to his own
plays, and there was only the 1660 *Théâtre* of Corneille to give
him courage. And he failed to establish the practice in England.
Dryden's detractors in *The Rehearsal* (1672) make fun of a dramatist who has to explain his plot in printed sheets: 'I have printed
above a hundred sheets of papyr, to insinuate the plot into the
boxes,' protests Bayes, when asked if the play will be understood;
and Swift, his cousin, probably represents an anti-critical majority
in his sneer in *A Tale of a Tub* (1704): 'He has often said to me in
confidence that the world would never have suspected him to be
so great a poet, if he had not assured them so frequently in his
prefaces that it was impossible they could either doubt or forget
it';[2] or again, in a poem of Swift's last years:

> Read all the prefaces of Dryden
> For these our criticks much confide in,
> (Though meerly writ at first for filling
> To raise the volume's price a shilling).[3]

To be any sort of critic in England, in the Restoration or long
after, was to work against the popular grain. And to write as a
descriptive critic, as Dryden intermittently did, was to defy two
of the mightiest intellectual fashions of the day.

[1] Ibid., I. 328.
[2] Sect. v.
[3] 'On Poetry' (1733).

First, there was neoclassicism. Dryden was lucky to absorb his classical theories, in the first instance, in the dilute and pragmatic form in which they appear in the *Discours* of Corneille, who was profoundly and intelligently aware of the difficulties of practising them; and, as early as the essay *Of Dramatick Poesie*, he quotes with emphatic approval Corneille's dictum in the 'Discours des trois unités': ''Tis easy for theorists to judge severely . . .' By the time the full weight of French neoclassicism fell upon English criticism, in Rymer's *Tragedies of the Last Age*, Dryden – though visibly shaken by Rymer's own speculative severity – had just enough courage to answer back and go his own way. And Rymer is proof enough that high-flying neoclassical doctrine and critical analysis cannot live together: *any* fiercely doctrinaire theory of criticism, indeed, is likely to reduce the poem to the level of a mere example.

The second intellectual fashion which might have defeated Dryden as a critic was that of experimental science under the influence of Bacon and Descartes. We know as a biographical fact how impressed Dryden was by the new philosophy of science. He was a founder-member of the Royal Society from 1662, and had been made a member of a committee it had created with the object of purifying the language. His prose is rich in scientific similes and indirect echoes of Hobbes. Aubrey called him a 'great admirer' of Hobbes, and added cryptically that Dryden 'oftentimes makes use of his doctrine in his playes'.[1] Much of the impoverishment of English imagery at this time, and perhaps the death of the Metaphysical style in poetry, must be laid to the door of a generation of scientists who, after Charles II's return, insisted that the language itself must be disciplined to suit the purposes of exact observation. It is worth adding that they were equally philistine in their opposition to history, and must certainly have despised any attempt, like Dryden's, to reinterpret the drama of a past age. Descartes, in the first part of his *Discours de la méthode* (1637), dismisses literary and historical studies in these terms:

But I thought I had given enough time to languages, and even to reading old books, their stories and their fables; for to converse with those of other ages is rather like travelling . . . When you spend too much time travelling, you become a stranger in your own country;

[1] *Brief Lives*, edited by Andrew Clark (Oxford, 1898), I, 372.

and when you are too curious of things done in the past, you usually remain exceedingly ignorant of what is done today.[1]

The New Philosophy was as contemptuously anti-historical as neoclassicism, though for different reasons, and some of its contempt for the past undoubtedly rubbed off upon Dryden, especially in his early years. But the severity of the new ideas did not suit his temperament, and the mellow moralism of Montaigne, who provided the acknowledged inspiration of his prose style, superseded them in the classical Lives of Plutarch (1683), Polybius (1693), and Lucian[2] (1711), all prefixed to translations of their works by other hands. History is now the consolation and the guide of the ageing critic: historians 'teach us wisdom by the surest ways', the ways of moral example, and history, he confesses, 'has always been the most delightful entertainment of my life'. In the same Life of Plutarch he uses the word 'biography' for the first time in English, and attempts for the first time the form of the literary life which Johnson was to establish as the chief mode of our criticism a century later, in the *Lives of the English Poets*.

And yet, though his mind, as he grew into 'the tattling quality of age', flowed with increasing ease in unfashionable historical speculations, his critical achievement looks all the more sadly frustrated by his early intellectual interests. Science and neoclassicism had not prevented him from saying important things, but they had prevented him from saying them soon and in formal order. His critical genius lies scattered in several dozens of documents. His perception of the importance of historical affinities in poetry grew stronger with the years, but remained unexplored to the end, a mere passing intuition, as in the priceless hint carelessly dropped in the last of his essays, the preface to the *Fables* (1700):

Milton was the poetical son of Spencer, and Mr Waller of Fairfax; for we have our lineal descents and clans as well as other families. Spencer more than once insinuates that the soul of Chaucer was transfus'd into his body, and that he was begotten by him two hundred years after his decease. Milton has acknowledg'd to me that Spencer was his original . . .

[1] For a discussion of this passage, see R. G. Collingwood, *The Idea of History* (Oxford, 1946), pp. 59ff.
[2] Written in 1695-6, during his work on the translation of Virgil.

The affectionate study of Chaucer that follows in the same preface is richly historical in the same sense: 'He liv'd in the infancy of our poetry, and . . . nothing is brought to perfection at the first. We must be children before we grow men.' A whole tradition of literary history, in such utterances, seems upon the point of being born. But for Dryden it was already too late, and the historical sense in criticism had to wait the greater part of a century, till the literary antiquaries, till the Warton brothers and Samuel Johnson, to take root in England.

The final estimate of Dryden as a critic must be cautiously stated. 'The favourite exercise of his mind', according to Johnson, 'was ratiocination'[1] – but the use to which he commonly puts his powers of argument is self-justification, almost never the impartial exploration of an idea. Much the greater part of his criticism, the prefaces to his plays and the essay *Of Dramatick Poesie*, represents a series of stages in his career as a dramatist; they are aspects of a continuing literary war that Dryden fought with his own critics, full of the bitter sound and fury of the Restoration theatres and coffee-houses; and his later critical essays, the prefaces to his translations of Juvenal, Virgil, and the *Fables* of 1700, are rather more reflective exercises in the same ephemeral vein. His interest in theoretical ideas is slight, confined almost entirely to the first years of his career, and largely derived from Hobbes. Johnson oddly divides his criticism into two kinds, the 'didactick' and the 'defensive', but it is the defensive that predominates at every period of his life except the last ten years. Compared with critics before and after, Dryden is refreshingly egotistical ('he may be thought to mention himself too frequently', Johnson complains) and free from any legislative intent upon other poets: only in the essay *Of Dramatick Poesie* does he get very near to a general literary manifesto, and he never attempted another. He wrote the first extended examples of descriptive criticism in English – but he analysed, not for the sake of analysis, but in order to generalize afterwards for his own purposes. The logical status of his criticism, then, remains puzzling and ambiguous. It looks backwards to the Elizabethans, and forward to Samuel Johnson, and hardly seems to know itself.

The Life of Dryden, in *The Lives of the English Poets*, edited by G. Birkbeck Hill (Oxford, 1905), I, 459.

And yet, we are bound to repeat, this uncertainty cannot possibly have been present to Dryden himself. No critic, not even Johnson, seems so perfectly sure of himself and of what he is saying at the moment when he says it – and if, a year later, he believes something else, he will say so with the same disarming candour. It is this supreme literary tact, this talent for evasion and equivocation, that allows him to play several critical roles at once. But the cost of such a sense of tact is crippling: for all the superficial vigour of his prose, real critical assertions are seldom made. (The contrast with Johnson here is sharp, and all in Johnson's favour.) His achievement, ultimately, lies not in analysing much or in doing it well, but in providing the inestimable example of showing that literary analysis is possible at all.

Chapter 3

THE AUGUSTANS

POPE

No Augustan criticism looks much like Dryden's, on the face of it. Its style is, in comparison, devitalized. It lacks audacity of judgement – the audacity, say, of Dryden's praise for Shakespeare and Chaucer. It is safe, and the hostilities it risks are personal rather than critical, as in Pope's devastating portrait of Dennis.[1] And yet it accepts and consolidates the revolution that Dryden made, and advances it cautiously on several fronts.

In the first place, the Augustan contempt for French neoclassical authority is much like Dryden's, even in its ambiguities. Dryden, as in his controversy with Rymer, never attacked the rules frontally: not, at least, in any essay he ever dared to publish. The attitude of the nineteen-year-old Pope, when he wrote the *Essay on Criticism* (written 1705-9), might be Dryden's cultural nationalism put to verse. In so far as the rules are French, Pope argues, they are bad; in so far as they are ancient, and judiciously interpreted by Englishmen, they are good. The Augustan critic, like Dryden, is in the happy position of eating his cake and having it too: his claim is to be more elastic than the French, and more truly classical as well. And admittedly there are sound reasons for claiming something like this: the French neoclassical critics really did misread Aristotle. But the Augustans, like Dryden, entirely fail to identify these misreadings, so that their assertions are not much better than bluster:

> But critic-learning flourish'd most in France:
> The rules a nation, born to serve, obeys;
> And Boileau still in right of Horace sways.
> But we, brave Britons, foreign laws despis'd,
> And kept unconquer'd, and unciviliz'd;
> Fierce for the liberties of wit, and bold,
> We still defy'd the Romans, as of old.[2]

[1] The Appius of his *Essay on Criticism* (1711), ll. 584ff.   [2] Ibid., ll. 712-18.

It is a brave, unsubtle joke, the notion of an uncouth Alexander Pope, painted in woad, throwing back legions of French critics from the shores of England. Pope is evidently a little ashamed of the cultural nationalism he has picked up from Dryden, and his language is defensively jocular. Such moments of disingenuousness are the price, apparently, that Englishmen in the reign of Louis XIV were ready to pay for self-respect.

The second heritage from Dryden is a historical sense. Dryden never wrote a literary history that was altogether his own, or a literary biography of any English poet; but his sense of a historical evolution in poetry intensified with age, and by the end of his life, in the preface to the *Fables* (1700), he possessed an untutored but certain conviction that the poetry of different ages calls for different standards of interpretation. Pope and Addison incorporate this radical intuition into their critical attitudes. Pope, indeed, calls for an impossibly high level of literary scholarship to aid the critic, and sets up an ideal of academic severity which, even two and a half centuries later, looks unattainable:

> Know well each Ancient's proper character;
> His fable, subject, scope in every page;
> Religion, country, genius of his age:
> Without all these at once before your eyes,
> Cavil you may, but never criticize.[1]

It is unfortunate that he should go on to mention Homer, of all poets, and to damn Homeric critics for their anachronistic judgements. Pope, inevitably, committed anachronisms enough when he joined the ranks of Homeric critics himself, in the preface to his own version of the *Iliad* (1715). Of course no Augustan critic can match Dryden for the fineness of his historical sense; but the new age after 1700 is generally aware that a sense of the past may be a useful part of the equipment of the critic. The work of seventeenth-century antiquaries was beginning to tell, to realize its full popular effect, decades later, in Scott's Waverley novels. But no English critic in the early eighteenth century had the industry or the training to use historical methods fully in the study of English poetry. The hack-writer Gerard Langbaine (1656-92) had re-

[1] Ibid, ll. 119-23.

garded source-reading as one of his duties in assembling his encyclopedic *Account of the English Dramatick Poets* (1691), but only for 'exposing our modern plagiaries by detecting part of their thefts'; and Johnson seems to be speaking the literal truth when he praised his Oxford friend Thomas Warton in a complimentary letter (16 July 1754) on Warton's *Observations on the Fairy Queen*, which had just appeared, for being the first English critic to consider a poet's knowledge of books: 'You have shown to all who shall hereafter attempt the study of our ancient authours the way to success, by directing them to the perusal of the books which those authours had read . . . The reason why the authours which are yet read of the sixteenth century are so little understood is that they are read alone . . .[1]' And Johnson adds that he hopes his *Dictionary*, which was to appear in the following year, may remove 'some part of this ignorance'. Of all such sophisticated arts of the literary historian as these, the Augustan critics were still utterly ignorant. Their historical sense is occasional, and it is nothing more.

The third debt to Dryden is a more positive one. The Augustans practise descriptive criticism much more casually and naturally than any Restoration critic had been able to do. Swift, in *The Tale of a Tub* (1704), even talks as if, by the end of the seventeenth century, there were already too many critics about in London, and all of them bad[2]; and Pope, of course, takes up this complaint – it is the subject of much of the *Dunciad*. Indeed, if we are to believe the youthful Pope of the *Essay on Criticism*, Augustan London was as over-supplied with reviewers as London is today. The *Essay on Criticism* begins with an assertion that there are ten critics for every poet:

> Ten censure wrong for one who writes amiss.[3]

For all our inadequate knowledge of the output of scurrilous literary pamphlets in the period, the claim seems absurd. Pope is surely

---

[1] *The Letters of Samuel Johnson*, edited by R. W. Chapman (Oxford, 1952), I, 56.

[2] Section III, 'Digression Concerning Critics', where Swift complains that commendatory and learned critics no longer exist, but only fault-finders, descended from Momus and Hybris (Censure and Pride).

[3] *Essay on Criticism* (1711), l. 6.

writing as the anxious young poet, eager to forestall contempt. In fact, the Essay might be read, in its opening section at least, as an attack on any sort of descriptive criticism, a demand for some sort of poetic exemption. Pope certainly poses impossibly difficult conditions, including the ridiculous demand that nobody should be allowed to criticize who has not already established himself as a poet:

> Let such teach others who themselves excell,
> And censure freely who have written well.[1]

This sounds like hurt dignity. And yet, on surviving evidence, the Augustan record in criticism is not much more impressive in its scope than the seventeenth-century one. Pope, Swift, Defoe, Richardson, Fielding all came and went without any memorable critical pronouncement being made upon their works. On the other hand, a tradition of periodical reviewing was in process of creation; and Addison's critical essays on Milton in the *Spectator* of 1712, which were unexpectedly popular, suggest that a new kind of critical market was growing up, impatient of legislative treatises on poetry and concerned with the useful and the particular. Addison (1672-1719) begins his first essay on Milton, in January 1712, with this bracing statement of policy: 'There is nothing in Nature so irksom as general discourses, especially when they turn chiefly upon words [i.e. upon the definition of general terms]. For this reason I shall waive the discussion of that point which was started some years since, whether Milton's *Paradise Lost* may be call an heroick poem?[2] And he goes on, in a freshly empirical mood: 'Those who will not give it that title, may call it (if they please) a Divine Poem. It will be sufficient to its perfection, if it has in it all the beauties of the highest kind of poetry; and as for those who say it is not an heroick poem, they advance no more to the diminution of it than if they should say Adam is not Aeneas, nor Eve Helen.' This is plain speaking against the whole decaying tradition of the legislative critics with their 'dull receits', as Pope had recently called them.[3] Dryden's first exercises in literary analysis have, by

---

[1] Ibid., ll. 15-16.
[2] *Spectator*, no. 267 (5 January 1712).
[3] *Essay on Criticism* (1711), l. 115.

the new century, partly pushed out the old Elizabethan and neo-classical tradition of considering poems purely in terms of *genre*.

The Augustans, if they can be called the School of Dryden, are certainly Dryden with a difference. The difference lies precisely in the rise of a new public avid for criticism, a public Dryden never enjoyed. Analysis begins as a fashionable activity in the England of Queen Anne. In such new conditions, descriptive criticism can throw off its wraps and appear for what it is. All of Dryden's analyses had appeared embedded in some other form, and claim, at least, to exist for the sake of some general argument. Pope's *Essay on Criticism* is not very different in this sense, a conservative verse-treatise both in form and content, containing general advice to critics – advice on sins to be avoided being marshalled in Section 2, and the positive advice on critical virtues to be emulated in Section 3. The attitudes are purely Drydenesque, if decidedly more explicit and bold than anything Dryden usually allowed himself; for where Dryden, as a critic, is almost always circumspect and diplomatic, even sage, the *Essay on Criticism* is the work of a cheeky young poet, brashly confident at having been invited, at the age of fifteen, to mend the verses of the elderly Wycherley,[1] and ambitious to stake out a claim for himself in the domain of poetry and to forestall destructive criticism. Where Dryden tends to let the Ancient-Modern controversy go by default, for example, Pope boldly calls it a red herring:

> Some foreign writers, some our own despise;
> The Ancients only, or the Moderns prize.
> Thus wit, like faith, by each man is apply'd
> To one small sect, and all are damn'd beside . . .
> Regard not then if wit be old or new,
> But blame the false, and value still the true.[2]

Such analysis as Pope does allow himself, like the final review of critics from Aristotle to his own day, is only summary, though

[1] Some of Pope's earliest letters to Wycherley and Walsh show how directly the Essay grew out of this commission. Cf. his letters of 26 December 1704, 2 July 1706, and 29 November 1707, where the distinction emerges between true wit ('a justness of thought and a facility of expression' or, later, 'propriety') and false wit ('conceit is to nature what paint is to beauty'); and *Essay*, ll. 289ff.

[2] Ibid., ll. 394-407.

his distinction between true wit and false, and his enthusiastic attack on the Metaphysical conceit (ll. 289ff.) suggest that only the occasion is lacking for a real critical exercise upon an actual poem. Wycherley was probably well served by this sorcerer's apprentice. And yet it is clear that Pope exploited his critical interests too early to exploit them well. The Essay is clever, but it is the indecent, puppyish cleverness of a precocious boy, and it does not represent an advance on Dryden except in terms of virtuosity.

ADDISON

Addison certainly does, if we are thinking in terms of a technical advance. His intelligence, beside Dryden's, is mean, and his careful prose looks flabby when compared with Dryden's modulated gusto and superb variety of pace and mood. But it is clear that, with Addison, something important has happened to English criticism. He may not have fathered much good work, or achieved much himself, but as a symptom he is extraordinary. With him the revolution is complete: a revolution from law to actuality, from interference with the poet in his act of creation to help and advice for the thousands who read. Admittedly from this concern with actuality, new generalizations arose at once. But they were generalizations about the reader, not about the poet, and it is the reader of poetry who firmly occupies the centre of interest betweeen the death of Dryden and the publication of the 1800 preface to the *Lyrical Ballads*. The Man of Taste is king: the consumer, at last, has won his right of choice. In theoretical criticism – and the eighteenth century is overwhelmingly the age of critical theory – the issue is now joined not on conformity to precept ('Is *Paradise Lost* an epic?'), but on the reader's response. By which of the five senses is the human imagination most gratified? How is true taste to be defined? And if a democracy of taste, a mere counting of heads, is not sufficient, what *does* constitute true taste in reading? These are issues which Dryden never once raises; and Pope raises them for professional critics only. Addison, in the *Spectator* essays, raises them for all polite society.

His programme, at least, is inviting: 'I shall endeavour as much as possible to establish among us a taste of polite writing.'[1] He had

[1] *Spectator*, no. 58 (7 May 1711).

already made it clear in the *Tatler* what he thought was the trouble with English taste – people could not see the wood for the trees:

> Ned [Softly] is indeed a true English reader, incapable of relishing the great and masterly strokes of this art [of poetry]; but wonderfully pleased with the little Gothic ornaments of epigrammatical conceits, turns, points, and quibbles which are so frequent in the most admired of our English poets, and practised by those who want genius and strength to represent, after the manner of the Ancients, simplicity in its natural beauty and perfection.[1]

This looks sound in principle, even if it is obviously designed to rule out the densely intellectual effects of the Metaphysical poets: it shows that Addison cares about general coherence and unity, that he has some interest in the structural properties of poems. And he is equally severe against the procrustean neoclassical critic who, though he attempts general judgements, does so only by rule-of-thumb: 'one that, without entering into the sense and soul of an author, has a few general rules which, like mechanical instruments, he applies to the works of every writer'.[2] At this very early stage, we seem to be promised something subtle and shrewd.

Addison's critical papers in the *Spectator* fall into four groups, two of them theoretical. First, there are the essays on 'wit', from April to December 1711 (especially nos. 35, 47, 61-3, 140, 249), where a theory of rhetoric is evolved out of Locke's distinction between 'wit' and 'judgement' in the *Essay Concerning Humane Understanding* (1690) (II, 2). It would be difficult to say whom Addison is addressing in these papers, whether poets or readers of poetry; but it is clear that his critical sense is more articulate than that of the Pope who wrote the *Essay on Criticism*, a poem which appeared in May 1711, while Addison's first critical series was in progress. True wit, according to Addison, is based on a 'congruity of ideas', and sometimes on their 'opposition'; false wit on a mere congruity of letters, syllables, and words (as in anagrams, puns, and figure-poems); with a third category of 'mixed wit' in between, 'a composition of pun and true wit' in which Cowley and Waller excelled – a remarkable identification of the special, alien

---

[1] *Tatler*, no. 163 (25 April 1710).
[2] Ibid., no. 165 (29 April 1710).

quality of pre-1660 poetry.[1] Addison's tolerance of the Metaphysical style is just wide enough to encourage us to feel that we
are already in a new world where the reader, and not the poet,
provides the audience of criticism, for his threefold distinction
admits not only of the 'true' and of the 'false', but of a third, historical category as well. He offers reasons for admiring the Metaphysical style without making any attempt to recommend it to
living poets. Secondly, there are the two essays of May 1711 on
the ballad 'Chevy Chase' (nos. 70, 74), where the shades of the
neoclassical critics are adroitly placated by a demonstration that a
medieval ballad may reveal Homeric and Virgilian influence and
possess the Aristotelian virtues. This clears the way for Addison's
work as a critic: he could not have analysed *Paradise Lost* in an
atmosphere so free of ancient precept without first poking mild
fun at the conservatives. (Dryden, after all, had used a similar
strategy against Rymer in his preface to *Troilus and Cressida* (1679)
by showing that even Sophocles had broken the rules.) The Chevy
Chase issues had a surprising sale, and may have encouraged
Addison to undertake the papers on *Paradise Lost*, from January to
May 1712.[2] And finally, there is the series 'On the pleasures of the
imagination' of June and July 1712 (nos. 411-21), an analysis of
taste in poetry, where the pleasures of the imagination are eccen-
trically defined as 'such as arise from visible objects, either when
we have them actually in our view, or when we call up their ideas
into our minds by painting, statues, descriptions . . .' (no. 411) – an
account that predicts in some measure the Augustan poetic neglect
of values other than visual ones.

Addison's analysis of Milton in the *Spectator* achieved notoriety
at once, and was collected into a volume as early as 1719, to become the foundation of orthodox views of Milton for the rest of
the century, and not only in England. According to Tickell, the
materials had been collected over many years, but the success of
the first papers evidently surprised Addison himself, encouraging
him to expand his scheme to eighteen weekly numbers – six on
general questions about *Paradise Lost*, followed by twelve papers,
one on each book of the poem. Even Addison cannot quite free

[1] *Spectator*, no. 62 (11 May 1711).
[2] *Spectator*, nos. 267-369 (weekly).

himself from the seventeenth-century habit of setting up a list of
rules by which the poem is to be judged. But at least the rules are
Addison rather than 'Aristotle', and the formality merely an opening strategy. Refreshingly, he dismisses the question as to whether
Paradise Lost is an epic or not at the outset – but goes on to contradict himself by analysing it according to the rules of the epic,
calling for a plot of which the action is one, entire, and great. The
last of the six general essays (no. 297) lists the defects of the poem:
the 'implex' plot, in which the fortunes of the hero, Adam, decline, is 'not so proper for an heroic poem' as for a tragedy such
as *Oedipus*; the hero is defeated, which is unheroic of him – but
then (striking out boldly in defence of an archaic theory), perhaps
the hero is not Adam at all, but Christ; there are too many digressions; the images ('sentiments') are too quaint and punning, the
heathen references inappropriate to a Christian poem, and the
technical terms indecorous. The book-by-book analysis that follows only confirms how very far from the text Addison is. At a
glance, its abundance of quotations looks impressive. But Addison's
comments on his quotations have all the vagueness of a schoolboy's ('wonderfully poetical', 'truly sublime'), and he almost
never ventures a strictly descriptive or interpretative statement.
Casual value-judgements are the only mode of proceeding. For
the Augustan Man of Taste, it soon appears, intelligent inquiry
concerning the meaning of a passage is barely a possibility. Whatever is obscure is merely bad; the critic's function is simply to
point and enthuse: 'to point out its particular beauties, and to
determine wherein they consist' (no. 369), as Addison explains in
his concluding paper. And 'wherein', for Addison, means only
'under what preconceived category' (the Sublime, the Soft, the
Natural). Much of the awful glibness of the Augustan aesthetic,
its pathetic readiness to take shelter behind a modish terminology
of criticism, is plainly visible in the language of this ambitious but
complacent critic.

FIELDING

The first century of descriptive criticism in English concerns itself
almost exclusively with drama and the epic, and other literary
forms are strikingly neglected. One youthful giant, the novel, is

largely overlooked until the age of the Victorians. Indeed anyone who still thinks that criticism has regularly existed to serve, as a secondary aid, the cause of literary 'creation' should be invited at once to look at two moments in our literary tradition. The first, in the early seventeenth century, is the Metaphysical poetry of Donne, Herbert, Crashaw, and others. We might expect a tradition that dominated English poetry for a half century and more to have left some substantial critical comment: the more so since that tradition was complex both in its learning and in its logical structure. But not at all. Metaphysical criticism is simply a blank in its own century, and not much better for two centuries after. Indeed hardly anyone thought it worth while analysing a Donne poem until, with Grierson's edition of 1912 and the new Imagist fashion in poetry, the case for analysis suddenly looked urgent. The second negative instance is the rise of the English novel in the decades that followed Defoe's *Robinson Crusoe* (1719), the age of Richardson and Fielding. The novel-form is an accomplished fact in England by the middle of the eighteenth century; the major form, at least by any quantitative estimate, from Scott's *Waverley* (1814). And yet where is the mass of novel criticism that, by any naïve expectation, we should look to find in the age of the Georges? It is simply not there. Richardson's novels provoked a few pamphlets devoted to the question whether they were calculated to corrupt public morals. The anonymous *An Examen of the History of Tom Jones* (1750), by the unknown 'Orbilius', is an abusive attack upon Fielding's moral system innocent of any notion of literary form. The contemporary debate over Sterne's novels was concerned with the propriety of a clergyman writing such works at all; Sterne's technical innovations passed without comment until seized upon by Virginia Woolf in the 1920s.[1] Whatever we may think the role of the critic should be, it is obvious that he has not in fact served as the poet's interpreter, forever at hand to inform and explain. The English poet has usually been forced to act as his own interpreter, and the circumstances in which he turns critic

---

[1] *Illustrations of Sterne* (1798), a study of Sterne's borrowings from Rabelais and Robert Burton by John Ferriar (1761-1815), a Scottish physician in Manchester, remains an exceptional study in the void of eighteenth-century criticism of the novel.

have been severely limited by his own temperament and by the uncertainties of finding a critical audience.

Criticism of the novel, especially, has proved the slowest of starters, and only Fielding among English novelists before Henry James felt the call strongly enough to yield to it. And Fielding's attempt (let us face it at once) was a false start. His own critical interests diminish steadily during his career as a novelist. He failed to create a tradition, and had no disciples. For some fifty years after his death in 1754, during the very years in which the novel established itself as a dominant form, criticism returned to poetry, as in Johnson's *Lives*, or expended itself on aesthetic theories like Burke's and Reynolds's. Journals such as *The Monthly Review* (1749-1845) and Smollett's *Critical Review* (1756-1817), it is true, frequently 'reviewed' current novels, but largely in terms of plot-summaries, and though the remaking of literary periodicals early in the nineteenth century improved the situation a little, it is still significant that Jane Austen's novels passed unnoticed by the re-viewers, apart from Scott's own generous welcome to *Emma* in the *Quarterly Review* (1816). Hazlitt's sixth lecture in his *Lectures on the English Comic Writers* (1819) and Scott's laborious imitation of Johnson in his *Lives of the Novelists* (1821-4) are feeble palliatives. Even the Victorian critics tended to avoid the novel: only one of Arnold's *Essays in Criticism* is about a novelist,[1] and that a Russian. Fielding apart, there is no attempt in England to give the novel a critical respectability until the articles of George Eliot and her companion G. H. Lewes in reviews in the 1840s and 1850s, and nothing we can begin to call an aesthetic of the novel until the present century, in the prefaces of Henry James (1907-9).

The claim of Henry Fielding (1707-54) to pioneer novel criti-cism in English, then, is beyond all challenge. Indeed he is so far ahead of fashion as to be not so much a pioneer as a lost and lonely explorer. This adventurer never returned. His criticism, which is

---

[1] 'Count Leo Tolstoi', *Fortnightly Review* (December 1887), reprinted in *Essays in Criticism: Second Series* (1888). At the beginning of this essay Arnold talks of the English and French novel as already a thing of the past: 'The famous English novelists have passed away, and have left no successors of like fame.' This is a fair comment on the immediate situation in the 1880s; but it does not explain why Arnold kept so quiet about Dickens, Thackeray, and George Eliot while they were alive.

almost entirely contained in the three prefaces to *Joseph Andrews* (1742) and in the eighteen prefaces to each 'book' of *Tom Jones* (1749), is an attempt, unique in its fullness, to respectabilize the novel by invoking and adapting neoclassical doctrines, such as those popularized in England by Rymer and Dennis, in its support. If this attempt was a failure – and I think that, by the time he was working on the second novel, it was already clear to Fielding himself that it was – there is something grandiose in the spectacle of this middle-aged magistrate, a full century before George Eliot, attempting to invest so parvenu a form with a classic dignity of its own.

Two great limiting factors forestalled success to Fielding's endeavours. The first was his training as a dramatist. His success on the stage cut short by the Licensing Act of 1737, at the age of thirty, Fielding laboriously adapted his talent for farce to the unaccustomed task of writing novels. The adaptation was never complete in the novels themselves, and the theatricality of a good deal of Fielding's fiction clashes oddly with his theories of classic form. You cannot indulge a taste for bedroom farce and pretend at the same time that a concern for society and for epic breadth are the motive-forces of your work. Second, Fielding suffers from a contemporary incoherence in theories of the comic. It is a little hard to call upon the first critic of the novel not only to advance a coherent account of the novel itself, but to concoct as well an explanation of why people laugh. And yet, if the novel is to be limited by definition, as Fielding limited it, to the *comic* epic in prose, there can be no doubt that some sort of account of the comic is called for. Earlier English critics had not helped much: Dryden's account of what constitutes good satire is exhilarating but not really helpful:

There is . . . a vast difference between the slovenly butchering of a man, and the fineness of a stroke that separates the head from the body, and leaves it standing in its place. A man may be capable, as Jack Ketch's wife said of his servant, of a plain piece of work, a bare hanging; but to make a malefactor die sweetly was only belonging to her husband.[1]

[1] 'A Discourse Concerning the Original and Progress of Satire' (1693).

'Fine raillery' was already a fine art when Pope was an infant. It was the supreme test of truth, God's cure for man's extravagant fancy, according to Shaftesbury's *Characteristicks* (1711). And a form of power, too: one remembers Pope's terrible moment of self-congratulation:

> Yes, I am proud; I must be proud to see
> Men not afraid of God, afraid of me.[1]

But it is useless to look to Dryden, or Pope, or Swift, for a realized theory of comedy; and Shaftesbury's doctrine that all evil is ridiculous is too remote from public opinion to be of much use to a popular novelist. Poor Fielding starts from scratch.

The deep contradiction in Fielding's theory of the novel appears in his first and most ambitious essays, the prefaces to *Joseph Andrews*. No doubt the novel itself contains its contradictions: it seems almost torn apart by its social and picaresque elements on the one hand, and its very 'literary' quality on the other, as a reply to (and part-parody of) Richardson's *Pamela* (1740) – the whole overlaid with a thick layer of moralism, largely in Parson Adams's mouth, so that there is unfortunately never any doubt as to what we are meant to think. Without the preface, we could only guess at what went wrong: with it, we know. Fielding has been sadly seduced by the neoclassical doctrine of generality into attempting two irreconcilable objects. On the one hand, the novels themselves suggest that Fielding wants to be what Scott Fitzgerald called a 'Marxian' novelist, or one deeply aware of the social context of the individual. In this sense Fielding is trying to be more of a Defoe than a Richardson, though he is too respectful of established society to explore deep. Against Richardson's conviction of the self-sufficiency of virtue, he insists upon virtue as conditioned by circumstance and experience: *Tom Jones* is set against the real and recent fact of the Jacobite Forty-Five, and the title-page insists that it is a 'History'. But, on the other hand, Fielding seeks to invest the novel with the dignity that Aristotle had accorded, in the *Poetics*, to all poetry – that of imitation – and his use of the word *history* is seriously equivocal:

Is not such a book as that which records the achievements of the

---

[1] 'Epilogue to the Satires' (1738), ll. 208-9.

renowned Don Quixote more worthy the name of a history than even Mariana's [i.e. a Latin history of Spain (1592-1605)]: for whereas the latter is confined to a particular period of time, and to a particular nation, the former is the history of the world in general . . .[1]

There is not much use arguing with a critic who will juggle so shamelessly with his own terms. We are left unimpressed by Fielding's ironic proposition in the rest of the chapter – it is entitled 'Matter prefatory in praise of Biography' – that novelists are biographers, or the kind of historian that describes not a whole period, but the life of an individual. Fielding's irony is laboured and flat, and the biographer-analogy reveals nothing that helps. In fact, for all his pretence at particularity, Fielding is putting a familiar neoclassical case: 'The lawyer is not only alive, but hath been so these 4,000 years . . . Mrs Tow-wouse is coeval with our lawyer; and tho' perhaps during the changes which so long an existence must have passed through, she may in her turn have stood behind the bar at an inn; I will not scruple to affirm, she hath likewise in the revolution of ages sat on a throne.' Such lawyers and landladies, existing out of time and place, are no subject for biographers.

Fielding's portentous theory of the 'comic epic in prose', elaborated in the preface to *Joseph Andrews*, is similarly familiar in its assumptions; but far more interesting in its conclusions. True, it is consistent neither with itself nor with the novel it exists to justify. But it is an honest attempt to define the new dignity of the novel. Fielding is very much aware of his own originality and of the probability of being misunderstood. *Joseph Andrews*, he explains in the opening paragraph, represents a 'kind of writing which I do not remember to have seen hitherto attempted in our language'. The Epic, he goes on, like the Drama, has a comic form as well as a tragic; Homer, according to Aristotle, wrote a comic epic the *Margites* (now lost) as well as the *Iliad*. Further, the epic may be in prose as well as in verse – though verse is natural to the epic. Such a form, the comic epic in prose, is not to be confused with stage-comedy or the serious prose romance. It differs from comedy in that 'its action is more extended and comprehensive, containing a much larger circle of incidents, and introducing a greater variety

[1] *Joseph Andrews* (1742), III, i.

of characters'; and it differs from the prose romance (and here Fielding lands himself in endless difficulties) in its ludicrous diction and its disposition to parody: 'In the diction, I think, burlesque itself may be sometimes admitted', chiefly in the battles, for the delectation of the classical reader. Fielding's love of 'burlesque', or parody, is his besetting sin. He had learned to love it in his mock-heroic play *Tom Thumb* (1730) before he abandoned the theatre – 'I have had some little success on the stage this way,' he confesses modestly – and he was fatally aware that nothing was better calculated to win a quick laugh. But, in the novels, it seduces him into spoiling effects: he introduces the very sympathetic Joseph Andrews in his eighth chapter with a mock-epic description of night which quite ruins the entrance of his young hero ('Now the rake Hesperus had called for his breeches . . .'); and he treats Sophia Western, the very pattern of feminine perfection, just as badly in *Tom Jones*: 'Hushed be every ruder breath. May the heathen ruler of the winds confine in iron chains the boisterous limbs of noisy Boreas . . .' (IV, ii). This is the facetiousness of the hearty classical scholar: Fielding probably felt a gentlemanly contempt for Defoe's demand for historical accuracy in the *Iliad* and for Richardson's priggish dislike of its 'savage spirit'. He calls for readers of stronger stomach, and his burlesque style in scenes of violence constitutes a kind of toughening course for moral greenhorns – as in *Tom Jones*, v, 8, where the village mob attack a pregnant Molly Seagrim in the churchyard. But parody is a tyrannous master unless, as in Joyce's *Ulysses*, it is skilfully handled within a firmly designed plan. In Fielding's case, only *Amelia* (1751), with its echoes of the *Aeneid*, shows much sign of a structural interest in parody – but by then the parody is too occasional to matter much. The uncomfortable question remains; is the comic epic essentially a work of literary pastiche, a parody of the classical epic, or is it full-blown moral comedy? Fielding wants to have it both ways, and in both theory and practice he seems oddly unaware that he cannot.

Fielding's theory of the Comic ('the Ridiculous', he calls it), which forms the second part of the Preface to *Joseph Andrews*, only confirms this sense of confusion. 'The only course of the true Ridiculous', he announces boldly, 'is affectation.' One supposes he cannot have read *Joseph Andrews*. The funniest character in the novel is beyond all question Parson Adams, whose simple-minded sincerity is unqualified. As a matter of fact, Fielding's honest characters are usually more ridiculous than his affected ones: Adams is much funnier than the nymphomaniac Lady Booby, who pretends to a 'niceness' of chastity she cannot live up to, and is rather frightening in the process. Jonathan Wild, too, that prince of hypocritical scoundrels, seems too terrible to be genuinely 'ridiculous', though other readers than myself have been drawn to laughter. And then, not content with a false theory of the source of the Comic, Fielding goes on to propose a further distinction that does not work: 'Now affectation proceeds from one of these two causes: vanity or hypocrisy. For as vanity puts us on affecting false characters, in order to purchase applause; so hypocrisy sets us on an endeavour to avoid censure, by concealing our vices under an appearance of their opposite virtues.' But, as he frankly adds, we tend to be hypocritical because we are vain, so that the distinction does not amount to much. In any case it is not observable in his novels, where hypocrites abound and pure vanity is scarcely ever in question.

No wonder Fielding's own critical certainties, as represented by the *Joseph Andrews* prefaces, seem to have crumbled in the seven years that divide this novel from *Tom Jones*. True, there is more criticism in the second novel, quantitatively, than in the first – all eighteen books lead off with a critical chapter. But it is all occasional. The *Tom Jones* prefaces make no attempt to erect a system. They occasionally make a gesture of acknowledgement to the old epic theory of the novel – 'prosai-comi-epic writing', Fielding calls it in Book v – but they make no attempt to defend or elaborate abstract issues in which the novelist seems to have lost all interest. And they diminish fairly steadily throughout the novel, both in length and in substance. By Book v – the most interesting of all in its preface – Fielding seems ready to throw in his hand, and few of the remaining prefaces are better than jokes. They are only there at all, Fielding explains in v, for an effect of contrast with the comedy of the novel itself: 'These soporific parts are so many scenes of Serious artfully interwoven, in order to contrast and set off the rest . . . In this light, then, or rather in this darkness,

I would have the reader to consider these initial essays.' Fielding's defensive facetiousness, as usual, fails to obscure the truth: he is finished with criticism. And yet his new distaste for analysis, as revealed in *Tom Jones*, is based upon a profound intuition that English criticism is on the wrong track. The legislative role of criticism, he insists, is an illusion, in so far as the neoclassical critics base their rules on observation of an alien literary tradition. The dramatic unities are a mere shibboleth, he contends, sixteen years before Johnson's Preface to Shakespeare (1765) exposed the same fallacy, and modern critics offend in that they 'adhere to the lifeless letter of law and reject the spirit'. 'We have not the profoundest veneration', he goes on, for 'the authority of *ipse dixit.*' This is spirited language, even when we remember that Fielding failed to devise a mode of analysis to compete with the arbitrary system he had grown to hate. His theories of the Comic and of the Novel-as-History are equally incoherent, and have no influence; his grandiose attempt, in *Joseph Andrews*, to give the novel classical status by re-defining its *genre* in terms of the epic is impressive only in its recognition that the novel needed status, and deserved it. No wonder, after such a false start, if the novel had to wait for a century or more before it found a critical tradition worthy of itself. But Fielding's attempt to explain and justify his own fiction in prefaces, as Dryden had sought to justify his plays, still looks audacious and brave. The silence all about it is so very profound.

Chapter 4

SAMUEL JOHNSON

WITH Samuel Johnson (1709-84), English criticism achieves greatness on a scale that any reader can instantly recognize. *The Lives of the Poets* stand four-square as the foundation-stone of our critical tradition, and they need no concessive defence of a 'historical' kind: the Life of Pope, for instance, is still the best general account of Pope in existence. The task is not to justify or recommend – Johnson's *Lives* need to be recommended about as much as the Odes of Keats – but to defend Johnson from his own fan-club of devotees. For in spite of several notable calls-to-order, the Johnson of the Johnsonian's imagination still exerts more influence than the Johnson of the *Rambler*, or even of the *Lives*: a burly, irreverent iconoclast, half Falstaff, half Winston Churchill, shouting down the pedants in the cause of common sense and seeking (as an American critic has put it) 'to subvert accepted critical dogmas and to deliver literature from the fetters of prescriptive criticism'.[1] This does not sound remotely like the Johnson of *Rambler*, no. 92: 'It is . . . the task of criticism to establish principles, to exalt opinion to knowledge, and to distinguish between those means of pleasing which depend upon known causes and rational deduction from the nameless and inexplicable elegancies which appeal wholly to the fancy . . .'

The tone of voice is positively schoolmasterly. And not only the tone: the sense, too, is deeply 'prescriptive' or legislative. Johnson certainly believed that the object of criticism was, in a very literal sense, to lay down the law, to ascertain and apply general principles of poetic excellence. Nor does the man-in-the-street image of Johnson, or that of the common man raised to a higher power, find much support in the texts. Boswell reveals one of his

[1] W. R. Keast, 'The Theoretical Foundations of Johnson's Criticism' in *Critics and Criticism Ancient and Modern*, edited by R. S. Crane (Chicago, 1952), p. 393.

terrors – that of death – and Reynolds another which we might have guessed from Boswell, and indeed from his very association with Boswell: his terror of loneliness.[1] And Johnson's neurotic sensibility is a significant element in his perception of literature. Boswell tells how 'he read Shakespeare at a period so early that the speech of the ghost in *Hamlet* terrified him when he was alone',[2] and we are at first tempted to dismiss the story as a childish phase. But not at all: some of Johnson's most mature criticism is conducted just this side of screaming-point. He is the only editor of Shakespeare one can imagine making a comment like this on the fifth act of *Othello*: 'I am glad that I have ended my revisal of this dreadful scene. It is not to be endured.'[3] Such sensitivities do not make Johnson a better critic. They merely make him a more interesting 'case'. But they do dispose of the *persona* which deceived few of his intimates.

Other misconceptions are more subtle. It is not much use, for example, to read Johnson in search of evidences of 'close reading'. It may be true that, of all eighteenth-century critics, he gets closest to his texts. He quotes liberally – but so did Addison in his Milton papers, and to small purpose. More than that, he actually comments upon quotations in language which is sometimes descriptive enough to admit of real distinctions. Still, it should be clear that Johnson would not shine in a modern practical-criticism class. His mind does not settle: it darts. In his passion for knowledge, including remote and useless knowledge, he is more of a Saintsbury than an Empson. On entering a strange house, we are told, he went straight to the bookcase and read the backs of books; and, antiquary-like, he recognized that knowledge was of two kinds: 'We know a subject ourselves, or we know where we can find information upon it.'[4] It was the second order of knowledge he excelled in. 'From his earliest years', Boswell tells us, 'he loved to read poetry, but hardly ever read any poem to an end,'[5] and he once asked an acquaintance incredulously: 'Sir, do *you* read books

[1] Sir Joshua Reynolds, *Portraits* (New Haven, 1952), p. 68: 'Solitude to him was horror. . . . Any company to him was better than none.'

[2] *The Life of Samuel Johnson* (1791), (the year 1729).

[3] *Johnson on Shakespeare*, edited by Walter Raleigh (Oxford, 1908), p. 200.

[4] *Life of Johnson* (18 April 1775).

[5] Ibid. (1729).

through?[1] This is not the language of the close critical analyst. It suggests virtues of quite another kind: momentary but brilliant insights, a gift for perceiving relationships, certainty of judgement, breadth. And these are precisely the virtues of Johnson's criticism.

And finally, Johnson is an unambiguously historical critic, and the true father of historical criticism in English. In him, Dryden's faint intuition of a historical order of 'schools' and 'influences' in English poetry is solidly realized. We do Johnson a resounding injustice in supposing that his greatest talent was for conversation. Pre-eminently, he was a scholar. Oxford's honorary doctorate was no accident: Johnson designed his career after arriving in London in 1737, after the first dreary years of hackwork, to pivot upon the *Dictionary* of 1755, the greatest work of English literary scholarship before that of the Victorian philologists; and he confirmed his reputation as a scholar ten years later, with the edition of Shakespeare (1765). Even in the *Dictionary* his purpose was a critical one, as he explained to Warton,[2] and its full title reveals how: *A Dictionary of the English Language: in which the words are deduced from their originals, and illustrated in their different significations by examples from the best writers.* This is a programme for editors; it opens out into vast inquiries involving textual criticism, source-studies, semantics. Not that Johnson himself foresaw all these possibilities, though the latter part of the preface to Shakespeare is an astonishingly comprehensive account of the duties of a critical editor. But a literary career that begins with the first historical dictionary in English, establishes itself with an annotated edition of Shakespeare, and ends with a collection of literary biographies, has about it an air of positively formidable solidity, and one wonders how Johnson's triumphs as a historical critic come to be mentioned so seldom. The answer, this time, is not only Boswell, though Boswell is always a large part of the answer to any question concerning the Johnson myth. The responsibility for this conspiracy of silence must rest squarely with critics of our own age. They have used Johnsonian criticism as if it were a schoolboy's idea of *Hamlet,* a ragbag of quotations to be discussed, at the point of an imperative, by hapless examinees. The sweep and scholarship

[1] Ibid. (19 April 1773).
[2] Quoted p. 60, above.

of any critic would vanish under so strangely selective a neglect.

So much for the myth. But certainly oddities in Johnson's career remain, such as may justifiably diminish any tendency towards 'prescriptive reverence'. The first is his laziness. This is not much in doubt: one thinks of the carelessness of detail in his scholarly works, the significant silences, years long, in his career, the bland facility of many of the *Lives*. In one of his last letters to Langton he talks of 'that voluntary debility' or indolence which 'will, if it is not counteracted by resolution, render in time the strongest faculties lifeless . . .' (12 July 1784). Johnson, it is true, had the wonderful ability to cultivate an indolence that did not kill his talents, but merely held them in suspension. His finest criticism was written in the last seven years of his life, after a writing silence of a dozen years. But again and again (and especially in the *Lives*, which were written at speed) we remark in the loose ends of his arguments the price that he paid.

And then there is his failure as a poet. Johnson's career is at least in the right order, in Baudelairean terms: his poetry turned to criticism. But whether it 'turned' in any very creative sense, as it did with Coleridge and Eliot, we may reasonably doubt. Even the eagerness of the twentieth century to find much in little where eighteenth-century poetry is concerned has not found a great deal to praise in the verse-satires *London* (1738) and *The Vanity of Human Wishes* (1749), and T. S. Eliot's essay puts one of them in the dock for its 'feigned indignation'.[1] I cannot see that Johnson's early years as a poet taught him anything that was critically useful to him: the very faults of his own poems, such as their excessive generalization, are among his own blind-spots as a critic in middle and later life. This failure accounts for, but does not excuse, a certain unctuous severity that occasionally reminds one of Rymer, and a very general lack of intimacy with the creative act. Whether Johnson praises or blames, he sits remotely in judgement, and everywhere except in the *Life of Richard Savage* (1744) we feel that his early literary struggles have been willingly forgotten. Admittedly, his criticism gains in dignity: Johnson is the first English critic who writes as if he were the equal of the greatest of modern poets. But dignity is no good substitute for sympathy.

[1] *On Poetry and Poets* (New York, 1957), p. 205.

Johnson's criticism, which was all written after the age of forty, falls into four groups. First, there are the periodical essays of his middle years, where the critical interest is largely concentrated in a dozen papers in the *Rambler* (1750-2).[1] Second, there is the *Dictionary* (1755), itself a critical endeavour as well as a programme and aid for future criticism. Thirdly, there is the edition of Shakespeare (1765), preceded by the *Proposals for Printing the Dramatick Works of Shakespeare* (1756). And fourthly and most substantially, there are the *Lives* of 1779-81, which crown his career. This career possesses a certain symmetry which is partly deliberate. The *Rambler* papers contain Johnson's critical theory: here, if only for a moment, he joins in the Augustan and post-Augustan battle of aesthetics, but in his own sceptical vein. The *Dictionary* and the Shakespeare preface establish his more novel pretensions to be not merely a man of taste but a literary scholar too. And in the *Lives* he exploits his learned reputation to evaluate the English poets of the past hundred years: an inquiry into taste, but in anti-Augustan style, since taste is founded now upon sound scholarship and wide reading. Johnson's ordering of his career is so good that it would be impertinent to depart from it.

First, the *Rambler*. After one or two occasional papers of a critical interest (such as no. 37, where his account of the pastoral is a good deal more sympathetic than in the Life of Milton a quarter of a century later), Johnson enters the lists of the aesthetic battle with no. 92 (2 February 1751). The search for good taste, he insists, can only be considered historically and relatively: what is beautiful to one generation is ugly to the next.

Beauty . . . is relative and comparative . . . and therefore Boileau justly remarks that the works which have stood the test of time . . . have a better claim to our regard than any modern can boast, because the long continuance of their reputation proves that they are adequate to our faculties, and agreeable to nature. It is, however, the task of criticism to establish principles. . . .[2]

Certain major elements in the Johnsonian aesthetic emerge at once.

[1] The principal critical papers are nos. 37 (on the pastoral), 92 (on onomatopoeia), 125 (against tragi-comedy), 156 (against some dramatic rules), and 158 (on the authority of the Ancients).

[2] The quotation is continued on p. 75, above.

First, Johnson accepts the Augustan revolution whereby (as in Addison's Milton papers of 1712) criticism is openly designed for the reader rather than for the poet; Johnson, like the Augustans, regards the formation of public taste as his first duty. Secondly, he is sceptical of current theoretical criticism in its attempt to define good taste. His argument, on this level, is impatient and dismissive: good books are books which have survived. It is not we who sit in judgement over great literature, but great literature – distinguished by its lasting power – that sits in judgement over us. To ascertain the essence of the Beautiful, he continues with airy scorn, 'would perhaps require a very great part of the life of an Aristotle and Plato'. The general cast of Johnson's mind is vigorously anti-theoretical. 'Definitions are hazardous':[1] such sentiments are in sharp defiance of an age much in love with abstract critical terminology. This is not to say that Johnson does not have his critical theories. But he is strongly averse to arguing them at length.

Johnson's theory of literary excellence, which we are obliged to snatch at as he runs, claims as its foundation the practice – but only the practice – of the Ancients. The authority of classical *criticism*, i.e. Aristotle, is largely dismissed. Ancient literature, simply by virtue of its survival, is a court of appeal of ultimate excellence, and laws of excellence are to be deduced from it by the conscientious critic. Moreover, whatever falls outside such laws is probably bad. Johnson does not even pretend to be a liberator from the critically prescriptive. Some laws, admittedly – such as the limit of two or three actors upon the stage at any one moment – are silly and ought to be discarded: Johnson is very hot against 'literary dictators', 'blind reverence',[2] and some aspects of 'the tyranny of prescription'. 'Many rules', he complains in no. 156, 'have been advanced . . . without consulting nature or reason.' But 'nature' means the practice of the ancient poets, and 'reason' the historical sense that enables the informed critic to interpret their practice in the light of existing conditions. Johnson is very far from seeking an end to rule. His object, as a theoretical critic, is not to repeal the neoclassical laws, but to amend them. The alternative to rule is,

---

[1] *Rambler*, no. 125 (28 May 1751).
[2] Ibid., no. 158 (21 September 1751).

for Johnson, merely awful: 'the anarchy of ignorance' and 'the caprices of fancy'.[1]

But the theory, tight and coherent as it looks, contains at least two escape-clauses, of which Johnson avails himself often in the Preface to Shakespeare and in the *Lives*:

1. The effective survival of ancient poetry is a debatable issue. Can the pastoral be said to have survived? In *Rambler* no. 37 Johnson believes it has, and suggests how ancient practice should be interpreted by the modern poet, and in what sense Spenser in the *Shepheardes Calender* has taken a false path: 'In writing or judging of pastoral poetry, neither the authors nor criticks of later times seem to have paid sufficient regard to the originals left us by antiquity; but having entangled themselves with unnecessary difficulties and advanced principles which, having no foundation in the nature of things, are wholly to be rejected . . .' Nature, as usually in Johnson, equals the Ancients. But the passage certainly suggests the modern pastoral is a viable form. A quarter of a century later, in the Life of Milton, *Lycidas* is roundly condemned for its pastoral frame: 'Its form is that of a pastoral, easy, vulgar, and therefore disgusting.' Evidently the survival of ancient practice is an issue where Johnson allowed himself a certain latitude.

2. The tradition, with its roots deep in classical poetry, is itself subject to alteration. 'Every new genius produces some innovation which, when invented and approved, subverts the rules which the practice of foregoing authors had established.'[2] Without this escape-clause, Johnson would indeed be in an embarrassing position in his defence of the Augustan poets: there is nothing much like Pope's *Rape of the Lock* in the literature of the Ancients. And certainly the concession is sensible. Too sensible. It admits exceptions vast enough to destroy any usefulness the original principle may have had.

Johnson's critical theory, conscientious and scholarly as it looks, is not in fact much better than an umbrella to shelter under in showery weather. It allows Johnson to praise what he likes, and condemn what he does not like. But this, after all, is precisely what we demand of a critic, especially of a critic whose intuitions are as

[1] *Rambler*, no. 92 (2 February 1751).
[2] Ibid, no. 125 (28 May 1751).

fine as Johnson's. And, moreover, it is a theory which leads him directly into descriptive criticism. Poetry is an evolutionary stream, a 'tradition': it invites examination as such. *The Lives of the Poets* only occurred at all by a happy publishing accident, but they do arise naturally out of Johnson's abstract convictions concerning the nature of art.

So, of course, does the *Dictionary*. Johnson would not have understood the twentieth-century battle between the conservatives who hold linguistics to be a prescriptive discipline, and the radicals who insist that it is a descriptive science. For Johnson, lexicography is both, and it is only one because it is the other. Of course usage varies from age to age, argues Johnson, and his *Dictionary* is proudly the first historical dictionary of English: 'As by the cultivation of various sciences a language is amplified, it will be more furnished with words deflected from their original sense,' he explains in his preface. But, like the critic in search of principles, the lexicographer selects as well as reports. 'I applied myself to the perusal of our writers,' he tells us, but in a critical spirit, and 'found our speech copious without order, and energetick without rules'. The *Dictionary* seeks to tidy up – there was 'perplexity to be disentangled, confusion to be regulated'. It illustrates by quotations, but only quotation from the 'best', so that it does not aspire to the impartiality of the Oxford English Dictionary. A word means, not what most men suppose it to mean, but what the finest authors have made it mean. Like his critical theory, Johnson's theory of language is only superficially democratic: it is not content to count heads.

The edition of Shakespeare (1765), long delayed, was embarked upon as soon as the *Dictionary* had been dismissed into the world 'with frigid tranquillity' – Johnson's incomparable phrase to describe his emotions as a lexicographer. It must have been far more congenial work, though less important, and the style of the *Proposals for Printing the Dramatick Works of Shakespeare* (1756) and of the 1765 preface suggests a certain gusto of mood. Johnson's Shakespeare is the sixth critical edition since the early folios – the others were by Rowe, Pope, Theobald, Hanmer, and Warburton – and we are only beginning to realize how closely Johnson followed his predecessors in form and even in substance. All wrote prefaces, which Johnson reprinted in his own edition, with Rowe's preface in Pope's revision. Johnson follows them, in his own preface, in insisting on his own labours in collating texts – there is nothing novel in this pretension – and in praising Shakespeare's genius as a sport of nature. But Johnson's preface is syncretic only in a respectable sense: we expect an editor to have studied his forerunners, and to have learned from them.

The preface is in essence a brilliant exercise in descriptive criticism – Johnson's first extended attempt at the form – with a major essay in theoretical criticism, the refutation of the unities of time and place, inserted midway, and a long appendix on editorial method. It falls, fairly clearly, into seven parts: Shakespeare considered as a poet of nature, followed by a defence of his tragicomedy, his 'central' style, his defects, the general attack upon the unities, the historical background, and the study of editorial method. The preface is firmly grounded, in its opening pages, in Johnsonian theory: Shakespeare happily occupies a classic position, like an Ancient, by virtue of his relative antiquity and 'continuance of esteem'. He *must* be great. (Johnson even dares speak of 'prescriptive veneration'.) And his greatness is of a familiar neoclassical kind, a mastery of generality: his characters are not 'individuals' but 'species'. All this is much of a piece with the earlier *Rambler* essays: 'Poetry cannot dwell upon the minuter distinctions . . .'[1] But, familiar as it looks, Johnson has some odd cards up his sleeve, and he will not scruple to play them, even at the cost of ruining his general strategy.

Three major inconsistencies emerge from the preface as a whole, though they are inconsistencies which, like the antitheses for which Johnson's syntax is famous, seem not so much defects as sources of energy – they provide power by which the argument may move. First, tragi-comedy is justified on conflicting grounds. This, the second section, is one of the most original parts of the preface. Dryden too had occasionally defended mixed plays, but only as occasion suited: he had condemned them too. And given that the neoclassical critics had abandoned, or forgotten, the Renaissance distinction between tragedy and comedy, it must indeed have seemed important to justify Shakespeare's mixture of 'crimes' and

[1] *Rambler*, no. 36 (21 July 1750); cf. *Rasselas* (1759), ch. x.

'absurdities'. But it will hardly do to justify tragi-comedy on Dryden's grounds that contraries set off each other, and then to excuse 'the rules of criticism' on the grounds that 'there is always an appeal open from criticism to nature', and that 'the mingled drama' can be shown to have instructed as well as pleased: this is a characteristically Johnsonian use of the escape-clause. Second, the extravagant (or at least unqualified) praise of Shakespeare as supremely 'the poet of nature' in the first part of the preface seems discredited in the light of some of his disparagements towards the end: 'As we owe every thing to him, he owes something to us; . . . we fix our eyes upon his graces, and turn them from his deformities, and endure in him what we should in another loath or despise . . . He has . . . perhaps not one play which, if it were now exhibited as the work of a contemporary writer, would be heard to the conclusion.'[1] This has the ring of sincerity: but, if sincere, it makes the veneration of the opening pages look prescriptive indeed. And finally, Johnson's somewhat Coleridgean praise for Shakespeare as the poet of the 'central' style, 'probably to be sought in the common intercourse of life, among those who speak only to be understood, without ambition of elegance', seems out of tune with the attack that follows, in the list of Shakespearean defects, upon his 'tumour', his weak declamation, his 'unwieldy sentiment'. More than once, the preface seems torn apart by Johnson's failure to qualify either his praise or his blame. But there are moments of scintillating perception. The refutation of the unities of time and place, and the assertion of the special status of dramatic illusion, is a model of logical demonstration, and rich in those effects of mock-simplicity which Johnson loved to affect: 'It will be asked how the drama moves, if it is not credited. It is credited with all the credit due to a drama. It is credited, whenever it moves, as a just picture of a real original.'[2] So he kicked the stone to refute Berkeleian idealism. The exposure of the unities that follows, 'not dogmatically but deliberately written', as he magnificently excused his own temerity, is one of the great moments of liberating intelligence in English criticism. And there

---

[1] *Johnson on Shakespeare* ed. cit., pp. 40-1.
[2] Ibid., p. 28. 'Moves'=moves emotion in the audience; 'credited'=believed to be real.

is a superb historical understanding implied, not only in the exposition of editorial principles with which the preface closes, but in the constant appeals to the study of background as an antidote to neoclassical rule-of-thumb:

Works tentative and experimental must be estimated by their proportion to the general and collective ability of man, as it is discovered in a long succession of endeavours.[1]

Every man's performances, to be rightly estimated, must be compared with the state of the age in which he lived, and with his own particular opportunities . . . Curiosity is always busy to discover the instruments, as well as to survey the workmanship, to know how much is to be ascribed to original powers, and how much to casual and adventitious help.[2]

Most nineteenth-century historical criticism, in its characteristic excesses as well as in its characteristic triumphs, seems foreshadowed here. However naïve Johnson's particular historical judgements ('The English nation, in the time of Shakespeare, was yet struggling to emerge from barbarity,' he goes on), there can be no doubt of his determination to view poetry as a tradition or evolution, 'a long succession'.

The *Lives of the English Poets*[3] (1779-81), a collection of fifty-two literary biographies, is a fitting climax to the career of our first great scholar-critic. It is a belated achievement – Johnson was sixty-eight when he began work on the *Lives* – but beyond all dispute his most brilliant. Boswell can hardly contain himself in his enthusiasm over the collection: 'the richest, most beautiful, and indeed most perfect production of Johnson's pen'.[4] 'Perfect' is an odd description: the *Lives* were written in haste, in the confidence of a great reputation, and there is a good deal in them that is formula-ridden and inconclusive. Their 'charm', as Boswell predicted in a letter to Johnson, owes something at least to 'the *magnum nomen*'[5] on the title-page.

---

[1] Ibid., p. 10.
[2] Ibid., pp. 30-1.
[3] So called since the second edition of 1781. The original title was *Prefaces Biographical and Critical to the Works of the English Poets*.
[4] *Life of Johnson*, op. cit. (May 1777).
[5] Ibid. (24 April 1777).

In 1777 a committee of some forty booksellers determined upon a new and superior collection of the works of the major English poets from Chaucer to their own times, and a deputation called upon Johnson to invite him to undertake the prefaces. He accepted promptly, but on his own terms. The whole of medieval, and almost the whole of Renaissance poetry, were eventually cut from the publisher's scheme and, of the fifty-two Lives that Johnson wrote, all but two – Milton and Cowley – are of post-Restoration poets. There is nothing to regret here. The Life of Cowley shows how alien pre-Restoration poetry was to Johnson, and if we could choose we should choose very much what we have – a review of the body of English poetry during the century that had elapsed since 1660, the period where Johnson is king.

Within four years the *Lives* were written – an average rate of about one Life a month, a terrible pace to maintain. Not enough thought, perhaps, has been given to the cost of this haste. It is clear, for instance, that Johnson felt obliged to adopt a formula, to save himself time. In his Advertisement to the first edition, he speaks of having first planned to write an 'advertisement' for each poet like those in what he calls the '*French Miscellanies*'. Sir John Hawkins, in his *Life of Johnson* (1787), identifies the source:

When Johnson had determined on this work, he was to seek for the best mode of executing it. On a hint from a literary lady of his acquaintance and mine [probably Charlotte Lennox], he adopted, for his outline, that form in which the Countess D'Aunois has drawn up the memoirs of the French poets, in her *Recueils des plus belles pièces des Poètes François*;[1]

and he adds that 'the foundation of his work', i.e. his chief sources of information, were the biographical dictionaries of Winstanley, Langbaine, and Jacob (1660, 1691, 1719). Hawkins is right about the *Recueil* (1692), though in attributing it to Mme d'Aunois he was misled by the title-page of an early edition ('Amsterdam',

[1] 'The Life of Samuel Johnson', in *The Works of Johnson* (1787-9), i, 532-3. For the suggestion of Mrs Charlotte Lennox (1720-1804), who translated several memoirs from the French, I am indebted to Hawkins's latest editor, Bertram H. Davis (1962), p. 301.

1692). An early biographer of Fontenelle[1] concludes that Fontenelle himself was probably the author of the *notices biographiques*, or biographical introductions, in the *Recueil*; and since these *notices*, and no other biographical model before Johnson, use the characteristic structure of Johnson's own *Lives*, it seems likely that Fontenelle is Johnson's source here.

In planning the *Lives*, however, Johnson can hardly have needed any advice. His hackwork in literary biography during his first and neediest days in London, between 1738 and 1756 – prefaces to booksellers' reprints, written on fee, and commissioned articles in the *Gentleman's Magazine* and elsewhere – had taught him Fontenelle's formula and how to use it. Two of the Lives, indeed (those of Roscommon and Savage) were written during these grim years and resurrected forty years later for insertion in the *Lives*. The anonymous 'Life of Dr Herman Boerhaave of Leyden',[2] for example, written by Johnson in his thirtieth year, already reveals the characteristic structure of a Fontenelle *notice*.

The structure is a tripartite one: biography, character, criticism. A Fontenelle Life, like a Johnsonian one, begins with a severely chronological account of the poet's life – ancestry, birth, education, and so on; in both critics, this is commonly by far the largest section. The second section, always the shortest, is a brief 'character' of the poet – his appearance and temperament. The third is purely critical, and usually of middling length. Digressions are admitted. But, on the whole, the formula is as rigorously applied by Johnson as by Fontenelle. Twenty-four of Johnson's fifty-two Lives, indeed, observe the tripartite arrangement absolutely, but even this figure gives a quite inadequate impression of the uniformity of his practice. Literally all of the Lives, for example, begin with biography, and all but four (Dryden, Smith, Halifax, and Hughes) end with criticism. Moreover, the divisions in Johnson are perfectly clear-cut. There is no question of over-simplifying his design: it really *is* simple. One striking aspect of the *Lives*

---

[1] N. C. J. Trublet (1697-1770), *Mémoires pour servir à l'histoire de la vie et des ouvrages de M. de Fontenelle* (Amsterdam, 1759) (second edition corrected), pp. 72ff. Trublet knew Fontenelle as an old man, and his biography is generally reliable.

[2] *Gentleman's Magazine* (January-April 1739).

is the total absence of bridge-passages, which might have been easy enough to invent, connecting the two major sections, the biographical and the critical. The character-section, for instance, might have been used as a link, as Fontenelle had sometimes done, but Johnson makes no effort to use it for this purpose. He is writing to a recipe, and he does not stir his ingredients.

Not that a Johnson Life is much like one by Fontenelle except in its bare bones. The French Lives are much shorter than any but the very shortest of Johnson's – often only a matter of a few hundred words. Johnson's immense facility – once the initial impulse had been supplied – must have led him astray here, and may account for the fact that the English lives, unlike the French, were published as a separate collection. They are much too weighty to be considered as mere introductions. Moreover, Fontenelle's criticism (his third section) is always far sketchier than Johnson's; it is often confined to a few valedictory phrases, and painfully general phrases at that. His criticism of Belleau may be taken as sadly representative: 'Ronsard l'appelloit le poète de la nature, parce que la nature règne dans tous ces ouvrages, qu'elle y peint et anime tout (1,267).' Johnson, in fact, expands the Fontenelle scheme generously, especially in its critical conclusion. His achievement is to turn the literary life into a vehicle of criticism.

An odd vehicle, none the less, and plainly a top-heavy one. Why does Johnson spend well over half his space on pure biography? And why does he throw up his formula in the face of his reader, neglecting every opportunity to disguise it? It would be tempting to argue, in the face of Johnson's reputation as a scholar-critic, that in the Lives he is creating the foundations of the nineteenth-century school of historical criticism by elevating the literary life to a new critical eminence. But Johnson is not a very biographical critic. His point of departure, it is true, is invariably in the poet's life, but he makes singularly little attempt to exploit biography for critical purposes. His notion of the creative act is not so much naïve as non-existent. He seems simply indifferent to the paradox (for Johnson the royalist) that Milton, with his outrageous republican sentiments, wrote the greatest of the English epics, and his formula allows him to evade this issue in a few dis-

missive phrases. His treatment of Gray, again, shows the opportunities he missed. The biography shows Gray leading the life of a
Cambridge scholar, the character reports him to be the 'most
learned man in Europe', and he is then appropriately rebuked for
his unscholarly 'Ode on Spring': 'I was sorry to see, in the lines of
a scholar like Gray, "the *honied* Spring".'[1] That the virtues and
failings of Gray's poems might be more closely defined by using
the biographical evidence he has just rehearsed does not occur to
Johnson. In modern terms, the *Lives* fall badly between two stools:
those who, like the New Critics between the wars, prefer their
criticism devoid of biography, will complain that Johnson is
largely biographical; and those who accept the critical relevance
of some biographical facts will wonder why Johnson uses his facts
so little.

It should be obvious, then, that Johnson is not at all a biographical critic in a manner that foreshadows Sainte-Beuve. He is rather
a critic who has discovered that criticism may usefully be practised
as an appendage to biography. Johnson's explicit interest in biography, like Dryden's before him, is moral and cautionary.[2] The
image of Gray's tranquil Cambridge existence really does reveal a
quality, and a lack, in his verse – but only, so far as Johnson can
see, by a kind of accident.

The Life of Milton is a monumental example of the characteristic triumphs and failures of Johnson's historical sense. Its design is
as formal as any – biography, character, criticism – except that the
middle section contains some oddly irrelevant material, including
an account of Milton's family. On this occasion, however, the two
principal sections of biography and criticism are in full collision:
the biography goes far beyond an attack upon Milton's political
views to the point of personal vindictiveness. Mere Toryism
would hardly account for Johnson's jibes against Milton's work
as a schoolmaster after his return from Italy in 1639: it is the
nastiest passage in the *Lives*,[3] though such real targets as Milton's
egotism and his easy talent for self-justification are surprisingly
overlooked. Animus, again, is the dominating mood of the early

[1] *Lives*, ed. Birkbeck Hill, III, 434.
[2] Cf. *Rambler*, no. 60 (13 October 1750).
[3] *Lives*, ed. cit., I, 98.

passages in the critical section: the short poems are 'distinguished by repulsive harshness'[1] and the celebrated denunciation of 'Lycidas' along with all modern pastorals fails to notice that most of the poem is scarcely pastoral at all. The progress of 'Lycidas' from the feebly particular to the magnificently general, from the dead youth to the Poet in his cosmic setting, is all dismissed by Johnson as an 'inherent improbability' polluted by 'irreverend combinations'.[2] He is not much more sympathetic to *Comus* and *Samson Agonistes*, but there are early signs of recovery in his critique of 'L'Allegro' and 'Il Penseroso', where he expertly recognizes the purely formal nature of Milton's distinction, designed to show 'how, among the successive variety of appearances, every disposition of mind takes hold on those by which it may be gratified'.

Johnson's critique of *Paradise Lost*, sixty years later than Addison's, is so far its superior that it is worth posing the contrast in reply to any question of Johnson's powers as an analyst. It is obvious that he is vastly nearer to Milton's text than Addison is, and worth noticing, at the same time, that he contrives to be so almost without quotation, 'because of selecting beauties there had been no end'[3] – there is only one in his whole account of the poem – whereas Addison loads his pages with extracts from the text. But Addison is concerned only with judgement, and snap judgement at that. Johnson attempts descriptive distinctions, even if by modern standards they are usually over-bold. The following passage, even to its initial hint of biographical intrusion, is a representative one. Milton

had considered creation in its whole extent, and his descriptions are therefore learned. He had accustomed his imagination to unrestrained indulgence, and his conceptions therefore were extensive. The characteristick quality of his poem is sublimity. He sometimes descends to the elegant, but his element is the great. He can occasionally invest himself with grace; but his natural port is gigantick loftiness. He can please when pleasure is required; but it is his peculiar power to astonish.[4]

[1] *Lives*, I, 162.
[2] Ibid., I, 163, 165.
[3] Ibid., I, 180.
[4] Ibid., I, 177.

One asks oneself, as so often in Johnson, just what the limiting factor in such language is. The set of antitheses upon which such a description of Milton's poetic talent is built (learning-provincialism; imagination-restraint; sublimity (*or* greatness, *or* loftiness) -grace; astonishment-pleasure) are not without their force. But their force would be the greater for precise illustration. And when Johnson does illustrate, he seems unwilling to test his principles closely in quotation. The following example is unusually precise in its language:

His similes are less numerous and more various than those of his predecessors. But he does not confine himself within the limits of rigorous comparison: his great excellence is amplitude, and he expands the adventitious image beyond the dimensions which the occasion required. Thus, comparing the shield of Satan to the orb of the Moon, he crowds the imagination with the discovery of the telescope and all the wonders which the telescope discovers.[1]

Milton's imagery, in fact, is sparser than that of Shakespeare and the Metaphysicals, and more readily extended in epic similes; Johnson oddly omits to mention the Homeric and Virgilian models that Milton is copying in his effort to attain epic dignity. The comment is just: but, as so often in Johnson, there is a certain failure to reconcile theory and practice. Is 'amplitude' in imagery, or the extension of the image beyond the limits of comparison, a virtue or not? Johnson's language suggests he has his doubts: the image in *Paradise Lost*, I, 284ff. passes 'beyond the dimensions which the occasion required'. But the fault may be a generous one ('He does not confine himself . . .'). The diagnosis is admirably just, but in his conclusion Johnson fumbles and fails. And yet this, after all, is vastly superior to the far commoner offence of eighteenth-century criticism, where judgements arise from no analysis at all.

Here, and often elsewhere, Johnson is clearly embarrassed by his own 'laws'. The ambiguity of his judgements, and the force that the 'prescriptive veneration' of established masterpieces always held for him, emerges almost as clearly in the Life of Milton as in the preface to Shakespeare. Johnson writes of *Paradise Lost* as if the

[1] Ibid., I, 179.

poem were a visit to the dentist, or a regrettable aspect of Sunday observance like compulsory church-attendance. His analysis is an act of self-persuasion, and one unconvincing and unconvinced reason after another is advanced why the epic has to be praised:

Every line breathes sanctity of thought . . .
Of human beings there are but two; but those two are the parents of mankind . . .
The poet, whatever be done, is always great . . .
There is . . . little opportunity for the pathetick; but what little there is has not been lost . . .[1]

until, at last, the truth is out: Johnson is determined, both as a patriot and a Christian, to assert a judgement he cannot feel; to 'lessen the reputation of Milton', as he confesses, might be to 'diminish in some degree the honour of our country',[2] and the fatal flaws in Milton's conception are finally conceded with an awful clarity:

The man and woman who act and suffer are in a state which no other man or woman can ever know . . .
These truths [of sin and redemption] are too important to be new . . . They raise no unaccustomed emotion in the mind; what we knew before, we cannot learn; what is not unexpected, cannot surprise . . .
The good and evil of Eternity are too ponderous for the wings of wit . . .[3]

The essential ambiguity of the Victorian attitude to Milton – one of bored and disingenuous reverence – is sufficiently represented by these two groups of quotations. As in the preface to Shakespeare, Johnson has not played quite fair with us. But the wonder is not that critics who, like Johnson, are at once patriots and Christians should feel obliged to relax their critical vigour before *Paradise Lost*, but that one of them contrived to define his objections so much more simply, more baldly, and more convincingly than Milton's modern detractors have done. Dr Leavis may well be right when he complained that Milton's Grand Style is 'incom-

[1] *Lives*, I, 179-80.
[2] Ibid., I, 181.
[3] Ibid., I, 181-2.

patible with sharp, concrete realization' and 'sensuous particularity'.[1] But, if we find the poem a bore, it seems much more likely we do so for Johnson's reasons than for these. For better or worse, most twentieth-century readers are simply not curious to know the answer to the questions that Milton poses in his greatest poem.

The Life of Milton shows Johnson uncomfortably poised upon a double contradiction: he respects Milton's poetry more than he respects Milton himself, and he respects it without loving it. The Life of Cowley, for all the notoriety of Johnson's attack upon the Metaphysical style, is a happier example of his genius for distinction. The knockabout abuse of the Metaphysical poets, so familiar in quotation, does not represent Johnson's purpose fairly: 'The Metaphysical poets were men of learning, and to shew their learning was their whole endeavour; but, unluckily resolving to shew it in rhyme . . .'[2] Johnson will have his little joke, and one of his favourite jokes is to pretend he cannot see beyond the end of his nose. We read on, happily eager to see him make more of a fool of himself: we are so certain, when he quotes (or misquotes) Pope's dictum on wit, that this must be the limit of his horizon too:

> What oft was thought, but ne'er so well expressed.

In the next two paragraphs he offers us two further accounts of 'wit', and in a moment we are panting to keep up with him:

that which, though not obvious, is, upon its first production, acknowledge to be just . . .
a kind of *discordia concors*; a combination of dissimilar images, or discovery of occult resemblances in things apparently unlike . . .[3]

Here is not one definition of wit, but three. And it is by the second test of the three that the Metaphysicals fail – their thoughts are 'not obvious, but neither are they just'. By the third definition they triumph, though their victory, in Johnsonian terms, hardly seems justifiable: 'the reader commonly thinks his improvement dearly bought and, though he sometimes admires, is seldom

---

[1] *Revaluation* (1936), p. 50.
[2] *Lives*, ed. cit., I, 19.
[3] Ibid., I, 20.

pleased'.[1] But the *nature* of the Metaphysical achievement is in
large part clearly defined, whatever we may think of Johnson's
view of it: 'The most heterogeneous ideas are yoked by violence
together; nature and art are ransacked for illustrations, compari-
sons, and allusions: their learning instructs, and their subtility
surprises . . .' This is an admirable account, in general terms, of
Donne's *Songs and Sonets*; and so is the sequel, framed as it is
as a rebuttal: 'Their attempts were always analytick; they broke
every image into fragments: and could no more represent, by
their slender conceits and laboured particularities, the prospects of
nature or the scenes of life, than he who dissects a sun-beam with
a prism can exhibit the wide effulgence of a summer noon.'[2]
Johnson is seeking in poetry something few readers now want;
but only a very perceptive reader of Cowley could have offered
such an analysis at all, and the concessions he is ready to make to
the Metaphysical mode are wide and generous: 'If they frequently
threw away their wit upon false conceits, they likewise sometimes
struck out unexpected truth: if their conceits were far-fetched,
they were often worth the carriage. To write on their plan, it was
at least necessary to read and think.'[3]

But the *Lives* are essentially a study of the Augustan mode in
English poetry, and the Lives of Dryden and Pope are its real
glories. At last the greatest of the English neoclassical critics finds
his own level: at last he speaks, and at length, of what he knows
and loves. To read these Lives is to realize how aberrant was the
task he had set himself in the preface to Shakespeare and in the
Life of Milton. With them, his best endeavour was to justify and
excuse; with Dryden and Pope, he is no longer on the defensive.
He is advocate; at times, he is almost mouthpiece. In Johnson the
Augustan poets found the most perfect of exponents: it is as if
Donne had written a treatise on the comedies of Shakespeare, or
Andrew Marvell a critique of *Paradise Lost*. No doubt too total a
sympathy can be a positive nuisance in a critic. You do not explain
what you know in your bones, and occasionally, it might be
objected against the Life of Pope, enthusiasm supplants discrimina-

---

[1] *Lives*, I, 20.
[2] Ibid., I, 20-1.
[3] Ibid., I, 21.

tion. But not often: Johnson is the kind of critic who hates to seem anyone's fool. He loves the qualifying phrase. The most rapturous paragraphs, such as those that conclude the critical section of the Life of Pope, are always balanced by a hint of detraction. A eulogy beginning: 'Pope had, in proportions very nicely adjusted to each other, all the qualities that constitute genius . . .' may end: 'The construction of his language is not always strictly grammatical; . . . nor was he very careful to vary his terminations or to refuse admission at a small distance to the same rhymes.'[1] The ferrule is always to Johnson's hand, ready for use. And, in any case, his enthusiasm for Dryden and Pope is limited to their technical achievement. He is no more impressed by their attitudes than the next man. They 'reformed our numbers' – but the 'metaphysical morality' of Pope's Essay on Man is relentlessly deflated: 'Never were penury of knowledge and vulgarity of sentiment so happily disguised.'[2] Dryden purified our diction and versification; but The Hind and the Panther is based on a fable 'full of absurdity', and though Absalom and Achitophel possesses, as a political poem, 'all the excellences of which the subject is susceptible: acrimony of censure, elegance of praise, artful delineation of character . . .', yet its construction is beyond repair:

We are alarmed by a faction formed out of many sects various in their principles, but agreeing in their purpose of mischief, formidable for their numbers and strong by their supports, while the king's friends are few and weak. The chiefs on either part are set forth to view; but when expectation is at the height, the king makes a speech. . . .[3]

The critical balance, in the Lives of Dryden and Pope, seems just right: a total sympathy with the artistic ends of the two poets, and a shameless scepticism concerning everything else.

Johnson's Lives mark the end of an era – an era that began with Dryden's essays of the 1660s, and which shared some common assumptions about the nature of poetry which are called neoclassical. But the more we talk about neoclassicism, the less interesting Dryden, Addison, Pope, Fielding, and Johnson will look.

[1] Ibid., III, 247, 249.
[2] Ibid., III, 243.
[3] Ibid., I, 436–7.

A common denominator of doctrine – any doctrine – is always likely to be uninteresting. It is, in any case, hardly more than a historian's tool: no European critic can be produced who believed in the whole of neoclassical doctrine as scholars have expounded it. And, ultimately, it does not matter whether Dryden, or Johnson, believed in it or not: the critic's strategy in the field, like any good general's, is likely to vary with the needs of the moment, and the study of theory is more likely to reveal his characteristic manner of excuse and justification than to produce any other result of intrinsic interest. Criticism is incurably pragmatic: Dryden will write blank verse if it suits him to do so, and Addison's love of *Paradise Lost*, or Johnson's admiration for the *Rape of the Lock*, is instinctive rather than principled. And, of course – overwhelming objection – theory has no future. The elaborate psychological and physiological theories of the Augustan aestheticians concerning the nature of beauty have now only the melancholy interest of deserted ruins. They are not even worth contradicting, for the most part, and (for the most part) no one ever troubled to contradict them. An occasional law, like that of the unities of time and place, finds its refutation, but on the whole Augustan aesthetic debates are neither talked out nor talked down: they simply fail to generate debate at all. For the solid achievement of this first continuous century in the English critical tradition, we must surely look beyond theory altogether.

That achievement may best, perhaps, be described as a historical one. Before Dryden, formal literary analysis had no purpose and therefore no existence, but Dryden's realization that an English tradition of poetry existed as a court of appeal against foreign laws, at a moment when French literary influence was almost overpowering, made criticism useful: his analysis of Jonson's *Silent Woman*, and his defensive prefaces, are stages in a literary war in which the chief prize is the English past, 'the giant race before the flood'. The assertion, once made, started a debate, and by Addison's time analysis had become almost a habit. The second stage, marked by the career of Johnson, is historical in a more precise sense: the endeavour now is a scholarly one. Johnson dominates this stage so completely that it is easy to forget he is not the whole of it, or even (in a strict sense) the pioneer. His *Dictionary*, and his editorial labours upon Shakespeare, are both deeply derivative. Thomas Warton's *Observations on the Fairy Queen* (1754) had, on Johnson's own generous admission, shown him the importance of the poet's background in its analysis of Spenser's Arthurian and (in its second edition of 1762) of his Italian sources. *An Essay on the Writings and Genius of Mr Pope* (1756-81), by Thomas's elder brother Joseph Warton, headmaster of Winchester College, was a laborious, poem-by-poem analysis of Pope's works on Longinian principles, devoted to the absurd task of showing that, if 'the sublime and the pathetic are the two chief nerves of all genuine poesy', then Pope does not belong to the highest rank of poets – a conclusion implicit in the premise, if conclusion ever was, but curiously attractive in its naïve solemnity. Johnson, no doubt seriously, called this schoolmasterly undertaking 'a book which teaches how the brow of Criticism may be smoothed, and how she may be enabled, with all her severity, to attract and to delight.'[1] From the 1750s onwards, the emotional as well as the sheerly cognitive foundations of historical criticism are rapidly laid: nostalgia for the past, as in Richard Hurd's *Letters on Chivalry and Romance* (1762); biography and gossip, in Horace Walpole's *Catalogue of the Royal and Noble Authors of England* (1758) and Johnson's *Lives*; edited texts like Bishop Percy's *Reliques of Ancient English Poetry* (1765), Thomas Tyrwhitt's *Canterbury Tales* (1775-8), and Malone's Shakespeare (1790); and full-scale literary history in Thomas Warton's *History of English Poetry* (1774-81) which, unfinished as it is, carried the story through three bulky volumes from the eleventh century to about 1600. And the Rowley controversy occasioned by Chatterton's *Poems* (1777), like the Ossian controversy of the 1760s, shows that for Johnson's day the poetry of the Middle Ages had become as disputed as the Elizabethan drama had been for Dryden and Rymer. The historians have happily labelled these names – Hurd, Walpole, Percy, the Wartons, Macpherson, and Chatterton – as 'transitional' and 'pre-romantic'. But is it so clear that their attitude to medieval poetry, at once affectionate, hesitant, and condescending, is in *any* way different from that of Coleridge in his loving parody of the ballad in 'The Ancient Mariner', or of Keats in buying his 'black-

[1] From the Life of Pope, in *Lives*, ed. cit., III, 236.

letter Chaucer', which he at once determined to 'bounden gothique'[1]? Percy is utterly at one with Coleridge when he presents his ballads, in the dedication to his *Reliques*, 'not as labours of art but as effusions of nature, shewing the first efforts of ancient genius, and exhibiting the customs and opinions of remote ages' (p. vi): he even interpolated modern, literary ballads into his collection, to make his medievalia tolerable to polite readers. Such precautions are as much 'romantic' as 'pre-romantic', and persisted well into the nineteenth century, until overtaken by German research techniques of history and the Higher Criticism. The great document of eighteenth-century medievalism, Gibbon's *Decline and Fall* (1776-88), lies outside the subject, but belongs utterly here in terms of chronology, and in terms of ethos too.

In face of such dates, Johnson's claim to be a pioneer of the historical method in criticism is thin indeed, and he never attempted to make it. But his is the only formidable critical intelligence in this parade of names. The writings of the Warton brothers, to whom he avowedly owed much, seem desperately lacking in intellectual pressure. Thomas Warton's *History* is just the kind of book a man does not finish, and it is no wonder either that his elder brother Joseph, who outlived Thomas by ten years, failed to finish it for him. When we consider that Thomas Gray[2] in the 1750s had planned to write a history of English poetry with his friend William Mason, and even detailed his plan in a letter to Thomas Warton (15 April 1770), based upon the Drydenesque theory of 'schools' of poetry – three 'Italian' schools of Chaucer, Spenser and Donne, and the 'School of France' initiated by Waller and Dryden – the loss seems nearly as great as the earlier loss of Dryden's history in favour of Rymer's. *The Observations on the Faery Queen* retains a certain pallid interest in its laborious attempt to create a sense of intellectual background, and it explains what would otherwise be unexplainable – how the nine-

---

[1] Letter to J. H. Reynolds (3 May 1818).

[2] *Correspondence of Thomas Gray*, edited by Paget Toynbee and Leonard Whibley (Oxford, 1935), pp. 1122-5. Gray admits to Warton that his scheme is based on 'a scribbled paper of Pope' discovered after his death by his friend Warburton, who sent it to Mason. Warton, in the preface to his *History* (1774), calls Gray's sketch 'that of Mr Pope, considerably enlarged, extended and improved'.

teenth century came to see Spenser as a romantic, visionary poet, Coleridge's 'mind constitutionally tender, delicate, and ... effeminate',[1] before Professor C. S. Lewis, in his *Allegory of Love* (1936), restored to us a poet of rugged Protestantism and almost muscular Christianity. 'Sensibility' is simply a quality invented by Thomas Warton and later romantic critics to justify Spenser's lack of architectonics:

> Spenser, and the same may be said of Ariosto, did not live in an age of planning. His poetry is the careless exuberance of a warm imagination and a strong sensibility.... Exactness in his poem would have been like the cornice which a painter introduced in the grotto of Calypso. Spenser's beauties are like the flowers of paradise.[2]

This is nonsense, and the wonder is that anyone can ever have read the *Faerie Queene* for long without realizing it to be nonsense. And yet there is no doubt that Warton has read the poem, and marshalled its qualities under such general headings as 'Of Spenser's stanza, versification, and language', where he is notably severe upon the Spenserian stanza, which 'led our author into many absurdities'.

Only two other eighteenth-century critics seem worthy of notice, and they are both Shakespeareans. Maurice Morgann (1726-1802) is credited, for his *Essay on the Dramatic Character of Sir John Falstaff* (1777), with the creation of the school of character-analysis in Shakespearean criticism later consummated in Bradley's *Shakespearean Tragedy* (1904). The title certainly belongs to Morgann more naturally than to Coleridge, whose claim to be a character-critic is based on a few familiar quotations torn out of context. And Morgann, in his pleasant, amateur fashion – the *Essay* was written for a dare, and apologetically offered to the reader as a 'mere experiment' and a 'novelty' (pp. 7-8) – is an impressive analyst of character, well aware, like Bradley, of the pitfalls of his own technique: 'But what have we to do, may my readers exclaim, with principles so latent, so obscured? In dramatic composition the impression is the fact; and the writer who, meaning to impress one thing, has impressed another, is unworthy

---

[1] *Biographia Literaria* (1817), ch. 2.
[2] *Observations*, op. cit., Sect. 1.

of observation (p. 4).' This is welcome assurance: but it is none the less true that Morgann's demonstration that Falstaff was not a 'constitutional coward' offends precisely in this way, by supposing the revealed 'facts' about Falstaff's career to be more important than our impression of what we see upon the stage.

The other Shakespearean is at once more interesting and more obscure. In Walter Whiter (1758-1832), Fellow of Clare College, Cambridge, and later a dissolute Norfolk clergyman, we have a critic whose claim to be considered the founder of imagery-analysis might be called unassailable, if it were not for the known fact that his work passed unnoticed until the present century. Coleridge, and G. Wilson Knight and Wolfgang Clemen in our own times, seem to have owed nothing to him,[1] though they might have owed the very principles of their technique. Because of this neglect – a neglect that Whiter himself bitterly resented – his 'Attempt to Explain and Illustrate Various Passages on a New Principle of Criticism, Derived from Mr Locke's Doctrine of the Association of Ideas'[2] is now merely a curiosity. Whiter's thesis was brilliantly original. It was that Locke's theory of association in the *Essay Concerning Humane Understanding* (1690) provided a technique for interpreting and emending the text of Shakespeare: 'Ideas . . . always keep in company, and the one no sooner at any time comes into the understanding, but its associate appears with it . . .'[3] Shakespeare's images, as Whiter shows by example upon example, are linked by just such subconscious associations. Hanmer, Johnson, Steevens, and Malone, for example, had all preferred the emendation 'mossed' to 'moist' in Apemantus's speech in *Timon*, IV, iii:

[1] The referenes to Whiter in the revised, English edition of Clemen's *The Development of Shakespeare's Imagery* (1951) (pp. 13, 74n.) are late additions, and are not to be found in the first, German edition of 1936. Wilson Knight does not mention Whiter at all. His rediscovery can be attributed to Professor J. Isaacs in *A Companion to Shakespeare Studies* (Cambridge, 1934), pp. 312-3, 320, and to a leading article in *The Times Literary Supplement* (5 September 1936), after the first studies by Wilson Knight and Caroline Spurgeon had appeared.

[2] The second part of *A Specimen of a Commentary on Shakespeare* (1794). The first part of the book is a commentary on *As You Like It*.

[3] Locke, *Essay*, II, 33.

>   What, think'st
> That the bleake ayre, thy boysterous chamberlaine,
> Will put thy shirt on warme? Will these moyst trees
> That have outliv'd the eagle, page thy heeles
> And skip when thou point'st out?

But, argues Whiter, '*warm* and *moist* were the appropriate terms in the days of Shakespeare for what we should now call an *air'd* and a *damp* shirt . . . Can the reader doubt (though he may perhaps smile at the association) that the image of the Chamberlain putting the shirt on *warm* impressed the opposite word *moist* on the imagination of the poet?' For some two hundred pages Whiter pursues his point with pedantic zeal: one can only wonder how different nineteenth-century Shakespearean criticism would have looked if Coleridge had read this book. But Whiter's refinement of the historical imagination, which almost involves the critic in the psycho-analysis of his poet, fell dead from the press.

Chapter 5

WORDSWORTH AND COLERIDGE

THE achievement of Coleridge is rightly held to be supreme among the English critics, but no one seeking to expound it can face his task with much confidence. Existing expositions, often by the most influential of modern critics, bear so little resemblance to one another that it is difficult to believe they are about the same thing, and the most famous of them all, I. A. Richards's *Coleridge on Imagination* (1934), seems to bear little relation to the text of Coleridge. And no wonder, since his criticism is only now in process of being adequately edited for the first time. Meanwhile, Professor Wellek has reconstructed the evidence for reaffirming that little, if any, of the philosophical doctrines on which Coleridge based his aesthetic were original to him, and that his chief importance was that of a 'mediator' between Germany and England.[1] And worst of all, the very nature of Coleridge's text forever defies clear analysis: of the seven major series of lectures he is known to have delivered, only three or four have substantially survived, and those in texts which he did not himself prepare for the press; his notebooks suffer from the usual confusions of notebooks; his first major critical essay (if one may so describe Wordsworth's 1800 preface to the *Lyrical Ballads*) was written by somebody else; and the only critical book which appeared in his own lifetime, the *Biographia Literaria* (1817), is so discursive and so sporadic in its argument as almost to merit its subtitle 'Biographical Sketches'. It is really not at all surprising if the commentators have failed to agree. The intriguing aspect of the msytery is that, while they have failed to agree on what Coleridge actually said, they are nearly all agreed that it was of the first importance.

Coleridge himself would have sympathized with the principle that the inductive process is an illusion, that one must begin with an affirmation. For all the diversity of Coleridge's criticism, we

[1] René Wellek, *A History of Modern Criticism* (New Haven, 1955), II, 151ff.

may safely begin by asserting that its object is not analysis, but a theoretical certainty – 'to reduce criticism to a system', as he put it in a letter to Byron (15 October 1815), 'by the deduction of the causes from principles involved in our faculties'; or, again, in the *Biographia Literaria*, 'to establish the principles of writing rather than to furnish rules how to pass judgement on what has been written by others' (ch. 18). This is the language of a theoretical critic – of one, indeed, operating on a level of abstraction remote even by the ordinary standards of aestheticians. For Coleridge, ultimately, only a theory of poetic creation matters: he analyses, not so much poems as they exist, but the creative act that makes them what they are. Now this is an interest of revolutionary significance. No English critic since Dryden had much concerned himself with the question of the poetic process, and Dryden's interest had been no better than a passing one, based on his acquaintance with Hobbesian psychology.[1] For eighteenth-century critics, a poem is simply there, and it is the variety or uniformity of human reactions to it that is worth discussing. But with Coleridge, creation is central. There is no hypothesis of the ideal reader, or of the average reader, in his criticism, corresponding to Johnson's consensus of informed opinion down the ages. There is just Coleridge. Whether he is reading Shakespeare or Wordsworth or Jeremy Taylor, we are frankly invited to see in them what Coleridge sees in them. There might be no 'problem of the reader' at all, so unaware he is of any such thing. But then, for Coleridge, a poem is not a machine, and you cannot write it off, as Johnson or I. A. Richards would do, by taking it to pieces and showing that it does not work. It is, for better or worse, evidence of a historical event, tempting inquiry into origins and sources. The question of values is scarcely an aspect of his criticism at all, and Coleridge hardly ever tells you whether he thinks a poem good or bad. The nearest approach to evaluation he is ready to make is to discuss some issue of category, such as in the eighteenth chapter of the *Biographia Literaria*, where he debates whether a mere 'metrical composition' is indeed a poem or some other thing.

[1] It is confined to three texts, two of them very early: the prefaces to *The Rival Ladies* (1664) and *Annus Mirabilis* (1667), and the 'Parallel betwixt Painting and Poetry' prefixed to his translation of Fresnoy's *Art of Painting* (1695).

Coleridge, then, unlike Johnson, is essentially a critic who practices descriptive criticism only as an illustration. His analysis of
Wordsworth's poems in the second half of the *Biographia Literaria*
is not gratuitous in the sense that Johnson's analysis of *Paradise
Lost* in his Life of Milton might be called gratuitous. It is not, that
is, based on any Johnsonian assumption that the analysis of existing
works of literature might be usefully pursued for its own sake. I
shall try to show later that the lectures on Shakespeare too have an
ulterior, theoretical purpose; though they were delivered on
commission, and suggest some concessions to the demands of an
audience. If this is right, it might easily be argued that Coleridge's
criticism represents a regression in the history of descriptive
criticism in English. It certainly represents an interruption, and it
should be honestly admitted at once that the interruption did not
have very fruitful consequences. There is no School of Coleridge
among the English critics. The young men who crowded to his
house in Highgate in the last years of his life, among whom (according to Carlyle) he enjoyed the reputation of a sage, sought
wisdom of a kind too generalized and too occult to turn them into
good critics – indeed, into any kind of critic. The Victorians could
not be expected to understand what he was talking about: some
of his texts had not been printed, most had not been edited, and
his criticism was nearly all of an order that would respond only to
close and concentrated exegesis. Coleridge's influence upon criticism is largely a twentieth-century one. He is a whole movement in
himself, the first and last of his line, the one English critic to try,
and to go on trying, to apply Kantian aesthetics to the past and
present of English letters.

For Coleridge, then, right theory is a cause – *the* cause. The
great defect of English criticism, he insists again and again, has
been its lack of fixed standards, and his repeated attacks on the
reviewers, tedious and self-interested as they undeniably are – the
uncertain logical progression of the *Biographia Literaria* is held up
several times because Coleridge cannot stay away from the subject
– have some justification when we remember that the personalities
in which journalists indulged were the far contrary of his own
critical ideal: 'Reviews are generally pernicious, because the
writers determine without reference to fixed principles . . . be-

cause they teach people rather to judge than to consider, to decide than to reflect.'[1] That is a very Coleridgean emphasis: he saw himself surrounded by impetuous dabblers, eager to know which were the good books and which the bad; whereas his own method presupposed a delicate and inquiring reverence for all of man's creation, and a passionate curiosity to explore its depths.

At its fullest extent, the whole body of Coleridgean criticism stretches over a period of more than thirty years, from the notes he scribbled in the autumn of 1800 for a preface to the second edition of the *Lyrical Ballads*, down to the last note made by his nephew H. N. Coleridge of his conversation shortly before his death in 1834. The beginnings sound uncertain, but there can be little doubt that the inspiration of the 1800 preface was Coleridge's. Wordsworth, years later, insisted it was so, and Coleridge, in a letter of 1802, talks of having turned over his notes for the preface, which he had originally intended to write himself. One of his notes, indeed, survives, containing the phrase 'the recalling of passion in tranquillity',[2] evidently the ancestor of the most famous phrase of the preface, 'emotion recollected in tranquillity'. On the other hand, there can be no doubt that Wordsworth was the actual author of the 1800 preface. Its language is of a plushiness, a rotundity, that is eminently Wordsworthian, and utterly different from the feverish, button-holing tone of Coleridge's prose. (It is one great rhetorical defect of the preface that, whereas its argument assumes prose to be stylistically more commonplace than verse, its own prose is of a polished stateliness that is the child of Johnson and Gibbon.) And in any case – final proof of Wordsworthian composition – it concerns itself solely with Wordsworth's own contributions to the *Lyrical Ballads*. To read the 1800 preface, you would never guess that the collection to which it is prefixed contains 'The Rime of the Ancient Mariner'.

There is no need, however, to father upon Wordsworth the logical incongruities of the 1800 preface. Coleridge's own think-

[1] *Shakespearean Criticism*, edited by T. M. Raysor (Cambridge, Mass., 1930), II, 57-8.

[2] *Notebooks*, edited by Kathleen Coburn (New York, 1957-), no. 787 and note. L. A. Willoughby has shown that the phrase echoes one by Schiller in an early review of 1791; cf. *German Studies Presented to H. G. Fiedler* (Oxford, 1938), pp. 443ff.

ing about aesthetics was confused in much the same way, as his early letters show, and the preface is as likely to be a distorting mirror of his own confusions as an example of Wordsworth's inability to theorize. It is, in all probability, both: Coleridge would never have tolerated such a formulation as this:

Poetry is the spontaneous overflow of powerful feelings: it takes its origin from emotion recollected in tranquillity: the emotion is contemplated till, by a species of reaction, the tranquillity gradually disappears, and an emotion, kindred to that which was before the subject of contemplation, is gradually produced, and does itself actually exist in the mind.

The idea of a double creative process could easily be Coleridgean, but the 'is' of the first sentence is utterly Wordsworthian – the verb 'to be' had a fascination for him that was sometimes fatal[1] – and, in combination with the word 'spontaneous', it leads the reader into endless difficulties: for, in the light of the claims that follow, 'is' must equal something like 'is the final product of', and 'spontaneous' must indicate something unforced and yet, paradoxically, deliberated. Wordsworth is badly out of his depth as a critic: to a mind so forcefully intent upon human observation, the writing of the preface, as he later admitted, must have been a most uncongenial distraction.

The movement of the 1800 preface is essentially a threefold one, though Wordsworth's revision and expansion for the third edition of 1802 introduces a fourth element – 'What is a poet?' – between the first and the second, and indeed a fifth in the form of an Appendix. First comes the notorious theory of the diction of poetry as 'a selection of language really used by men' – a cautious restatement of the phrase in the introductory note or 'Advertisement' to the first edition of 1798, which was almost entirely absorbed into the 1800 preface, 'the language of conversation in the middle and lower classes of society'. The history of this re-

[1] Cf. his 1800 note on 'The Thorn': 'Poetry is passion, it is the history or science of feelings'; or, magnificently, from the 'Song at the Feast of Brougham Castle' (1807), ll. 163-4:

The silence that is in the starry sky,
The sleep that is among the lonely hills.

vision, from 1798 to 1800 to 1802, is one of increasingly defensive vagueness and, alas, of increasing logical incongruity: Wordsworth, in trying to extricate himself, only succeeds in getting in deeper and deeper. For his theory of language leads him into a discussion of metre which, he is forced to admit, is a merely 'superadded' and 'adventitious' attraction, exposing himself in an assertion as vulnerable as any critic ever made: 'There neither is, nor can be, any *essential* difference between the language of prose and metrical composition.' From this the preface moves into the third, most positive, and (perhaps) most Coleridgean section: an attempt to analyse the creative act of the poet. But by now the difficulties of reconciling the parts of the argument are so vast that it seems embarrassing to begin to pose them: in what sense, for example, can the process of linguistic selection which Wordsworth began by recommending be reconciled with the rapt condition he now suggests as proper to the poet? Coleridge's attack on the preface, culminating in chapters 17-20 of the *Biographia Literaria*, seems positively graceless in its determination to pursue its quarry to the end: the more so, when we remember that Coleridge had been its chief begetter. But his careful and sensible insistence upon the differences that do properly distinguish the language of poetry, and his call for 'a certain aloofness', is all fumblingly anticipated by Wordsworth himself in his revision of 1802. The Appendix completes the drift away from the purely imitative, almost photographically naturalistic, theories of the Advertisement in its self-contradictory admission that 'the first poets . . . spake a language which, though unusual, was still the language of men'. (But if men really spoke it, in what sense was it unusual?) Wordsworth knew that something had gone wrong. He may also have sensed, and rightly, that it was not his fault. After all, he had never wanted to be a critic.

Coleridge's *Biographia Literaria* (1817), hastily written in the summer of 1815, is a summary attempt to marshal objections against the preface that had been growing up in his mind over the past fifteen years, and to provide criticism with a systematic basis of its own. Its curious structure – largely metaphysical in its first half, largely critical in its second, and (in spite of its title) only sporadically autobiographical – may be accidental, or the result of a hasty decision: but at least it has the merit of balancing the two great interests of his career, philosophy and poetry. Indeed, the structure of the book might have been its greatest triumph, if only the connexion had been well and truly made between the two sections, at chapters 12 and 13. As it is, Coleridge fails to make clear the vital link between Kantian metaphysics and his distinction between Imagination and Fancy; and when he takes up the story again, in Chapter 14, with an account of the genesis of the *Lyrical Ballads*, its 1800 preface, and the ensuing controversy, the reader may be forgiven for failing to grasp where the connexion lies. Chapter 13, indeed, is the Waterloo of English aesthetics – oddly enough, it was probably written within a few weeks of the battle – in that, at the very moment when Coleridge is propounding his theory of 'counteraction', he breaks off *in mid-sentence*, and calls off the chase with a childish joke: a pretended letter from a friend urging him not to publish the present chapter in the *Biographia* at all, but to hold it over for some later work. The result, of course, was that it was never written at all.

Still, it seems unjust and unwise to lay the emphasis elsewhere, and to read the *Biographia* primarily for its *obiter dicta* or its occasional biographical revelations. There is no doubt that, for Coleridge, the heart of the book lay in Chapter 12 and its ten 'theses', and a reconstruction of Coleridge's argument in this neglected chapter will carry us further towards the heart of his critical preoccupations than anything else will do. The movement of his argument is away from an initial, tentative dualism, much of it based upon his study of Schelling. 'All knowledge', he begins, 'rests on the coincidence of an object with a subject . . . The sum of all that is merely objective we will henceforth call *nature* . . . The sum of all that is subjective we may comprehend in the name of the *self* or intelligence.' But this assertion, common to all eighteenth-century aesthetics and indeed to all Cartesian logic, is set up only to be knocked down. For if truth presupposes a knower and a known (Thesis I), it is also clear that many truths, far from being immediate and original, are derived from others (II). There must, he suggests rather hastily, be an ultimate truth, 'self-grounded, unconditional, and known by its own light' (III), and it must be unique (IV). Neither objective nor subjective, it is a fusion of both (v), a fusion Coleridge calls the Self or I AM (VI), which has a will to act (VII) and is neither finite nor infinite (VIII). 'In the reconciling and recurrence of this contradiction', Coleridge goes on, 'consists the process and mystery of production and life.' At this point philosophy passes into religion (IX), a theism based on the conviction that the individual must be a modification of the higher consciousness (X).

Theses I-IV, then, are the philosophical groundwork of the system, IX-X a religious superstructure that does not concern us here. Theses V-VIII, however, are a revealing summary of Coleridge's view of the creative act. They show that, for Coleridge, the truth that the poet seeks is neither objective nor subjective; that is to say, it exists neither in the mind of the poet nor in what he sees about him, but in 'the identity of both', the one acting upon the other in 'a perpetual self-duplication'. 'The spirit, in all the objects which it views, views only itself'; or, as he had put it in verse a dozen years before:

> O Lady! we receive but what we give,
> And in our life alone does nature live:
> Ours is her wedding-garment, ours her shroud![1]

This Kantian 'counteraction' of forces, as Coleridge calls it – the poet informing nature, even as he is informed by it – is driven or guided by the imagination, that 'essentially vital' force which, unlike the fancy, 'dissolves, diffuses, dissipates' the world around us.

The achievement of Kantian aesthetics, of which Coleridge is the one considerable English spokesman, was to convert our notion of the creative act from the poet/nature dualism of eighteenth-century aesthetics and the 1800 preface into a puzzlingly circular process of endless counteraction. It follows, for Coleridge, that the outcome of such a process, the poem itself, is of a bafflingly difficult logical status. Coleridge, in the fragmentary Chapter 13, calls it a '*tertium aliquid*', being neither subject nor object but 'an interpenetration of the counteracting powers, partaking of both'; it is neither a thought nor a thing, but what Coleridge later called

---

[1] 'Dejection: an Ode' (1802), st. IV; cf. *Notebooks*, op. cit., no. 921.

'a middle quality'[1] between the two. By the very equivocation of its status, it is unique, answerable to no laws but its own. The debt to Kant is clear, and yet we should hesitate long before denying Coleridge his originality as a critic; a reading of Kant, which he probably did not begin until his visit to Germany in 1798-9, only helped him to formalize his deepest intuitions concerning poetic creation. According to his own account of his school-days, he learned as a boy from his schoolmaster that 'poetry . . . had a logic of its own as severe as that of science; and more difficult, because more subtle, more complex, and dependent on more, and more fugitive causes'.[2] And 'Kubla Khan', probably written in May 1798, and surely the greatest triumph in English of what Mr F. W. Bateson would call 'the Critical Muse', shows how far a pre-Kantian Coleridge had felt his way towards this revolutionary position. For the Khan too, like the poet, is intent on reconciling a contradiction, and the pleasure-dome that he decrees lies within 'twice five miles' of ordered gardens which yet contain a 'deep romantic chasm', where the river Alph is paradoxically forced, for all its violence, into a decoration for a despot:

> A mighty fountain momently was forced:
> Amid whose swift, half-intermittent burst
> Huge fragments vaulted like rebounding hail . . .

The roar of the 'fountain' and the caves is tamed into the 'mingled measure' of a work of art. The equation with poetry, in the last stanza, is almost explicit:

> I would build that dome in air,
> That sunny dome! those caves of ice!
> And all who heard should see them there . . .

Coleridge's poet certainly re-creates, in some sense, the 'objects' which he sees and hears, but in a sense which Coleridge already felt to be unusual and terrifying:

> And all should cry, Beware! Beware!

[1] 'On Poesy or Art' (lecture XIII, 1818), reprinted in *Biographia Literaria*, edited by J. Shawcross (Oxford, 1907) II, 254.
[2] *Biographia Literaria* (1817), Ch. I.

The mass of descriptive criticism – notes, lectures, and published works – that Coleridge erected upon this grandiose theoretical foundation are less impressive, in themselves, than has sometimes been claimed, and hardly intelligible when divorced from his theory. Many an innocent reader, directed to read 'Coleridge on Wordsworth' or 'Coleridge on Shakespeare' as major texts of illumination, must have left them with a sense of puzzlement. What has all the fuss been about? How has such a discursive and inconclusive analyst of poetry won the reputation of the greatest English critic? Dr F. R. Leavis has summed up such commonplace reservations with a frankness that is still unique:

> Coleridge's prestige is very understandable, but his currency as an academic classic is something of a scandal. Where he is prescribed and recommended, it should be with far more by way of reservation and *caveat* (I have come tardily to realize) than most students can report to have received along with him. He was very much more brilliantly gifted than Arnold, but nothing of his deserves the classical status of Arnold's best work.[1]

But then Leavis begins the same examination with a rigorous exclusion of Coleridge's 'philosophy of art' as being merely 'Coleridge's philosophy' and, as such, not worth the attention of the literary student. This neatly poses the difficulty all English aestheticians have encountered in winning serious attention since Coleridge's day. Coleridge's philosophy (as Leavis rightly suggests) is no longer worthy of study by philosophers; and simply because it is philosophical it is not worthy of study by critics either. That seems to leave it without readers of any kind. The result of this strange departmentalizing has been that Coleridge's descriptive criticism has tended to be divorced from its foundations, studied as if it were something other than variations upon a given theme, and not unnaturally found to be disappointing.

Coleridge's descriptive criticism, in terms of subject, falls into three groups. First, there is the confused body of his Shakespearean criticism, principally in the 1811-12 lectures on Shakespeare and Milton, as well as various marginalia and notes; together with

[1] *Scrutiny*, IX (1941), reprinted in *The Importance of Scrutiny*, edited by Eric Bentley (New York, 1948), pp. 86-7.

Chapter 15 of the *Biographia Literaria*, largely a revision of one of his lectures of 1811-12 and entitled 'The specific symptoms of poetic power elucidated in a critical analysis of Shakespeare's *Venus and Adonis* and *Lucrece*.' Second, there is the critique of Wordsworth in the *Biographia Literaria*, chapters 14, 17-20, and 22. And third, there is a vast miscellany of comments on various poets, mainly of the English seventeenth century, in lectures, marginalia, notes, and even formal treatises, such as the tribute to Samuel Daniel in the eighteenth chapter of the *Biographia*, or to Herbert's *Temple* in the nineteenth. The modern reputation of these, and some other, poets stems from such passing recommendations, though it is worth noticing at once that Coleridge is not much more sympathetic to the Metaphysical style than Johnson had been: the Herbert he discovered and loved is a 'well-bred gentleman' in his expressions whose language possesses a 'simple dignity', in spite of a 'too frequent quaintness of the thoughts'. Characteristically, Coleridge does not recommend the older English poets for their own virtues: his concern, as he explains at length in the sixteenth chapter of the *Biographia*, is to unite their 'characteristic merits' with those of his own age in an ideal poetic language.

Coleridge's view of Shakespeare survives, unfortunately, mainly in the form of lecture-notes of varying authenticity. His whole career as a lecturer deserves a quick review. He is known, for certain, to have delivered seven major series or groups of lectures, of which only three or four substantially survive. The first, delivered in Bristol between January and November 1795, on historical and political questions, survives only sketchily. The second, given in London at the Royal Institution from January to June 1808 and entitled 'Principles of Poetry', being mainly on Shakespeare and Milton, is largely lost: a profoundly complicating factor, since A. W. von Schlegel was delivering his own course on the drama in Vienna at the same time, and the loss leaves the question of Coleridge's alleged plagiarism of Schlegel forever uncertain. The third course (18 November 1811 to 27 January 1812) is the chief single source of our knowledge of Coleridge's Shakespearean criticism, being delivered near Fetter Lane, in London, under the inaccurate title 'Shakespeare and Milton in Illustration of the Principles of Poetry, and the Applications as Grounds of Criticism . . . to the Later English Poets'; it has survived in two reports by members of his audience. As in 1808, he hoped to reach the poets of his own age and, as in 1808, he failed to do so. Fourthly, Coleridge gave at least two series of lectures in the course of 1812 on classic and romantic drama, largely lost. Fifthly, he gave several courses in Bristol in 1813 and 1814 on Shakespeare, Milton, and various political issues, of which we have only notes and newspaper reports. Sixthly, from January to March 1818 he delivered, again near Fetter Lane, a course which remains our chief source of his non-Shakespearean criticism, a survey of English poetry from the Middle Ages to the eighteenth century, which survives in autograph notes and in reports. And seventh, from December 1818 to March 1819, in the Strand, he delivered a course of lectures on the history of philosophy, which has survived in shorthand notes,[1] and, concurrently, two successive literary courses that have not survived at all.

We are fully entitled to feel confused. In spite of the efforts of his nephew Henry Nelson Coleridge, and of his daughter Sara, to collect such material and render it continuous, and in spite of the more scrupulous efforts of modern editors, the form in which Coleridge's analysis of Shakespeare and other poets has survived does not invite. It is not surprising if a good many strange notions are abroad concerning the nature of this material, based on repetitious quotations of a few extracts. The oddest, perhaps, is that Coleridge should be called a character-critic, a follower of Maurice Morgann and an ancestor of A. C. Bradley, based on his famous remark, 'I have a smack of Hamlet myself, if I may say so.' More recently, an attempt has been made to represent him as an ancestor of G. Wilson Knight and the post-1930 school of imagery-analysis.[2] The second is certainly nearer the mark, but Coleridge, though interested in imagery, can hardly be said to analyse it; he never examines the text of an entire play or poem with a view to isolating single images or systems of imagery. As

---

[1] First published as *Philosophical Lectures*, edited by Kathleen Coburn (1949).

[2] Barbara H. Hardy, 'A Smack of Hamlet', *Essays in Criticism*, viii, (1958), and M. M. Badawi, 'Coleridge's Formal Criticism of Shakespeare's Plays', ibid., x (1960).

for character-analysis, the claim is absurd. Bradley's style of criticism was based upon an assumption that Shakespearean characters
are as naturalistic as the characters of nineteenth-century novels;
and if there is one species of literature Coleridge is not interested
in, it is the novel. All the novels of Jane Austen and Walter Scott
appeared during his working life, and yet there is scarcely a mention of one of them in his books and lectures. The whole quality
of his mind was too abstract and too humanly disinterested to make
it imaginable for him to pose such questions as 'How Many
Children Had Lady Macbeth?' (Bradley, to do him belated justice,
was well aware of the absurdity of this question, and said so.)
The essential nature of Coleridge's Shakespearean criticism defies
classification in terms of the great modern schools. It comes near
to defying it in any terms, but if sense is to be made of it at all, it
can only be in terms of Coleridge's own aesthetic principles.

The 1811-12 lectures on Shakespeare are a very explicit attempt
to illustrate the principles of 'counteraction' and 'organic growth'
in relation to the greatest of all the English poets. The poet, in
Coleridge's view, does not create – he becomes; a poem is not
created – it grows, like a tree, as if with an inner life of its own.
Shakespeare's works are handled as a vast illustration of the failure
of Aristotle's principle of art as an imitation of nature, and the
theoretical foundations are firmly laid before the illustrations are
offered. This is what he is reported to have said in Lecture III:

Of Shakespeare he had often heard it said that he was a close copier
of nature, that he was a child of nature, like a Dutch painter[1] copying
exactly the object before him. He *was* a child of nature, but it was of
human nature and of the most important of human nature. In the
meanest characters, it was still Shakespeare: it was not the mere Nurse
in *Romeo and Juliet*, or the Dogberry in *Much Ado about Nothing*, or the
blundering Constable in *Measure for Measure*, but it was this great and
mighty being changing himself into the Nurse or the blundering Constable that gave delight . . . Compare it to Proteus, who now flowed, a
river, now raged, a fire, now roared, a lion . . .

The attack upon the whole neoclassical tradition of Shakespeare
criticism, and especially upon Johnson's 1765 preface, is as plain as

[1] 'Dutchified' is a term of contempt in Coleridge for an excess of poetic
detail. Cf. *Shakespearean Criticism*, op. cit., II, 174.

can be – upon Johnson's assertion that 'Shakespeare is, above all writers . . . the poet of nature; the poet that holds up to his readers a faithful mirrour of manners and of life.'

The most sustained attempt to analyse a Shakespeare play according to the new mode is to be found in Coleridge's account of *The Tempest* in the ninth lecture of the 1811-12 series. The lecture, in Collier's report, is a comprehensive attack on neo-Aristotelian dramatic criticism, including the three unities; and especially against the French neoclassical critics, such as Voltaire. 'These creatures', Coleridge observes acidly, 'have informed us that Shakespeare is a miraculous monster, in which many heterogeneous components were thrown together, producing a discordant mass of genius – an irregular and ill-assorted structure of gigantic proportions.' He then analyses *The Tempest* 'by way of example'. It turns out to be an example of 'organic', as against 'mechanic', regularity – Coleridge is, of all the English critics, the fondest of abstract distinctions – and this distinction is very like the one R. G. Collingwood was to draw, more than a century later, between 'art' and 'craft'; for while a 'mechanic' object is moulded in identical form to its prototype, an 'organic' one, such as a Shakespearean character, conceals 'a law which all the parts obey, conforming themselves to the outward symbols and manifestations of the essential principle'. A Shakespearean character, in fact, is not pre-determined: it shapes itself according to circumstances, and the poet acquires knowledge of how his puppets would react by an act of empathy. Gonzalo's surprisingly moderate reaction to the Boatswain's rudeness during the storm in the first scene of the play, Coleridge continues ('I have great comfort from this fellow . . .'), shows how Shakespeare 'transports himself into the very being of each personage'; and so does Miranda's first sight of the ship ('A brave vessell, Who had, no doubt, some noble creature in her, Dash'd all to peeces'), since Shakespeare has felt his way into the mind of an unknowing girl who has seen only Prospero and Caliban. This is the characteristic tactic of analysis employed by Coleridge throughout his sporadic examination of Shakespeare's plays and poems, and his conclusion may be simply stated. It is that Shakespeare's supremacy among the English poets lies not, as Johnson supposed, in the richness and detail of his observation – no 'mere observation' of old women, he concludes, could in itself have produced the portrait of the garrulous Nurse in *Romeo and Juliet* – but in the wide sympathy that enables him to identify himself at will: 'The great prerogative of genius . . . is now to swell itself to the dignity of a god, and now to subdue and keep dormant some part of that lofty nature, and to descend even to the lowest character – to become everything, in fact . . .' (Lecture VII, 1811-12). Everything 'but the vicious', Coleridge adds, with an unexpected intrusion of simplicity. It is easy to forget that he believed in his theory of counteraction in a literal sense, and not as metaphor.

We should expect Coleridge's aesthetic to find its ideal illustration in the critique of Wordsworth that dominates the second half of the *Biographia Literaria*, following immediately upon the most comprehensive account we have of that aesthetic in chapters 12-13. He has a perfect – indeed, all too easy – target in the 1800 preface, where neo-Aristotelianism achieves its final *reductio ad absurdum*. And the poety of Wordsworth lends itself to the kind of distinction-making in which Coleridge delights. Its inequalities provoke a reasoned explanation, and the imagination-fancy distinction defined in chapter 4, and again in chapter 13, was never used to better purpose than here:

I challenge for this poet the gift of imagination in the highest and strictest sense of the word. In the play of fancy Wordsworth, to my feelings, is not always graceful, and sometimes recondite. The likeness is occasionally too strange, or demands too peculiar a point of view, or is such as appears the creature of predetermined research rather than spontaneous presentation (ch. 22).

This account is fairly precise, when we recall that, whereas the imagination is given to 're-create, . . . idealize, . . . unify,' the fancy 'has no other counters to play with but fixities and definites' and is a mere 'mode of memory' (ch. 13). Here, indeed, are the two Wordsworths, and Coleridge was the first critic to demonstrate how oddly they co-exist, and how intimately:

> 'Once I could meet with them on every side,
> But they have dwindled long by slow decay;
> Yet still I persevere, and find them where I may.'

> While he was talking thus, the lonely place,
> The old man's shape, and speech, all troubled me:
> In my mind's eye I seemed to see him pace
> About the weary moors continually,
> Wandering about alone and silently.[1]

It is the leech-gatherer who speaks, and the first stanza is 'fanciful' indeed, the merest reportage. The second stanza, as Coleridge notes, belongs to another order of experience.

Still, the entire critique suffers from its status as a mere illustration. The linguistic theories of the 1800 preface are efficiently exploded, and the case is made in chapters 19 and 20 for a new poetic diction, based upon a study of some of the older poets, notably Chaucer, Daniel, and Herbert: a diction based on *lingua communis* or 'neutral style', which is 'natural', 'unstudied', and 'logical'. For a moment Coleridge flirts with a legislative purpose in his criticism. But the role of an arbiter of literary fashion was never a congenial one to him, and his repeated failure in lectures to consider the state of contemporary poetry surely suggests a strong distaste for the part. And descriptive criticism, too, is sent to the tradesmen's entrance. For an analysis of Wordsworth's verse as such, we have to wait till chapter 22, with its long catalogue of Wordsworth's 'defects' and 'beauties'. And even here, the approach is abstract: poems are marshalled under eleven heads – five defects and six excellences – and provided with illustrative texts from the *Lyrical Ballads* and the poems of 1807 and 1815. Only this chapter, in the whole book, deserves the title of extended analysis, and it is the longest single analysis that Coleridge ever ventured in print. Hasty as its composition evidently was, and extravagant in its wealth of quotation, the critique is scattered with evidences of an analytical delicacy and insight that deserve the title of greatness, though they are too occasional and too sporadic to unite into a major critique. Coleridge's rich capacity for perceiving and identifying distinctions is at last directed to a particular end, though his judgements are still more generalized than we should think proper today – more generalized, even, than Johnson's had been. The five defects, and less clearly the six excellences, are ranged in

[1] From 'Resolution and Independence' (1807), quoted in ch. 22 of the *Biographia*.

ascending order of generality: both lists begin with questions of style, and end with questions of subject, so that the very ordering of Wordsworth's trial, admirably inclusive as it is, is weighted in favour of a certain kind of philosophical amplitude. Not that Coleridge over-values the philosophical element in poetry: he is almost uncharitably funny about his old friend's endless solemnity when he protests that 'the feelings with which, as Christians, we contemplate a mixed congregation rising or kneeling before their common Maker, Mr Wordsworth would have us entertain at all times, as men and as readers.' The five defects are 'inconstancy' of style, 'matter-of-factness' (or a 'laborious minuteness' of detail), 'an over-fondness for the dramatic form', 'an intensity of feeling disproportionate to such knowledge and value of the objects described as can fairly be anticipated' or 'verbal bombast', and 'thoughts and images too great for the subject' or 'mental bombast'. It does not matter that the list of Wordsworth's excellences that follows contradicts much of this indictment; Coleridge's whole case is based on the conviction that there are two Wordsworths, and that his poems are marked by incongruity on every level. 'An austere purity of language' is the first, followed by 'a correspondent weight and sanity of the thoughts and sentiments', 'the sinewy strength and originality of single lines and paragraphs', 'truth of nature in his images and descriptions', 'a meditative pathos', and 'the gift of imagination'. The scheme allows him opportunities for closer analysis than one might expect: not, in general, in the wealth of quotations, which are offered merely as illustrations of general qualities, but in Coleridge's loving concern for the quality which distinguishes a Wordsworthian poem from any other: 'a sympathy with man as man; the sympathy indeed of a contemplator, rather than a fellow-sufferer or co-mate ... but of a contemplator from whose view no difference of rank conceals the sameness of the nature; no injuries of wind or weather, of toil or even of ignorance, wholly disguise the human face divine ...'

It is difficult to summarize, in historical terms, the achievement of a critic whose influence has been as delayed, and as dubious, as that of Coleridge. His overriding interest in the creative process was one which later nineteenth-century critics did not share, and it is not clear that, in our own century, he has taught I. A. Richards, T. S. Eliot, or G. Wilson Knight anything they would not have thought of for themselves. Most modern parallels are decidedly *post facto*: the alleged likeness of Coleridge's Shakespearean criticism to the modern school of imagery-analysis was not suggested until nearly thirty years after the appearance of *The Wheel of Fire* (1930). Coleridge's aesthetic could not appeal to a generation of Victorians to whom no system of aesthetics was of much interest. As a descriptive critic, his achievement is brilliant but sporadic, and offers no single example worthy to be advanced as a model. If his criticism survives, as it vigorously does, it is not by virtue of what it demonstrates but by virtue of what it abundantly suggests, for no English critic has so excelled at providing profitable points of departure for twentieth-century critics. Perhaps there is something perverse about a professional pundit who had so little to say that was comprehensible to his own century; but, a hundred years later, his manuscripts, as they belatedly see print, seem among the richest of our capital assets. They are the relics of a mind passionately in love with free inquiry, concentrated and disciplined in its determination to decipher the secret of poetic discourse. The obsession is an eccentric one, in English terms: a culture as intensely literary as that of England has little reason to pose questions about literature as abstract and as sceptical as those which Coleridge, for thirty years, struggled to answer.

Chapter 6

LAMB, HAZLITT, DE QUINCEY

THERE is no School of Coleridge in nineteenth-century English criticism, and the achievement of Charles Lamb (1775-1834), Coleridge's friend since their schooldays at Christ's Hospital, suggests in its minor distinction how difficult and confusing a master Coleridge must have seemed. Lamb's criticism, almost all descriptive apart from a late essay on 'Stage Illusion', is tiny in its scope. It could be collected – and has been collected[1] – into a slim volume of less than fifty thousand words, and survives as something altogether desultory, scattered through his letters, the apparatus of the *Specimens* (1808) and other editions of his favourite authors, the monthly and quarterly reviews, and of course *The Essays of Elia* (1823-33). Unmistakably Coleridgean in its subject-matter – it concerns itself overwhelmingly with such favourite subjects of Coleridge's as Elizabethan and Jacobean drama, the prose of Sir Thomas Browne, Jeremy Taylor, Fuller, and Walton, and contemporary romanticism – it looks timid and cautious when set beside the revolutionary assertions of some contemporary critics. Everything points to a lack of confidence. But Lamb is one of those rare authors who can make a virtue of timidity and amateurishness. Throughout his long clerkship in East India House (1792-1825) he would never have pretended to be an 'important' critic, and only asks that he should be seen lucidly for what he is: a good friend and a good disciple whose critical intuitions possess, at the best, a delicacy unknown to more vigorous and ambitious intelligences than his own.

There are moments, none the less, when we feel that Lamb's real mentor is not Coleridge but Samuel Johnson, and it comes as a start, in view of Lamb's reputation as leader of the nineteenth-century vogue for the quaint and the baroque, to watch him inveigh as heavily as Johnson might have done against medieval

[1] *Lamb's Criticism*, edited by E. M. W. Tillyard (Cambridge, 1923).

and Tudor extravagances, both literary and moral. The following judgement against Marlowe could easily belong to some neo-classical critic:

Tamburlaine . . . comes in, drawn by conquered kings, and re-proaches these 'pampered jades of Asia' that they can 'draw but twenty miles a day'. Till I saw this passage with my own eyes, I never believed that it was any thing more than a pleasant burlesque of mine ancient's. But I can assure my readers that it is soberly set down in a play which their ancestors took to be serious.

and 'Barabas the Jew, and Faustus the conjurer, are offsprings of a mind which at least delighted to dally with interdicted subjects.'[1] Only the 'quaint' reference to 'mine ancient' belongs to the beloved Lamb of the Elians, forever tolerant and (in spite of personal tragedy) forever good-humoured. The sentiments belong to the world of Johnson's sound Anglican moralism that makes no bones about being shocked and will have no truck with the fanci-ful. There is much more of this sort of thing in Lamb than is commonly remembered. The moral assumptions of his criticism are not exactly stern. But they are conventional, a part of that con-tinuum of English prudery that has its roots in eighteenth-century middle-class piety and looks forward to the great Victorian censor-ship. The fact is that his taste for Renaissance quaintness is only a degree or two more developed that Johnson's, and hardly different at all from that of the Wartons or of his friend Coleridge. It is rather a sympton of the growth of a popular historical sense, of the vogue for the 'Gothic' past, than of any determined critical analysis. Lamb's taste for the seventeenth century is sentimental, and scarcely more than sentimental: he could no more abide the Metaphysical conceit than Coleridge could, and preferred Wither, who 'lays more hold of the heart', to Quarles's 'wretched stuff': 'Religion appears to him no longer valuable than it furnishes matters for quibbles and riddles; he turns God's grace into wan-tonness. Wither is like an old friend . . .'[2] On the other hand, he can see virtues in Renaissance poetry less baroque than the imagery of Quarles, and yet too particular to have appealed to

---

[1] Ibid., pp. 16, 17 (from the *Specimens* of 1808).
[2] Ibid., p. 67 (letter to Southey, 8 November 1798).

Johnson. Sidney's sonnets struck the mean that he loved best, 'full, material, and circumstantiated', in healthy contrast to late eighteenth-century verse, where there are too many 'vague and unlocalized feelings'.[1] Poetry *may* number the streaks of the tulip, in Lamb's view – perhaps ought to do so. The Johnsonian term 'Nature' resounds through his criticism, but it is a Nature strangely elastic in its scope, and includes even the matter of visions and of waking dreams:

> Where he [the true poet] seems most to recede from humanity, he will be found the truest to it. From beyond the scope of Nature if he summon possible existences, he subjugates them to the law of her consistency. He is beautifully loyal to that sovereign directress, even when he appears most to betray and desert her . . . Caliban, the Witches, are as true to the laws of their own nature (ours with a difference) as Othello, Hamlet, and Macbeth.[2]

This is to liberalize neoclassicism out of existence. But it is very characteristic of Lamb that, in offering his own version of the Coleridgean doctrine of organic growth, he should clothe it in the familiar but incongruous language of eighteenth-century aesthetics.

A sound Johnsonian critic, then, partly romanticized by his reverence for Coleridge: this seems an apter summary of Lamb's quality as a critic than any view that conceives of him as the perfect prototype of the romantic critic. Wordsworth, Coleridge, Hazlitt, and De Quincey are all more romantic critics than Lamb, and all of them reject more firmly than he did the 'Aristotelian' criteria of critical judgement. Compared with them, Lamb's position seems wavering and uncertain, and his belief in a clear, moral light and his affection for the obscure and cavalier are often in mild, unworried conflict. But he is not the kind of critic who takes himself seriously or thinks consistency to be any sort of virtue, and the doubleness of his vision is on the whole a matter for complacent pride. His attitude to Restoration comedy provides a perfect illustration. He has no doubt that, ultimately, it deserves the moral condemnation it has already received ('The business of their dramatic characters will not stand the moral test'). But, on

---

[1] *Lamb's Criticism*, p. 13 ('Some Sonnets of Sir Philip Sydney', in *Last Essays of Elia*).

[2] Ibid., p. 5 ('Sanity of True Genius', in *Last Essays of Elia*).

the other hand, 'I am glad for a season to take an airing beyond the diocese of the strict conscience . . . I come back to my cage and my restraint the fresher and more healthy for it. I wear my shackles more contentedly for having respired the breath of an imaginary freedom.'[1] The spiritual tourist is all the better for his little spree, though even on his day out he observes some essential rules, abandoning himself to Congreve and drawing the line at Marlowe. Such tolerances would not have been admitted by Addison or Johnson: but they have a future, they make sense in Victorian terms, in the liberal morality of Leslie Stephen, Walter Pater, and the Bloomsbury Group.

Lamb's attraction to Jacobean tragedy, which he sought to revive through the slightly bowdlerized *Specimens of English Dramatic Poets Who Lived about the Time of Shakespeare* (1808), is all of a piece with this readiness to enjoy new and alien experiences. The attraction is one of opposites. Lamb's very gentleness is drawn to the Webster of *The Duchess of Malfi*: 'To move a horror skilfully, to touch a soul to the quick, to lay upon fear as much as it can bear, to wean and weary a life till it is ready to drop, and then step in with mortal instruments to take its last forfeit: this only a Webster can do.'[2] The distance between Lamb and Webster is so vast that we are surprised he can see him even with a telescope; yet he defines Webster's essential quality with notable accuracy, if only by generalities. Lamb's analysis is rarely more particular than this, and its chief virtue is the virtue of sound characterization. He loves to tell you, in a few phrases, what a whole author is like. And the taste that moves him is conservative but self-indulgent, in love with quaintness if it is not too quaint, and romanticism if it is not too romantic, but above all impressed by the abiding worth of sober virtue. The middle-aged critic who welcomed Wordsworth's *Excursion* (1814) in the *Quarterly Review* for its devotional seriousness rejected much of the work of the second generation of romantic poets, including all of Byron and Shelley, and much of Keats. 'They are for younger impressibilities. To *us* an ounce of feeling is worth a pound of fancy.'[3]

[1] Ibid., p. 75 ('On the Artificial Comedy of the Last Century', in *Essays of Elia*).   [2] Ibid., p. 23 (from the *Specimens*).
[3] Ibid., p. 110 (from the review of *Lamia*, *New Times*, 19 July 1820).

The criticism of William Hazlitt (1778-1830) is at once more ambitious and less satisfying than Lamb's: it is not content to be judged as minor. Hazlitt is the first English writer to make a major career out of descriptive criticism; following upon the double failure of his early career – after declining to follow his father into the Unitarian ministry, he tried to be a painter, and then a philosopher, and did not satisfy himself in either part – his concern is uniquely with the English poets past and present. His criticism is purely descriptive, with no motive beyond analysis and judgement: or rather judgement and then analysis, for he understood perfectly what some later critics have laboured to deny, that evaluation is rather the starting-point of criticism than its aim and object. If you are any sort of reader (let alone a professional critic) you begin with an opinion – it is nonsense to talk of 'arriving' at one: 'to feel what is good and give reasons for the faith that is in me', as Hazlitt defined his task. He was, at any rate, good at getting his priorities right.

To feel well, however, implies a wide and delicate sensitivity, and to give reasons that matter calls for analytic gifts. Hazlitt's criticism has enjoyed a sizeable reputation for more than a century, but it is doubtful if it will bear examination on either count. For sensitivity, he possesses only a familiar clutch of *a priori* notions of a romantic radical born a little too late; and since he never pursues analysis beyond a few phrases, we are not entitled to suppose that he was capable of it.

The range of his interests is superficially impressive. At the age of thirty-eight he turned to criticism with a study entitled *Characters of Shakespear's Plays* (1817), in which he attempted to 'vindicate the characters of Shakespeare's plays from the stigma of French criticism', allowing some credit to August Wilhelm von Schlegel as a precursor. But Hazlitt's account of Shakespeare is as simple-minded as his title suggests, and he commits the elementary offence of detaching figures from their dramatic contexts, as Schlegel and Coleridge rarely do. In the same year appeared a collection of essays entitled *The Round Table*, including his review of Wordsworth's *Excursion*, and in 1818 a collection of his dramatic reviews, *A View of the English Stage*, and the eight *Lectures on the English Poets*, a synoptic view of the major poets from Chaucer to the contemporary scene. In 1819 the *Lectures on the English Comic Writers* were published, mainly on eighteenth-century literature, and in 1820 the *Lectures on the Dramatic Literature of the Age of Elizabeth*; and finally, after the period of his marital crisis of 1823-4, *The Spirit of the Age*, or essays on writers of the previous half century, which appeared anonymously in 1825. The achievement is no doubt deliberately comprehensive: so far as verse and drama are concerned, little or nothing that he valued highly in modern English escapes this battery of essays and lectures, all composed in the last fifteen years of his life.

And yet, when all is said, what are the merits of it all, beyond a few telling phrases? Hazlitt's language has at times a certain splendour, but a splendour flyblown and empty of significance, like a schoolboy in a hurry with his homework anxious to impress a master with a taste for rhetoric. His language abuses meaning: look, for instance, at the famous 'general notion' of poetry in the introductory lecture of 1818, 'On Poetry in General': 'the natural impression of any object or event, by its vividness exciting an involuntary movement of imagination and passion and producing, by sympathy, a certain modulation of the voice, or sounds, expressing it'.[1] This is hopeless confusion – whose impression (poet's or reader's?); and how does anyone's impression 'produce' modulations? Or consider the pompous claims for poetry in the paragraphs that follow, father to so many confusions; 'wherever there is a sense of beauty, or power, or harmony, as in a motion of a wave of the sea . . . – *there* is poetry, in its birth . . . Fear is poetry, hope is poetry . . .' Does 'is' mean 'equals', or 'is the subject of'? But no use the machinery of siege – there is nothing to be taken. Hazlitt, as usual, is not saying anything, he is simply making a noise to suggest to us that he is, or has been, excited about something. He is eminently the kind of descriptive critic who flaunts his own personality at the expense of his subject, and finds in poetry an admirable and infinitely various excuse for the favourite exercise of self-exposure. He is the father of our Sunday journalism. We are in pursuit of nothing when we ask for evidence and elucidation of his impression of Chaucer, which (as it happens) looks just enough – 'his poetry reads like history. Everything has a

[1] *Complete Works*, edited by P. P. Howe (1930-4), v, 1.

downright reality' – or of Spenser, which is riotous nonsense – 'In
reading the *Faery Queen*, you see a little withered old man by a
woodside opening a wicket, a giant, and a dwarf lagging far
behind, a damsel in a boat upon an enchanted lake, wood-nymphs,
and satyrs . . .'[1] His quotations, which (as in many of our early
critics) are nearly all misquotations, do not illustrate passages before or after, and De Quincey was surely justified in condemning
as 'indolent' and 'dishonest' his habit of using quotations and misquotations in irrelevant abundance to advance his own argument.[2]
His criticism is void of scholarship even in the most elementary
sense, and he commits, as a professional critic, elementary errors
(such as attributing the Spenserian stanza to the Italians)[3] which we
should hesitate to forgive in the hurried work of such good poets
as Dryden and Coleridge. We realize very soon what the biographers' evidence confirms to the hilt; that Hazlitt's criticism is
not about the English poets, but about Hazlitt's memory – years,
sometimes decades, old – of the English poets as he first knew
them. A friend reports that 'unless what he was employed on was
a review, he never had a book or paper to any kind about him
when he wrote',[4] and his confessions in *The Plain Speaker* that 'I
hate to read new books', and that 'books have in a great measure
lost their power over me'[5] is one of the frankest statements of
incompetence in the record of literary journalism. 'I know how I
should have felt at one time', was his sad comment on Keats's
'Eve of St Agnes'.[6] And at no time did he have patience for difficulties. 'Of Donne', he wrote in the fourth lecture of 1818, 'I know
nothing but some beautiful verses to his wife, dissuading her from
accompanying him on his travels abroad, and some quaint riddles
in verse, which the Sphinx could not unravel.'[7] This suggests a

[1] *Complete Works*, op. cit. v, 35-6.
[2] *North British Review* (November 1848), reprinted in *De Quincey's Literary Criticism*, edited by Helen Darbishire (Oxford, 1909), p. 256.
[3] *Complete Works*, op cit., v, 43.
[4] Quoted by P. P. Howe in his *Life of William Hazlitt* (1947) (new edition), p. 259.
[5] *Complete Works*, op. cit., XII, 220, 225 ('On Reading Old Books'), first published in *London Magazine* (February, 1821), rather *early* in Hazlitt's career as a critic.
[6] Ibid., XII, 225.
[7] Ibid., v, 83.

mind closed to critical endeavour. The contrast with Coleridge's sensitive, compassionate regard for what is strange, as in his hesitating but just recommendation of Herbert's *Temple* in the nineteenth chapter of the *Biographia Literaria*, seems unchallengeable. Unless one looks to criticism for a few portable phrases – such phrases as Dryden's 'magnanimity of abuse', or Scott's 'pleasing superficiality' as a poet – Hazlitt is not even of pass quality as a critic of English. His gustiness and vigour may, as rhetoric, approach the virtues; but they also serve to mask a coarseness of apprehension and a conservative hatred of ideas which the nineteenth-century reader tolerated with alarming readiness. Only Leslie Stephen, in a brilliant essay on Hazlitt, has troubled to expose his philistinism: 'He recognized and denounced, but he never shook off, the faults characteristic of small sects,' he pointed out, concluding: 'To claim to have learnt nothing from 1792 to 1830 is almost to write yourself down as hopelessly impenetrable.'[1] Hazlitt may not have been hopelessly impenetrable. But the obstinacy of his Bonapartism long after Napoleon's crimes had been exposed to Europe, and his stubborn refusal to reread and reappraise English poetry, are lamentably alike.

The youngest of the three, Thomas De Quincey (1785-1859), suffered from no such intellectual obstinacy. He is, in fact, the most impressionable, and impressionistic, of all the English romantic critics, and marvellously retained a sense of enthusiasm and wonder for what he loved best in English poetry – the Elizabethans and Wordsworth – until the last, poverty-stricken years of a long life. His faults are not the faults of the doctrinaire, but simply those of a good man in a hurry, anxious to be fair, remarkably judicious, and too eager for his monthly cheque to be careful of fact and detail.

De Quincey's discipleship to Wordsworth was the starting-point of his critical career – the *Lyrical Ballads* appeared when he was only thirteen years old, and he settled in Grasmere eleven years later, in 1809; and though it grew discriminating with the years, and though his friendship with the older man ceased with De Quincey's unworldly marriage in 1817, it was a discipleship that never wavered in its ultimate loyalty. The final criterion of

[1] *Hours in a Library: Second Series* (1876).

excellence in all De Quincey's criticism, which is contained mainly in periodical essays of the 1820s and 1830s, is the 'moral sublime' of the poet whom, as late as 1845, he called 'not only supreme, but unique'.[1] De Quincey is the most Wordsworthian of critics. He is, in a way, more Wordsworthian than Wordsworth himself, whose 1800 preface is too Coleridgean to fit the quality of his genius, as De Quincey saw, or to be anything better than a 'needless embarrassment'[2] to the Wordsworthians. De Quincey's rebuttal of the 1800 theory of diction is intellectually almost as impressive as Coleridge's, and leaves a much better taste in the mouth. It is full of eloquent sympathy for a great poet who is out of his depth: 'How *could* a man so much in earnest, and so deeply interested in the question [of poetic diction], commit so capital an oversight?' he exclaims in affectionate indignation at Wordsworth's failure, half a century before, to cite examples of which past styles in English poetry he was for, and which against. As it is, he goes on, in a memorable passage that might stand as an epitaph on many controversies in aesthetics, 'no man, in this dispute, steadily understands even himself; and, if he did, no other person understands him, for want of distinct illustrations. Not only the answer, therefore, is still entirely in arrear, but even the question is still in arrear: it has not yet practically explained itself so that an answer to it could be possible.'[3]

Most of De Quincey's criticism, hasty and sporadic as it all is, looks like an attempt to rectify Wordsworth's unfortunate 'oversight' in failing to be a great critic as well as a great poet. His critical essays are mostly about his contemporaries, the romantic poets, rich in reminiscence and unreliable anecdote. Their quality is not easy to describe. They appear in a relaxed, playful, exuberant prose that none the less allows for strict organization and a firm, argumentative pressure. There is an underlying austerity in De Quincey's criticism, a faculty for reasoning at length of which Wordsworth and Hazlitt were utterly innocent, and a conscientious determination to get the right answer which Hazlitt did not

[1] *De Quincey's Literary Criticism*, op. cit., p. 221 (*Tait's Magazine*, September 1845).
[2] Ibid., p. 225.
[3] Ibid., p. 226.

share at all. His most famous critical essay, 'On the Knocking at the Gate in *Macbeth*', which appeared in the *London Magazine* as early as October 1823, not long after the successful series *Confessions of an English Opium Eater* (September–October 1821) that made his reputation, is as neatly organized a demonstration as the logician could wish, beginning with a posing of the question which looks chatty and is in fact wonderfully precise: 'From my boyish days I had always felt a great perplexity on one point in *Macbeth*: it was this: the knocking at the gate, which succeeds to the murder of Duncan, produced to my feelings an effect for which I could never account . . .' and proceeding by way of a 'digression' which is nothing of the kind towards a finely perceptive conclusion:

In order that a new world may step in, this world must for a time disappear. The murderers, and the murder, must be insulated . . .; we must be made sensible that the world of ordinary life is suddenly arrested – laid asleep – tranced – racked into a dread armistice; time must be annihilated; relation to things without abolished; and all must pass self-withdrawn into a deep syncope and suspension of early passion. Hence it is that when the deed is done – when the work of darkness is perfect, then the world of darkness passes away like a pageantry in the clouds: the knocking at the gate is heard; and it makes known audibly that the reaction has commenced; the human has made its reflux upon the fiendish; the pulses of life are beginning to beat again . . .

De Quincey has posed a question and then answered it with wonderful accuracy. But, in a way, the question is more original than the answer. No doubt it is modishly suspect, and modern critics who worry about something they call 'the Affective Fallacy', or the 'confusion between the poem and its results' are certain to be embarrassed by De Quincey's excellence as a critic – no critic could be more frankly 'affective' – and certain too to be puzzled why it is that *Macbeth* does not 'tend to disappear'[1] under such analysis. But the problem has been falsely defined. Certainly the affective reactions of some critics to some poems may be too

[1] W. K. Wimsatt and Monroe C. Beardsley, 'The Affective Fallacy', *Sewanee Review*, lvii (1949), reprinted in Wimsatt, *The Verbal Icon* (Lexington, Kentucky, 1954).

eccentric and too extravagant to be worth analysing (Arnold's personal fallacy[1]); and again, an irresponsible critic may tiresomely insist upon his own emotional response to a given poem to the extent of neglecting or denying its intelligible content. Both offences arise from a failure in the critic's historical sense, and both can be rebutted, if at all, only by an appeal to history. Swinburne's impressionistic *Study of Shakespeare* (1880), for example, calls for the expert historical study of Elizabethan theatrical convention to prove that Swinburne is writing not about Shakespeare but about himself. But to admit all this is not to deny that it is ever proper for the critic to analyse his own emotional reactions. In a sense, there is nothing else he can ever do. It is simply to insist that such reactions should be historically informed as well as deeply experienced. Much of De Quincey's criticism shows how good 'affective' criticism can be: he *feels* Wordsworth to be the greatest of contemporary poets, and then seeks reasons for his unique quality. He feels the knocking on the gate in Macbeth to be magnificently theatrical, and twenty years later he discovers why. To pose such questions at all, and so frankly, is to make descriptive criticism one degree more honest and more sane. The danger of eccentricity, in principle, remains – what if a reader were to object that he felt nothing of De Quincey's 'peculiar awfulness and depth of solemnity'? Such a critic can only help to sharpen the reader's own reactions to a given work – he cannot create a reaction out of nothing. And yet, given that his premise is generally shared, his analysis is likely to reveal more of Shakespeare's stagecraft than Johnson's remoter generalizations. It is the great merit of De Quincey as a critic that he trusts his own instincts enough to test them rigorously; and though he is modern enough to think analysis worth doing for its own sake, his favourite form of criticism begins in description and ends in generality. A beam of light touches the poem, and passes through it; and, for an instant we see its strange transparency, and understand in some part how it came to be made.

[1] 'The Study of Poetry' in his *Essays on Criticism: Second Series* (1888).

Chapter 7

MATTHEW ARNOLD

... the method of historical criticism, that great and famous power in the present day ... The advice to study the character of an author and the circumstances in which he has lived, in order to account to oneself for his work, is excellent. But it is a perilous doctrine that from such a study the right understanding of his work will 'spontaneously issue'.

THIS quotation from one of the last and best of the critical essays of Matthew Arnold (1822-88)[1] suggests at once how untypical a Victorian critic he was, and how proudly he knew it. The 'great and famous power' of historical criticism, against which no other Victorian critic before the nineties raised his voice, seemed to him implausible and over-rated almost before it had established itself. 'The old story of *the man and the milieu*' – that is how, in the same essay, he dismissed by misquotation the grandiose theories of Taine concerning 'race, milieu, moment' as the occasion for creative energy. Each civilized age has its favourite discipline from which special enlightenment is expected to flow. Today it is sociology; for Arnold's age it was undeniably history, and the new techniques of historical research summed up for the heroine of George Eliot's *Middlemarch* (1871-2) by the dread word 'German'. The amateur English tradition of Gibbon and Hallam had fallen back before the systematic researches of Niebuhr and Ranke. The techniques of the new scientific criticism of texts ('the Higher Criticism', as it came impressively to be called) had invaded the study of the Bible, and with the publication of seven *Essays and Reviews* in 1860 was shown to have established itself inside the Church of England. For the President of Mark Rutherford's nonconformist seminary in the 1850s, the word 'German' was 'a term of reproach suggesting something very awful, although nobody knew exactly

[1] 'A French Critic [Edmond Schérer] on Milton' (*Quarterly Review*, January 1877), reprinted in his *Mixed Essays* (1879).

what it was'.[1] Germany led: France followed only a little behind. A French reviewer confidently wrote as early as 1825 that the absolute study of texts was already dead in French criticism, and the day of historical criticism at hand: 'After long considering literature as something invariable and absolute, capable of submitting itself to prearranged forms, criticism now regards it as the variable and changing product of its own society.'[2] That was written when Arnold was three years old; in France, at least, the battle for history was already won. But England was submitting very fast. G. H. Lewes (1817-78) hailed the new 'scientific' historiography in his articles in the *Westminster Review* in the 1840s as the foundation of a future 'science of man'.[3] Years later, in a lecture delivered at St Andrews University in 1887, Leslie Stephen (1832-1904), whose long, rambling essays in criticism represent something of a triumph for his own relaxed, anglicized version of continental historicism, cautiously admitted that 'the historical method is now in the ascendant', affecting 'not only history in the old sense, but philosophy, political and social theory, and every other branch of inquiry which has to do with the development of living beings'. 'I will not say', he went on, that the study of literature can be 'made truly scientific'. But literature can be 'treated in a scientific spirit'.[4] A year later, Arnold was dead. He had spent a good deal of his energies for thirty years in denying it all.

The spirit of denial in Arnold's criticism is, on the face of it, the most striking thing about it. He is the great gainsayer of English criticism, the most insistent and professional of nonconformists.

[1] From his autobiographical novel, *The Autobiography of Mark Rutherford* (1881), ch. 2.

[2] H.R., 'De la littérature des Hébreaux,' *Globe* (2 April 1825), p. 467.

[3] 'Modern French Historians' (*Westminster Review*, XXXVI, September 1841), pp. 276-7. The utilitarians were among the most enthusiastic claimants for the new historiography of France and Germany as the basis of all future humane studies, and the early *Westminster Review* is full of such assertions. The battle was soon won. 'From this time,' wrote John Stuart Mill, twenty years later, on Comte's sociological discoveries, 'any political thinker who fancies himself able to dispense with a connected view of the great facts of history, as a chain of causes and effects, must be regarded as below the level of the age' (*Auguste Comte and Positivism* (1865), p. 86).

[4] Leslie Stephen, *Men, Books, and Mountains*, edited by S. O. A. Ullmann (Minneapolis, 1956), pp. 19, 25.

His characteristic strategy is, like Pope's Atticus,[1] to 'hesitate dislike'. He delights in sapping confidence. But in all this, paradoxically, he is only behaving after the convention of the Victorian intellectual: rude as he is against established literary values, he is no ruder than Carlyle and Ruskin against established society and morality. Iconoclasm is the strongest and deepest of currents among the Victorian intelligentsia. It was they, after all, who conceived the revolutionary doctrines by which the twentieth century lives and dies, and Arnold in his criticism is just such a spirit of contradiction incarnate. The literary values he recommends are those that the poetry of his day was least able to achieve; his cultural values are everything that cultivated opinion in his own day was not. Both are revolutionary alternatives to the *status quo*; for Arnold, like his contemporary Marx, challenged his own world to suicide and rebirth. The urbanity of his manner is not even superficially a conservative gloss; it was a red rag to a bull in a society that suspected urbanity, it sharpened the challenge.

Arnold's defiance of the Victorian tradition of poetry began in reaction against himself. In 1849 he had startled his friends with a first collection of poems, *The Strayed Reveller*, where the bright young man just down from Oxford revealed himself as a melancholy romantic in love with solitude. Three years later he issued a new collection of poems as *Empedocles on Etna*, and in 1853 replaced this drama of suicide with the miniature epic *Sohrab and Rustum*, and a preface written during the summer in reply to an anonymous and deprecating review of *Empedocles*.[2] The preface to the *Poems* of 1853, written at the age of thirty-one, is the first of Arnold's prose works, and oddly stiff and graceless it is when we think of the ironic elegance of his later prose. 'It is far less *precise* than I had intended,' he complained in a letter to his old schoolfriend Clough. 'How difficult it is to write prose.' For the remaining thirty-five years of his life he wrote hardly anything else.

Arnold's criticism measures the distance between his ambition as a poet and his performance. A poet in the tradition of Keats, he seeks in his prose to extricate himself from a romanticism he both loves and despises. Nothing, in the history of criticism, is more

[1] The Addison of the 'Epistle to Dr Arbuthnot' (1735), l. 204.
[2] *North British Review* (May 1853).

familiar than the spectacle of a poet turning in early middle age to justify his achievements and rationalize his failures, as Dryden had done – or, like Baudelaire and Eliot, to explore in prose notions for which, as poets, they felt themselves unready. Arnold's criticism begins in a more hostile spirit, in self-disgust, and his attack upon the rejected *Empedocles* in the 1853 preface, upon its extravagant subjectivity and its lack of action, is not much less than an attack upon the whole of his brief career as a poet.

The conscientious distaste for his own poetry which is the starting-point of Arnold's criticism began very early, before he had published his first volume of verse. 'What a brute you were', he wrote to Clough in the winter of 1848-9, 'to tell me to read Keats's letters . . . What harm he has done in English poetry. As Browning is a man with a moderate gift passionately desiring movement and fulness, and obtaining but a confused multitudinousness, so Keats, with a very high gift, is yet also consumed by this desire: and cannot produce the truly living and moving, as his conscience keeps telling him. They will not be patient, neither understand that they must begin with an idea of the world in order not to be prevailed over by the world's multitudinousness: or, if they cannot get that, at least with isolated ideas,' and he goes on to condemn the influence upon young writers of Keats, Tennyson, 'yes, and those d—d Elizabethan poets generally'.[1] In October 1852, in a further letter to Clough, he returns to the same point – that the greatest poets may be the worst influences:

Keats and Shelley were on a false track when they set themselves to reproduce the exuberance of expression, the charm, the richness of images, and the felicity, of the Elizabethan poets. Yet critics cannot get to learn this, because the Elizabethan poets are our greatest, and our canons of poetry are founded on their works . . . Modern poetry can only subsist by its *contents*: by becoming a complete *magister vitae* as the poetry of the Ancients did: by including, as theirs did, religion with poetry, instead of existing as poetry only, and leaving religious wants to be supplied by the Christian religion.[2]

The demand that poetry help to fill the spiritual void felt by a faithless age carries us, with surprising suddenness, into the heart

[1] *Letters of Matthew Arnold to Arthur Hugh Clough*, edited by H. F. Lowry (Oxford, 1932), pp. 96-7.
[2] Ibid., p. 124.

of a conviction he spent many years in justifying: that the poet in an open society and in conditions of expanding literacy must, like priests in the age of priests, offer guidance and instruction, and that the language of such poetry 'must be very plain, direct, and severe: and it must not lose itself in parts and episodes and ornamental work, but must press forward to the whole'. No wonder he felt his own poetry to be worse than useless, a mere addendum to the vicious, or at best irrelevant, Keatsian tradition. 'The Scholar-Gipsy', written in 1852, he confessed to Clough, 'at best awakens a pleasing melancholy. But this is not what we want.'[1] What we do want – and the 1853 preface might almost be considered a manifesto, if the savour of Arnold's own sense of failure did not hang so thickly over it – is a flat rejection of the poetry of the romantics and Elizabethans in favour of poems that are 'particular, precise, and firm', dealing with human actions not rooted in one time or place, but which 'most powerfully appeal to the great primary human affections: to those elementary feelings which subsist permanently in the race'. Here, in its grasp of essentials, lay the virtue of the civilization of the Greeks: 'They regarded the whole; we regard the parts.'

The demand is highly reminiscent, and in two ways. It is reminiscent, first, of Coleridge's call, provoked by the 1800 preface, for a new dignity or 'neutrality' of style in contemporary poetry. And secondly, it sounds a little like the defunct seventeenth-century obsession of English poets and critics with the 'heroic poem'; *Sohrab and Rustum* and *Balder Dead*, indeed, are little epics, as oddly isolated in time as those epigones of English pastoral poetry, 'The Scholar-Gipsy' and 'Thyrsis'. But both echoes are accidental: Arnold nowhere shows any sign of having absorbed Coleridgean aesthetics, and he is evidently conscious only of the classical epic of Homer and Virgil, while remaining noticeably indifferent to such neoclassical epics as *Paradise Lost*. It was part of the price he paid for rejecting the fashionable historicism of his day that he rarely knew who his own intellectual ancestors were.

In 1857, at the age of thirty-five, Arnold was elected to the Chair of Poetry in Oxford, a position of dignity he held for ten years, with the distinction of being the first incumbent to lecture

[1] Ibid., p. 146.

in the English language. But to say that is to create a false impression at once: a brilliant poet and man-about-town, still young and contemptuous of academic pedantry, blowing away the cobwebs of Latin scholarship in a mood of intellectual liberation. To realize how wrong all this is, one only has to turn to his inaugural lecture of 1857, 'On the Modern Element in Literature'.[1] It is a lecture against the modern element in literature, in which Arnold seeks an alliance with the classical dons in his audience against the prevailing tide of middle-class romanticism. Oxford University, he declared in the preface to the first series of Essays in Critisicm (1865), 'is generous, and the cause in which I fight is, after all, hers'. This is the voice not of modernity and liberation, but of neo-conservatism, of the candidate for Establishment honours. Arnold might almost be angling for a knighthood. It is true, of course, that the projected alliance between Arnold's New Hellenism and the Old was never effected, and involved too many incongruities ever to be effected; and Arnold may have felt a little ashamed of his Inaugural, with its measured warnings against romantic modernity in favour of ancient classical severity. He did not collect it. Indeed, the first three years of his ensuing Oxford lectures are largely lost (1857-60), and he reappears only in 1860-1, when he delivered three lectures On Translating Homer (1861), an attempt to define more closely the qualities of the 'excellent action' of the 1853 preface by means of a summary of the Homeric qualities that any English translator must achieve – rapidity of action, plainness of language, plainness of thought, and nobility – involving himself in controversy with F. W. Newman, whose own version of the Iliad (1856) provided Arnold with his whipping-boy. Shortly after, from 1862, he began to publish a series of articles on single authors, which he collected in 1865 under the title of Essays in Criticism; and for this he wrote, as a provocative opening, 'The Function of Criticism at the Present Time' – his first formal statement of his critical position since the 1853 preface, and logically continuous from it. The 1865-6 lectures On the Study of Celtic Literature (1867) were an uninformed attempt to apply racial, anthropological standards to literary studies.

[1] Macmillan's Magazine (February 1869), posthumously collected in the so-called Essays in Criticism: Third Series (Boston, 1910).

The first series of the *Essays in Criticism* marks the end of the initial stage in Arnold's career as a critic and publicist – the second, indeed, had already begun. The 1860s were perhaps the most controversial of nineteenth-century decades: the religious controversy was taking on a new pugnacity in such debates as that between Charles Kingsley and John Henry Newman. Ruskin half-deserted art-criticism to write *Unto this Last* (1862), and reviewers thought it mad. And in 1862 the Anglican Bishop Colenso of Natal produced a treatise to prove that the Pentateuch 'is not historically true'. It was pre-eminently the age of head-on intellectual collisions, and Arnold met Colenso, as nearly as he ever met any antagonist, head-on. This second phase of his critical career, which carried him far into theology, politics, and educational and social controversy, lasted till the late 1870s, when he returned, for the last few years of his life, to literary studies, including the articles ultimately collected to form the second series of *Essays in Criticism* (1888). The second, and most controversial, phase had confirmed Arnold's intellectual isolation. His attack on Colenso's liberal Christianity had alienated latitudinarian opinion, he had never permanently endeared himself to conservatism, and he now found himself pushed onwards and upwards into that position of exalted independence that accorded so aptly with his temperament. 'Conservatism, like Liberalism, taken alone,' he solemnly assured Eton schoolboys years after, 'is not sufficient, is not of itself saving.'[1]

It is a matter of convenience to consider the first and third phases together, as those in which literary interests predominated. The two series of *Essays in Criticism*, though separated in time by twenty years, are neatly complementary, and their coincidence suggests how little Arnold's critical attitudes evolved. If criticism led him into social interests, which led him in their turn back to poetry, it is not clear that he learnt much that was critically useful in the process. The first and second series of essays are, in outlook, all of a piece: they are contrasted only in subject. In the first series, he considers authors either minor in themselves (Joubert, Maurice de Guérin and his sister Eugénie), or remote from English readers (Spinoza, Marcus Aurelius, Heine). The list of names looks like an appeal to intellectual snobbery, and so it is – these are not

[1] 'A Speech at Eton', in *Irish Essays* (1882).

authors any English critic had tackled before, and they are offered now as a cure for intellectual isolationism. With Arnold, indeed, snobbery enters English criticism with a vengeance, and it has never been eradicated since. The Arnoldian critic invites the reader to enter a charmed circle of connoisseurship, as Johnson and Coleridge had never done, to separate himself from a brute mass of Barbarians, Philistines, and Populace. In 'The Function of Criticism at the Present Time' a programme of connoisseurship is offered, and in a manner of high-bred disdain which is almost as significant as the programme itself. Consider the language of the 1865 preface – and the present passage was not among those excised or subdued in the second edition of 1869: 'One cannot be always studying one's own works, and I was really under the impression, till I saw Mr Wright's complaint, that I had spoken of him with all respect.' Perhaps it is simply bad for people to be invited to lecture at Oxford. At all events, this combination of academic hauteur and lazy man-about-town insolence enlivens, and disfigures, much of his criticism and all of his controversial writings forever after. Both the romantic young poet, and the austere young critic of the 1853 preface, are dead: the new pose is adult, scintillating, intriguingly decadent: one is, he complains languidly, 'but the last sparkle of flame before we are all in the dark, the last glimpse of colour before we all go into drab – the drab of the earnest, prosaic, practical, austerely literal future.' No one, since Johnson in his *Lives*, had so nearly succeeded in writing a work of criticism that was also a bedside book: the unctuous grace of the *Essays* of 1865, even when recognized and exposed, still seduces the reader to answer the call to a 'critical effort' in England that will match the continental. For it is of the first importance that not one of the mediocrities singled out for commendation in the first series is an Englishman. For this English critic, the grass on the other side of the Channel was always greener. The English romantics, the staple reading of every literary Englishman, for all that they possessed 'plenty of energy, plenty of creative force, did not know enough' – but Goethe, unlike Byron, did, for his poetry is deeply informed by a 'great critical effort'. The French Revolution was 'a more spiritual event than our Revolution', as French intelligence is superior to mere English common sense, as France herself is 'the country in Europe where *the people* is most alive'. The ensuing attack on the criminal complacency of English society reminds us that the second, social phase of Arnold's interests has already begun.

'The Function of Criticism' establishes itself as a major document not only by embodying a literary programme and a new infectious tone of voice. Like most successful intellectual influences, Arnold provides slogans which give his arguments a memorable, even a portable, quality. They are, appropriately, borrowed largely from the French and German, for Arnold is an adapter rather than a coiner of terms. His final, question-begging definition of the function of criticism, 'a disinterested endeavour to learn and propagate the best that is known and thought in the world', lifts a word from an essay of Sainte-Beuve, who had spoken of the critic's task of introducing '*un certain souffle de désintéressement*'. 'Philistine', a word he first uses in the Heine essay,[1] is avowedly borrowed from the German *Philister*; and 'sweetness and light', of later usage, is (curiously enough) borrowed from Jonathan Swift. But Sainte-Beuve's influence is more thorough-going; his biographical-critical essays, which had begun to appear in French journals in 1824 to continue till his death in 1869, are the source of critical inspiration that Arnold always appealed to, and he twice acknowledged his debt to this 'perfect one' among European critics. It is obvious, indeed, that Sainte-Beuve's *portrait littéraire* is the structural model for an Arnoldian essay in criticism. Here, as in Johnson's *Lives*, most studies begin in biography and end in criticism; but now the two principal components are utterly merged, so that we should seek in vain the moment of separation, and both subserve a mysterious end superior to biography and critical analysis alike. A Sainte-Beuve portrait has a symbolic function, and his heroes, like Arnold's, are saints in a secular canon of excellence. The *portrait* is a pursuit of individual personality which is far more than a sum of biographical details: 'The day, the moment, when one hits upon the familiar gesture, the revealing smile, the indefinable blemish, the sad, intimate wrinkle that seeks in vain to hide itself under the already thinning hair – at this moment analysis vanishes into creation, the portrait

[1] *Cornhill Magazine* (August 1863), reprinted in *Essays in Criticism* (1865).

speaks and lives, you have found the man.'[1] This, on the face of it, is the very ecstasy of historical enthusiasm, and it seems incredible that any critic as bored as Arnold was with historical scholarship should have had any patience with it. But two considerations may have made this doctrine seductive to him, along with the carefully worked *portraits* and *causeries* which it inspired. First, it was French; and second, it was a doctrine not of history but of super-history. Arnold was too discursive an intelligence, and too amateur a scholar, to find any use for the new German tradition of historical research, or for such austere ambitions as Ranke's to re-discover the past 'as it really happened'. Sainte-Beuve's prescription is different from Ranke's in a subtle but important respect. It seeks to re-create the past, not as it was, but as it is for us: 'to see the object as in itself it really *is*',[2] as Arnold defines the critical function, suggests a certain unconcern for the poem as a document in time, 'as it really *was*'. Nineteenth-century historicism on the Continent generated its own special mysticism so fast that it is impossible to draw distinctions between historical scholars and historical re-creators: Ranke himself believed in such mystical realities as the 'inner life' of past political systems as surely as Sainte-Beuve held that 'the man' is more than a sum of biographical facts. What distinguishes the Arnoldian essay-in-criticism is the novel disproportion of fact and re-creation. There is a great deal of icing and not much cake. The essays are usually constructed on a similar plan to Sainte-Beuve – an interpenetration of biography and criticism, often with a brief, generalizing opening – but Arnold's pocket-biographies do not, like Sainte-Beuve's, suggest toil in libraries or a passionate concern for facts. They plagiarize heavily – sometimes upon an essay by Sainte-Beuve. And their manifest purpose lies elsewhere, in directing us, by a series of exemplary and cautionary tales, how, and how not, to behave. The first, continental series of 1865 teaches us what to be; the second, English series of 1888 teaches us what not. The national antithesis – mainly, but not entirely, a French-English one – is explicit in 'The Function of Criticism', where the ignorance of the

---

[1] 'Diderot' (*Revue de Paris*, June 1831), collected in *Portraits littéraires* (1844).
[2] *On Translating Homer* (1861), Lecture II. Arnold quotes his own phrase in the first paragraph of 'The Function of Criticism at the Present Time'.

English romantics is essentially an ignorance of continental ideas and poetry: 'this makes Byron so empty of matter, Shelley so incoherent, Wordsworth . . . so wanting in completeness and variety.' It is not simply their lack of reading, which was no worse than Sophocles's or Shakespeare's, but the fact that English society since the Puritan Revolution has been rootedly provincial. The very mediocrity of the Continentals selected for praise in the first series establishes the point that the distinction is not one of individual talent but of social maturity. A second-rate Frenchman like Joubert takes precedence over a first-rate English intelligence such as Coleridge. Arnold's Joubert is not a figure in history, a largely forgotten author of maxims in Napoleonic France: he is a 'French Coleridge' who, 'with less power and richness than his English parallel, . . . had more tact and penetration. He was more *possible* than Coleridge . . .' Enthusiastic as some of the praise for the English romantics may seem in the second series, when quoted out of context, it is too heavily hedged about with qualifications to soften the antithesis, and too condescending in tone to count for much in itself. Keats was 'a great spirit', true, but 'not ripe' for the creation of enduring works such as the *Agamemnon* or *King Lear*; Wordsworth lacks style; Byron emerges as a kind of infant prodigy, Shelley a crazed, angelic clown. This multiple indictment of the English achievement represents no kind of advance in principle upon the twenty-year-old demand, in 'The Function of Criticism', for a period of critical consolidation in English thought. It is a judgement in depth of the inadequacy of the whole range of English romanticism.

And yet, between the two series of essays, falls the great body of Arnold's work as a publicist: the educational treatises of the early sixties, the attack upon English social and cultural complacency in *Culture and Anarchy* (1869), and the religious treatises of the seventies such as *St Paul and Protestantism* (1870), *Literature and Dogma* (1873), and its sequel *God and the Bible* (1875). Increasingly irrelevant as it looks, the effort was not discontinuous from Arnold's career as a critic. For Arnold is very Victorian in his refusal to accept formal limitations. Johnson and Hazlitt, even Coleridge, would have thought it improper for a critic to venture so far; but for Arnold it was obvious that poetry and religion are aspects of a wider entity called 'culture', or the total current of ideas in which a given society lives. They are, for Arnold, different versions of human awareness of the human condition, but both T. S. Eliot and Lionel Trilling have surely falsified his purpose in suggesting that he ever sought to substitute poetry for religion.[1] The misunderstanding rests largely on a key passage from 'The Study of Poetry' (1880): 'Without poetry, our science will appear incomplete; and most of *what now passes with us* for religion and philosophy will be replaced by poetry' [my italics]. It is the sham religion of dogmatic assertion which will be replaced by poetry, not the true religion of Christian humanism. Arnold's real purpose is to defend what he considered the essentials of Christianity by means of a tactical retreat involving the abandonment of dogma. Colenso's 'weak trifling' against the historical truth of the Pentateuch seemed to him based upon 'a total misconception of the essential elements of the religious problem'. These 'essential elements' are never closely defined: the most we can say is that for Arnold, as for the young Newman years before, poetry and religion are similar in their humanist emphasis: 'Poetry then is our mysticism,' as Newman had argued in his early, Anglican days, 'and so far as any two characters of mind [the poetical and the mystical] tend to penetrate below the surface of things, and to draw men away from the material to the invisible world, so far they may certainly be said to answer the same end; and that is a religious one.'[2] Poetry and religion are not alternatives or competitors: for Arnold they are twin currents, and he sees their relationship as one of analogy. Each must purge itself to meet the new, continental challenge of criticism: poetry of its subjectivism, its provinciality, its indifference to new ideas; Christianity of its absurd infallibilities, whether the Papal infallibility of the Catholics or the Biblical infallibility of the Protestants, 'the notion that every syllable and letter of the Bible is the direct utterance of the Most High'. His own role, accordingly, he conceives as one of tactful midwifery, 'to ease a severe transition', as he puts it in *God and the Bible*, towards 'a Catholicism purged, opening itself to the light

---

[1] Cf. Eliot, 'Arnold and Pater' (1930), in his *Selected Essays* (1932); and Trilling, *Matthew Arnold* (New York, 1939), ch. 7.

[2] J. H. Newman, 'Prospects of the Anglican Church' (*British Critic*, April 1839).

and air, having the consciousness of its own poetry . . .' – a 'liberal'
Christianity, in fact, admitting a ritual whose significance, like
that of poetry, is accepted as analogical. The 'liberalism' of
Arnold's Christianity is extreme, in the sense that it involves a
total rejection of the supernatural; the Incarnation, according to a
mock-catechism in his 'Comment on Christmas', is not a historical
fact but 'a homage to the virtue of pureness', and the 'kingdom of
God' exists not in another world but in an 'ideal society of the
future'. Arnold's *religion*, a dogmatic Christian might plausibly
object, is a religion-substitute, whatever his notion of poetry may
have been. It is based upon a will to be Christian rather than upon
any real conviction; its motive seems hardly more respectable than
that of saving something out of the wreck. It certainly apes Christian observances, like other Victorian religious systems, including
Positivism and Marxism. It is a rehabilitation-school for honest
doubters, pseudo-Christian in a sense that is as likely today to
disquiet the reverent agnostic as the believer.

Such a religious philosophy would have no place in a history of
criticism, were it not for the fact that it brings us as near as we are
ever likely to get to a notion of Arnold's aesthetic. He is a critic
who disdains theory – which means, of course, not that he lacks
theoretical preconceptions, but that they can only be guessed at.
But his religion-poetry analogy is instructive enough to encourage
us to define an Arnoldian aesthetic by inference. The opening
passage of 'The Study of Poetry', which heads the second series of
Essays in Criticism (1888), concluding with the surprising statement
that 'the strongest part of our religion today is its unconscious
poetry', follows upon a still more surprising chain of argument:
'Our religion has materialized itself in the fact, in the supposed
fact; it has attached its emotion to the fact, and now the fact is
failing it. But for poetry the idea is everything; the rest is a world
of illusion, of divine illusion. Poetry attaches its emotion to the
idea; the idea *is* the fact.' The most astonishing aspect of this display of Poor Man's Platonism is that Arnold should think it called
for so little defence. He offers none. The utterly staggering assertion that poetry assumes the real world not to exist is made as
casually as if two and two were being added to make four. But the
doctrine that poetry is unworldly and evanescent is not just

Arnold's – it is Victorian, and could certainly be paralleled in the writings of Newman and Mill, and traced back to the poems and letters of Keats. It is no doubt too incoherent to be dignified by the title of an 'aesthetic'. Unlike the neo-Aristotelianism of Dryden, Pope, and Johnson, and unlike Coleridge's forgotten attempt to create for poetry a unique logical status of its own, the Victorian mind possessed, and sought to possess, no definable doctrine of the nature of art. It despised abstraction. It was insistently obscurantist, as Arnold is here, in all issues of critical theory. Saintsbury's *History of Criticism* (1900) disposed of 'the more transcendental' aesthetic, in his first chapter, as mere 'cloud Junos'. But at least it is clear from such passages that, for Arnold, the essence of poetry lay in its analogical character. The 'unconscious poetry' of Victorian religion refers, of course, to Arnold's view that what many Christians believed to be literally true (e.g. the Incarnation) was in his view only metaphorically so. 'Poetic', in fact, means 'metaphorical'. The damage done to Christianity by the Pauline Epistles derived, among other causes, from the fact that Paul 'orientalized', or used a language which made no distinction between statement and analogy:

The Hebrew genius has not, like the Greek, its conscious and clear-marked division into a poetic side and a scientific side; the scientific side is almost absent; the Bible utterances have often the character of a chorus of Aeschylus, but never that of a treatise of Aristotle. We, like the Greeks, possess in our speech and thought the two characters; but so far as the Bible is concerned, we have generally confounded them . . . [1]

The Jewish Paul, expressing himself 'by a vivid and striking figure', he claims to have been misinterpreted again and again by the literal Puritan intelligence. The claim anticipates I. A. Richards's distinction of the 1920s between 'emotive' and scientific statements; and most Victorian critics write as if poetic statements belong, indefinably, to some special order. But it is one thing to admit the force of poetry to be, like liberal Christianity, analogical, and another to show it to be so by the deliberate analysis of individual poems. The oddity of Arnold's criticism is that, while we are repeatedly enjoined to choose 'the best, the really excellent'

[1] *St Paul and Protestantism* (1870), ch. 1.

and to adopt 'a high standard and a strict judgement' and to eschew 'the historic estimate and the personal estimate',[1] we never see Arnold doing any of these things himself.

A historical estimate of Arnold must always conclude him to have been the most influential force among the Victorian critics. But there seems no good reason now for accepting his claims to greatness as a critic. Those who see civilization as a cause rather than a condition of mind will always be attracted to this most insistent and eloquent of its advocates. But to enjoin and encourage men to be critical is no more like being a good critic oneself than to urge men to be good is to be a serious contributor to the study of ethics. Those who see in Arnold's essays evidence of a major critical intelligence should set themselves to consider the following objections. Where, first, in the entire corpus of Arnold's criticism, do we see 'the great critical effort' at work upon any English text – upon a single play of Shakespeare or poem of Milton, Wordsworth, or Keats? The admirers of Johnson, Coleridge, even Hazlitt, can point to demonstrations of critical finesse. The admirer of Arnold's criticism has to accept the word for the deed. Again, Arnold's critical programme of a 'disinterested endeavour' to seek out and advocate the best is not only hopelessly question-begging: it is also hopelessly out of key with Arnold's own achievement. The *Essays in Criticism* and the Biblical reinterpretations are not even remotely disinterested. They are works of passionate partisanship by a skilful, urbane, not always candid controversialist with a zest for opposition. Their virtues, which are considerable, are essentially polemical. If Arnold had seriously tried to be 'disinterested', his career as a critic would not have happened at all. And it is no defence to argue that Arnold's passionate partisanship is all in favour of such *désintéressement*. There are Arnoldian values clearly implicit in his preference for French civilization over English, Joubert over Coleridge, Renan over St Paul, Wordsworth over Shelley, and Goethe over both. Those who cannot see such values as especially and distinctively Arnoldian disqualify themselves by their very discipleship from the task of judicious appraisal.

More than that, there is no coherent theory of poetry in Arnold's

[1] 'The Study of Poetry', op. cit.

criticism. This might not matter at all if, as in Johnson, a certain incoherence of ideas were compensated for by vigorous critical demonstration. As it is, Arnold's notion of a poetry purged, like religion, of fact and dealing in analogical truths is explored in vacuous and tautological language. There is far too much of this kind of thing in the *Essays in Criticism*:

> In poetry, as a criticism of life under the conditions fixed for such a criticism by the laws of poetic truth and poetic beauty, the spirit of our race will find . . . its consolation and stay.   But the consolation and stay will be of power in proportion to the power of the criticism of life.   And the criticism of life will be of power in proportion as the poetry conveying it is excellent rather than inferior, sound rather than unsound or half-sound, true rather than untrue or half-true.[1]

Does this really mean more than that, all things considered, good poems are better than bad poems?

For a critic who enjoyed the benefits of a public career, and who spent a dozen years in writing essays on religious and social questions, Arnold is culpably vague concerning the proper subject of poetry. The 1853 preface is free with advice to poets to be 'particular, precise, and firm' – about what? Arnold's own answer, in this first of his critical essays, is as 'general, indeterminate, and faint' as could well be. The true subject of poetry, he claims, is 'an excellent action' appealing to 'the great primary human affections'. This account, surprisingly, is never enlarged upon in the religious essays, though an image of perfection emerges in the 'sweetly reasonable' Jesus of *Literature and Dogma* (1873), a figure that combines the virtues of a liberal Protestantism with the Hellenist ethos of Rugby School. It may be – and reference to the poems would, on the whole, support this claim – that an action is 'excellent' to the extent that it recommends such values as loyalty and open-mindedness. But, given Arnold's generous use of such terms as 'good', 'true', 'sound', and 'sweet', it is hardly fair-minded of him to leave us so profoundly in the dark concerning the nature of light.

The deep voids and gaping incongruities of Arnoldian criticism are so evident that they call for explanation rather than analysis. It

[1] 'The Study of Poetry', op. cit.

is well worth asking how it happened: Arnold remains in most respects the most seductive of the great Victorian pundits, more variously and wittily intelligent than those great juggernauts Ruskin and Carlyle. He is almost never dull. And the vast contradictions that underlie his programme for the poetry and the civilization of England do not in any way diminish its fascination. The first impulse of Arnold's criticism, in the 1853 preface, was his own sense of incongruity as the author of poems that 'are not what we want'. This gap remains: we feel certain to the end that Arnold's head and heart are never likely to say the same things. The prophetic Wordsworth of his 'Memorial Verses' of 1850 who 'spoke and loosed out heart in tears' belongs to another world from that of the qualified praise of the essay of 1879. The poems of the last quarter-century only confirm our image of an incurably romantic poet pushing his own talent hard against the grain. One critic has already found 'a shadowy personal significance' in *Sohrab and Rustum*,[1] where 'the strong son is slain by the mightier father', and the hint is worth pursuing to explain the paradox of his prose. The great themes of the poems are of solitude and isolation in the midst of men ('The Scholar-Gipsy', 'Thyrsis', the Marguerite poems), most fittingly portrayed in *Sohrab and Rustum*, where the young Sohrab seeks his father through the world and meets him only in mortal combat. Arnold's father was also his headmaster, Thomas Arnold of Rugby, himself a propagandist for the classical tradition in English schooling, and Arnold's fast-fading, self-questioning career as a young romantic poet may have found its apt model, at the age of thirty, in the Persian fable of the young warrior who dies at the hand of the very father he has long sought out, while his dying injunction to Rustum reads like Arnold's injunction to his own society to revive the classical mode:

> Do thou the deeds I die too young to do.
> And reap a second glory in thine age (ll. 775-6).

And old Rustum's answer, not less aptly, seems to acknowledge the hopelessness of the task:

> And the great Rustum drew his horseman's cloak
> Down o'er his face, and sate by his dead son (ll. 858-9).

[1] Trilling, op. cit., ch. 4.

Chapter 8

HENRY JAMES

THE three decades between Arnold and Eliot (c. 1890-1920) defy useful generalization. It is the age of the aesthetes, such as Pater and Wilde, with their self-conscious attempt to demoralize criticism (in a peculiarly literal sense) by belittling the importance of meaning; but it includes the birth of an intensely moralistic tradition of novel-criticism in the reviews and prefaces of Henry James, and the triumph of motive-analysis in the *Shakespearean Tragedy* (1904) of A. C. Bradley. And all the while, in a less original key, the triumph of historical criticism is completed in the works of academic journalists such as George Saintsbury, Arthur Quiller-Couch, and Edmund Gosse, and with the establishment of chairs in English literature at Oxford and Cambridge around the turn of the century. Edwardian criticism is an odd compound of these several elements – the aesthetic, the moralistic, and the biographical. But then the quality of the age is confused and eclectic, heartily indifferent to dogmatic consistency, and delightedly aware of the variety of uses to which literature can be put. The immense mass of critical essays and literary histories of George Saintsbury (1845-1933), for instance, is built upon the assumption that no critical law is ultimately worth observing through thick and thin. Obviously the tradition in which he writes is, in one sense, continuous from the biographical tradition of Saint-Beuve: 'The essential qualities of literature, as of all art, are communicated by the individual, they depend upon idiosyncrasy.' But, paradoxically, 'biographical and anecdotic detail has, I believe, much less to do with the real appreciation of the literary value of an author than is generally thought. . . . If they are not allowed to shoulder out criticism altogether, there can be no harm in them.'[1] Such unconfident historical criticism is already vulnerable in its sheer lack of principle: biography has turned to gossip, and gossip is

[1] *Essays in English Literature, 1780-1860* (1890), pp. xii, xxviii-ix.

now defended on the only ground on which gossip can ever be defended – that it is amusing for its own sake. This is a whole world away from the serious Victorian enthusiasm that had seen in history the key to all knowledge, and though literary history has enjoyed a few belated triumphs, as in the works of R. W. Chambers (1874-1942) and C. S. Lewis, it has still failed to recover from the lack of confidence occasioned by late Victorian disparagement. Before T. S. Eliot and I. A. Richards were schoolboys, the ground for anti-history was being prepared by academics who could find no better excuse for information than Saintsbury could find, and by ninetyish aestheticians with an open contempt for the human values of literature. In this complicated story, the criticism of Walter Pater (1839-1894) occupies an ambiguous position: it is almost as moralistic as Arnold's and James's, and we are rarely allowed to forget for long that Pater was an Oxford don of serious Christian inclinations. But the doctrines which, in all seriousness, he offers are fatally trivializing, and no good critic could afford to swallow them. For Pater, the content of literature is an embarrassing necessity, 'mere matter' and 'nothing without the form', which is, ideally, 'an end in itself'. 'All art constantly aspires towards the condition of music'[1] is a slogan bound to reduce descriptive criticism to the level of unfalsifiable statements, for analysis only flourishes where content is seriously regarded and where the text is respected by critic and reader as a common point of reference. Pater's uncertain attack was quickly reinforced. Oscar Wilde (1854-1900), in a few flimsy essays on critical issues, popularized anti-history in epigrams that turned the historical sense on its head and had no difficulty in making it look old-fashioned. 'All bad poetry springs from genuine feeling'[2] – the fal-

---

[1] 'The School of Giorgione' (*Fortnightly Review*, October 1877), collected in the third edition of *The Renaissance* (1873, 1877, 1888). Pater is a tentative, unsystematic critic, and contradictory statements could easily be found. In the later essay on 'Style' for instance, in *Appreciations* (1889), he looks more like a disciple of Arnold than an ancestor of Wilde, 'the distinction between great art depending immediately, as regards literature at all events, not on its form, but on the matter'.

[2] From the dialogue 'The Critic as Artist'. There is surviving evidence of Wilde's early, conventional historicism in the prize-essay *The Rise of Historical Criticism* (Hartford, Conn., 1905), probably written at Oxford in 1879, which is full of the usual Victorian enthusiasm: 'Historical criticism . . . is part of that

lacy is not worth exposing, but its vogue in the nineties and after suggests how close the critical tradition came to total collapse.

The monumental exception lies in the criticism of Henry James (1843-1916), the American expatriate who, almost alone in his age and adopted country, continued to see literature intensely as a human and moral concern, and who dared to apply his critical talents, with immense seriousness, to the analysis of the novel. The revolution was extraordinarily sudden and complete. The English novel, as we have seen, had to wait an extravagantly long time – well over a hundred years – for a body of criticism to match its own dignity. It is even more surprising to find how suddenly and how powerfully the first mood of critical curiosity made itself felt. As late as 1884, Henry James, already a middle-aged novelist, called the English novel 'undiscussed': twenty years later he 'discussed' it so thoroughly in eighteen prefaces for the New York edition of his *Novels and Tales* (1907-9) that we are left asking what critical instrument peculiar to the novel he has failed to use. No critical revolution can ever have been so total as that represented by the New York prefaces. It is as if the horseless carriage had been invented at one stroke as a race-track model. Novel-criticism in English does not grow, as the art of analysing poetry grows painfully over the three centuries that separate us from Dryden. It just happens; for whatever importance we attach to the mid-Victorian reviews of novels by George Eliot, G. H. Lewes, and Walter Bagehot,[1] it is as clear today, as it was to James himself, that they were written without an assured technique and without an assured audience.

And yet a silent need there must have been to meet the 'contemporary deluge' of novels, as James called it in 1899: the novel, by the eighties, was self-evidently the pre-eminent literary form in England, and still longer and more firmly established in France and Russia. Critics like Pater and Wilde who looked elsewhere

---

complex working towards freedom which may be described as the revolt against authority. . . .' Cf. facsimile in Stuart Mason, *Bibliography of Oscar Wilde* (1914), p. 471.

[1] Cf. Richard Stang, *The Theory of the Novel in England, 1850-70* (1959), where greater importance is attached to the work of these pioneers than I have felt able to allow.

did so out of a deliberate, fastidious denial of the taste of their own time and place. James, an older man and a provincial American in origin, looked firmly to the present. For all the sophistication of his criticism, it was a characteristically naïve decision. For the first time since Fielding – that curious false-starter among critics of the novel – an English-speaking novelist writes memorably of his art.

The publication of James's notebooks in 1947 has established what was never worth doubting, that this art was deeply conscious and articulate from the start. Almost from the beginning, from the age of thirty-five until his death, James soberly set down his rational choices as he worked, and consciously, articulately, made up his mind on paper. It is in these notebooks, from the year 1878 onwards, that novel-criticism as we know it was born. Every novel and every story was willed into existence in an almost uniquely self-conscious sense, and the eighteen prefaces he wrote at the end of his career, in his mid-sixties, knowingly celebrate a great career. Those who believe good criticism to take its rise most naturally from the failure of a creative life should be directed here, where the balance between criticism and creation seems almost designedly perfect. Certainly the dominant tone of James's criticism is not, like that of Dryden's, apologetic. James's prefaces are in no sense works of self-justification. They are modestly confident, paradoxically buoyed up by a respect for the ultimate obscurity of all great works of art. Indeed, as James early emphasizes, his early novels were so remote from his elderly recollection as to be almost the work of another man.

Notebooks apart – and they must always remain apart, inevitably unique, studio-talk rather than analysis – James's criticism falls into three stages. Its scope is not wide; or to put it in another way, James concentrated his critical energies from the start. Almost all his criticism is about contemporary authors, almost all are English, American, and French, the great majority are novelists. First come the early reviews written from the age of twenty-one, some as early as a decade before his final settlement in Europe in 1875; at which early age, he tells us later, 'the verb *to contribute* took on at once to my ears a weird beauty of its own,'[1] and he

---

[1] 'The Founding of the *Nation*', *Nation*, New York (8 July 1915), reprinted in his *American Essays*, edited by Leon Edel (New York, 1956).

contributed articles to the newly-established *Nation* and elsewhere on any sort of book – including an attack on Dickens's *Our Mutual Friend* (1865).[1] His first review, indeed (October 1864), appeared only a few months after his first story, and he collected some of them early as *French Poets and Novelists* (1878). Secondly, there is the magnificent central phase that opens with a manifesto-like 'The Art of Fiction' (1884),[2] a review of a published lecture of this title by Walter Besant, and followed by major essays on Trollope (1883), R. L. Stevenson (1888), Maupassant (1888), Zola (1903), and Balzac (1905); while the early, deeply generous tribute to Hawthorne in the English Men of Letters volume (1879) may be added here, and late reviews such as 'The Younger Generation' on Conrad, Arnold Bennett, and Hugh Walpole.[3] Thirdly, there are the prefaces of 1907-9, composed in a single, confined period of preparation for the collected edition of his works. They are so nearly a total statement of his view of the novel that it is convenient to consider them at once, adducing evidence from the earlier reviews and essays as they seem helpful.

The New York prefaces occurred half-accidentally, arising out of a publisher's contract. In 1904-5 James revisited his native America for the first time in twenty years, and arranged the terms of a definitive edition of his fiction with Scribners of New York during the visit. Perfectionism prompted a revision of the novels, and the impulse to write prefaces at all may have taken its rise from a desire to explain the case for revision in the light of the genesis of each work. They must have been written mainly in the course of 1906-7, though James did not complete them all, or even know how many there were to be, until the appearance of the twenty-four-volume edition was well advanced. In a letter to Grace Norton, probably written as late as the beginning of 1908, he promises twenty-three volumes, and fifteen prefaces only, adding that the latter 'are difficult to do – but I have found them

---

[1] *Nation* (21 December 1865), reprinted in *The House of Fiction*, edited by Leon Edel (1957). Cf. Edel and Dan H. Lawrence, *A Bibliography of Henry James* (revised edition, 1961), pp. 289ff.

[2] *Longman's Magazine* (September 1884), collected with many of the following essays in *Partial Portraits* (1888) and *The House of Fiction*, op. cit.

[3] *Times Literary Supplement* (19 March and 2 April 1914), revised as 'The New Novel' in his *Notes on Novelists* (1914).

of a jolly interest'. The revising of the text of his fiction and the proof-reading were bad enough, but the prefaces were 'the real tussle'; he dictated them, according to his secretary Theodora Bosanquet, every morning over many weeks, in the rich, luminous style of his last period. We may guess that James surprised himself with the wealth of his own theoretical interests, and that the design grew under his hands as he wrote: why else should so methodical a genius set down so much of critical interest in a series of eighteen overlapping and interrelated essays, when their interest so far exceeds the merely prefatorial? There is a hint of missed opportunity in the letter to W. D. Howells (17 August 1908): 'They ought, collected together, . . . to form a sort of comprehensive manual or *vademecum* for aspirants of our arduous profession. Still, it will be long before I shall want to collect them together for that purpose and furnish *them* with a final Preface,' a hint usefully taken up by R. P. Blackmur in his collected edition of the prefaces, *The Art of the Novel* (1934). As a manual of novel-writing they are, inevitably, hopelessly disorganized, since each novel and each group of tales dictates its own set of critical questions. Besides, the very choice of stories for the New York edition now seems capricious. Six novels – *The Europeans* (1878), *Confidence* (1880), *Washington Square* (1880), *The Bostonians* (1886), *The Other House* (1896), and *The Sacred Fount* (1901) – were omitted altogether from the collection and, accordingly, have no preface. The case of *The Bostonians*, rejected by Scribners on prudential grounds, is especially regrettable, and was openly regretted by James himself. Chaotic, then, the material admittedly is, but we ought to feel grateful for what we have. At all events, the nine novels and the nine groups of tales which together compose the New York edition provide material assorted enough to call out most of James's resources as a critic.

James's object in his criticism, as it develops, is ambitious and clear: it is to create from nothing an English tradition in the criticism of the novel. He is very certain that no such criticism exists. In 'The Art of Fiction' of 1884 he complains that

only a short time ago it might have been supposed that the English novel was not what the French call *discutable*. It has no air of having a theory, a conviction, a consciousness of itself behind it – of being the expression of an artistic faith, the result of choice and comparison . . . There was a comfortable, good-humoured feeling abroad that a novel is a novel, as a pudding is a pudding, and that our only business with it could be to swallow it.

And in the previous year he had noticed, in the essay on Trollope, that in English terms 'it is rather dangerous to be explicitly or consciously an artist — to have a system, a doctrine, a form'. The English novel, unlike the French, was not discussable, but James set out to make it so. His own account of what it means to discuss or criticize – 'to appreciate, to appropriate, to take intellectual possession' – fits the eighteen prefaces, but in a rather unusual sense. It is not only that the novels so discussed are James's own, as the plays of Dryden's prefaces are Dryden's plays. James's prefaces are only doubtfully self-criticism, for he sees his own stories distantly, through a nostalgic haze. The first of the novels, *Roderick Hudson* (1876), was already thirty years old when he came to revise it, and though the first part of each preface is concerned with reconstruction and recollection, 'the story of one's story', time has thrown the author himself now into the role of a mere reader, now into that of the elderly sage whose past life, as he reads and revises, returns irresistibly over the passage of the years. There are stories which, he admits in the preface to *The Reverberator*, 'become in the highest degree documentary for myself', and there are moments of passionate evocation as the greatest of all American tourists seems to see, smell, and touch the cities of his early manhood. 'There are pages of the book', he wrote of *The Portrait of a Lady* (1881), which had been partly composed in Venice, 'which, in the reading over, have seemed to make me see again the bristling curve of the wide Riva . . . The Venetian footfall and the Venetian cry – all talk there, wherever uttered, having the pitch of a call across the water – come in once more at the window'; and of *The Tragic Muse* (1890) he writes: 'I catch again the very odour of Paris, which comes up in the rich rumble of the Rue de la Paix.' James's great critical effort begins as a labour of love, his 'remembrance' is in itself 'a great romance'.[1] And the evocation

[1] Letter to A. C. Benson (24 February 1895); *Henry James: Letters to A. C. Benson*, edited by E. F. Benson (1930), p. 5.

is useful, in a double sense: first, it sets the stage for isolating the novel's point of departure, its 'germ'; and second, it serves to remind us, as James seeks to do, that the artist himself must entertain no arrogant certainty that he can reconstruct the work of his own past as it once grew under his hands. The author is a privileged, uniquely well-informed reader of his own works – but he is a reader too, with a reader's due uncertainties. The very form of the novel, indeed, forbids any possibility that we can ever feel certain we have said everything: 'The private history of any sincere work, however modest its pretensions, looms with its own completeness in the rich, ambiguous aesthetic air, and seems at once to borrow a dignity and to mark, so to say, a station.'[1] The professional critic has something to learn in humility from James's fastidious uncertainties: 'The sunk surface has here and there, beyond doubt, refused to respond: the buried secrets, the intentions, are buried too deep to rise again . . .'[2] The disclaimer reminds us of neo-critical theories that urge the critic not to waste time over the author's intention.[3] The resemblance is only superficial. For James is perceptive enough to see that mere impossibility does not rule out an endeavour, and that no species of criticism is ever likely to enable us utterly 'to take intellectual possession'. There are kinds of criticism that lead us to within shouting distance of the work, and kinds that lead us further and further away; and James is clear that 'the buried secrets, the intentions' of the novelist are what the imaginary novelist Vereker in 'The Figure in the Carpet' (1896) called 'the thing for the critic to find'. This story, from James's middle period, insists with brutal frankness on the propriety of historical interpretation. It is the naïve narrator who protests that the critic 'was like nothing . . . but the maniacs who embrace some bedlamitical theory of the cryptic character of Shakespeare. To this he replied that if we had had Shakespeare's own word for his being cryptic, he would at once have accepted

---

[1] *The Art of the Novel*, edited by R. P. Blackmur (New York, 1934), p. 4 (preface to *Roderick Hudson*).

[2] Ibid., p. 11.

[3] W. K. Wimsatt and Monroe C. Beardsley, 'The Intentional Fallacy', *Sewanee Review*, liv (1946), reprinted in Wimsatt, *The Verbal Icon* (Lexington, Kentucky, 1954).

it.'[1] Even the Baconians, then, are right in principle, though of course idiotic in the particular case: good poems really are what poets mean them to be, whatever they may be besides. It is important to recognize that the ironic force of the story lies not, as some critics have supposed, in any assumption that Vereker's secret is not worth having – there is no hint of this in the notebooks, and it is explicitly denied in the preface – but in the narrator's simple-minded attempt to discover the novelist's secret in any way except by a careful reading of the novels. Each interview takes him further away from the intelligence of the dead genius – whereas a 'close or analytic appreciation' might have led him straight to the secret. The story repeats James's protest against the lack of effective novel-criticism in England, what he calls 'this odd numbness of the general sensibility'. 'How strangely and helplessly among us all', he exclaims in his preface to the story, 'what we call criticism . . . is apt to stand off from the intended sense of things.'[2] On the historical issue, then, James is simply a romantic critic, as intently concerned with the creative art as Coleridge himself. Of course design may, in this view, grow under the artist's hands, but it is not less the artist's design because he modifies it in the course of creation. The characters of *The Portrait of a Lady* (1881), we are told, behaved as if they were in search of an author, and answered their novelist as he worked 'that if I would trust them, they would show me' what the heroine Isabel Archer was to do; and he urges us, in the preface to *The Ambassadors* (1903), never to underesimate 'the energy which [a story] simply makes for itself.' Coleridge's theory of the organic form of works of art seems only just around the corner, though I cannot pronounce on the question of a direct debt. Some of James's analogies, certainly, sound startlingly familiar: in 'The Art of Fiction' he had called the novel 'a living thing, all one and continuous, like any other organism, and in proportion as it lives will it be found, I think, that in each of the parts there is something of each of the other parts.'

The central obsession of the prefaces is the issue of 'form',

[1] 'The Figure in the Carpet', ch. 5; in his *Embarrassments* (1896).
[2] *The Art of the Novel*, edited by R. P. Blackmur (New York, 1934), pp. 227, 228, 229.

obsessional because based upon the intractable paradox that stories never fit their author's purposes like pints in pint pots. The perfectionist in James accepted the challenge: 'art', he proudly concluded in his preface to *The Golden Bowl* (1904), 'is nothing if not exemplary.' Without form, novels are mere 'fluid puddings', as he called the novels of Tolstoy and Dostoyevsky: 'form alone *takes*, and holds and preserves, substance.'[1] He dreamed of himself, incongruously, as a ruthless technician of the novel – 'art should be as hard as nails' and the artist 'an absolutely Roman father'[2] – and summoned up French novels whose morality shocked him to teach the English novel a sense of competence. And still the paradox defeated him: you cannot pin down life (that echoing word in the prefaces) like a butterfly upon a board. All art, ultimately, has this element of falsity, pretending to a tidiness that is quite unreal:

Really, universally, relations stop nowhere, and the exquisite problem of the artist is eternally but to draw, by a geometry of his own, the circle within which they will happily *appear* to do so. He is in the perpetual predicament that the continuity of things is the whole matter, for him, of comedy and tragedy; that this continuity is never, by the space of an instant of an inch, broken, and that, to do anything at all, he has at once intensely to consult and intensely to ignore it.[3]

This is screwing the problem up to a high pitch, and it is not obvious that 'the continuity of things', or causality in human relations, is 'the whole matter' in a novel. It counts for very little in Fielding; though it is an indispensable part of all novels that aspire to psychological truth, the only kind James ever wanted to write. Such novels, inevitably, are something of a cheat, but James insisted that the cheat must at least be professionally contrived, 'only by delicate adjustments and an exquisite chemistry, so that there will at the end be neither a drop of one's liquor left nor a hair's breadth of the rim of one's glass to spare'. A novel, at

---

[1] Letter to Hugh Walpole (19 May 1912); *Letters of Henry James*, edited by Percy Lubbock (1920), II, 246.
[2] Letter to A. C. Benson (26 February 1895); *Letters to A. C. Benson*, op. cit., p. 7.
[3] Preface to *Roderick Hudson; Art of the Novel*, op. cit., p. 5.

its technical best, is a 'successfully *foreshortened* thing',[1] selecting from 'clumsy Life' and 'the fatal futility of Fact'[2] what is revealing and significant – 'life being all inclusion and confusion,' as he put it in the preface to *The Spoils of Poynton* (1897), and art 'all discrimination and selection'. It is in this sense, as he explains at length in the same preface, recounting how he had heard the 'germ' at a London dinner-table, that life is a nuisance: it does not know where to stop.

A fruitful confusion of terms, of which James nowhere seems conscious, emerges at this point: for life is not just an untidy aggregation of facts in James's criticism: it is also, as in the stories themselves, a moral imperative. From the ardent young Roderick Hudson to the tentative Strether of *The Ambassadors* (1903), James's heroes make their bid for Life and meet defeat at its hands, and are yet justified in the attempt: 'Live all you can; it's a mistake not to. It doesn't much matter what you do in particular as long as you have your life. If you haven't had that, what *have* you had . . .?' This is Lambert Strether's advice to little Bilham, approvingly quoted by James in his preface to the novel. The ambiguity is significant. James's fascination with form and his tragically agnostic vision meet in verbal ambiguity at this point: life is supremely worth the telling, for it is all that we have.

And yet its essential complex remains, to the end, a technical challenge. James developed the technique we now call 'the central intelligence' – the technique of viewing the action of a novel through the eyes of a character whose subtlety of mind equals that of the novelist himself – as early as *Roderick Hudson*, though his account of Rowland Mallet in his preface of thirty years after is surely, as analysis, characteristic of his later years: 'The centre of interest throughout *Roderick* is in Rowland Mallet's consciousness, and the drama is the very drama of that consciousness – which I had of course to make sufficiently acute in order to enable it, like a

---

[1] Preface to *The Tragic Muse*; ibid., p. 87. Cf. his account of the even more stringent demands of form made by the drama, which 'needs a masterly structure. It needs to be shaped and fashioned and laid together', like packing a coffer: 'it closes perfectly, and the lock turns with a click; between one object and another you cannot insert the point of a penknife' (*Views and Reviews* (1908), pp. 181-2).

[2] Preface to *The Spoils of Poynton; Art of the Novel*, op. cit., pp. 121-2.

set and lighted scene, to hold the play.' This 'most polished of possible mirrors', as he calls Mallet when he returns to the subject in the preface to *The Princess Casamassima* (1886), is to be set 'right in the middle of the light' or the thick of the action. The technique is genuinely new, for previous 'central intelligences', such as some heroines of Jane Austen and George Eliot, had been protagonists too. But James's fascination with problems of perspective in the novel carried him beyond this technique into the far more intricate design of multiple vision, as in *The Golden Bowl* (1904), which 'abides rigidly by its law of showing Maggie Verver at first through her suitor's and her husband's exhibitory vision of her, and of then showing the Prince, with at least an equal intensity, through his wife's; . . . these attributions of experience display the sentient subjects themselves at the same time and by the same stroke . . .' By the new century, even the subtleties of the technique of a 'central intelligence' had come to seem limiting and mechanical.

The extent of James's revolution in the criticism of the novel is difficult to over-state. Before he wrote, none of the ordinary assumptions of twentieth-century novel-criticism were current; and James not merely made them current but even added many of the delicate qualifications which we expect a pioneer to leave to his successors. It was James who, in the deceptively mandarin prose of his prefaces, made us look for a total, unifying meaning in novels by identifying the points of departure of his own; it was James who taught us to see such significances as being organized part by part, and to study the interrelations of such parts; it was James who defined for us the role of morality in the novel as having nothing to do with 'special precept' or the demands of social conformity, and James who pointed to the inevitable falsity of fiction as well as to its essential truth. And – as if this were not enough – it was James who first convincingly explored the technical problems of the novel in English, though his demonstration lacks comprehensiveness and omits many a familiar academic issue such as the place of the narrator and the virtues of the first-person singular. And all this is effected with no Arnoldian imperatives, no open injunction but that of 'life' itself, and no obtrusive aspiration to legislate for other novelists. His private name for the New York prefaces, a '*vademecum*', proves after all to be not quite a joke; for with all proper reservations concerning their lack of sustained argument and neatly formulated principles, they may serve the patient reader very well as that.

Chapter 9

THE EARLY TWENTIETH CENTURY

T. S. ELIOT

THE question sounds eminently reasonable, but remains un-answerable: what is revolutionary in the criticism of T. S. Eliot? Everyone except, apparently, Mr Eliot himself, can see that the critical tradition of the whole English-speaking world has been turned upside down by the trickle of articles and lectures – there has never, strictly, been a critical book – issuing from his pen since the First World War. But the nature of Eliot's influence as a critic has always been felt to be mysterious and indefinable. E. M. W. Tillyard, in his history of the Cambridge English School, has told how the essays in *The Sacred Wood* (1920), when they first appeared, 'made me uncomfortable, and I knew they could not be ignored'.[1] Disciples – even enemies – have hardly succeeded in identifying what is new and special in Eliot's criti-cism, though they have been loud in praise and censure. The most discreet of major English critics, he has practised evasion and reticence with determined skill. In his earliest period, positions are tentatively stated and argument disarmed by a certain irony; in his middle years, argument is openly spurned; and in the later years, since the Second World War, he has elaborately pretended never to have been a major critic at all. Altogether, his critical career might almost have been planned as a vast hoax to tempt the historian into solemnities for the sport of Philistines.

The key to Eliot's reticence as a critic surely lies in the relation-ship between his criticism and his poetry. In a sense, his criticism is a smoke-screen to the rest of his career. It misleads as much as it reveals about the quality of his poems, and the smoke-screen grows thicker as the years pass. By the 1950s Eliot's determination to hide himself from the devotees of his poetry by means of critical red-herrings had grown so obvious as to suggest a motive: the intense love of privacy, perhaps, of a fastidious New Englander

[1] *The Muse Unchained* (1958), p. 97.

whose poetry has led him into the indignity of spiritual self-exposure. We fear something of the kind as early as a Harvard lecture of 1932, where he attempted to disarm analysis of *Ash-Wednesday* (1930), a poem intimately tracking the path of a religious conversion, by suggesting the addition to the poem of a Byronic motto:

> But the fact is that I have nothing planned,
> Except perhaps to be a moment merry . . .[1]

The mask of the sage slips at such moments of embarrassing whimsy, to reveal the face of injured piety.

The formal properties of Eliot's criticism, at least, are clear enough, and may be summarily described. An Eliot essay is a statement of an attitude, a *prise de position*, an evaluation. It does not even pretend to be biographical, in the sense that an Arnold essay so pretends: Arnold's fiction that he is a disciple of Sainte-Beuve gives way, with Eliot, to a frankly unhistorical insistence upon the relevance of certain poets here and now, and Eliot hardly ever stoops to purvey information. Secondly, 'relevance' means relevance to modern poets rather than to modern readers, and Eliot even commits himself openly to this object in the 1935 lecture on Milton: 'Of what I have to say I consider that the only jury of judgement is that of the ablest poetical practitioners of my own time.'[2] Thirdly, Eliot eschews close analysis in favour of general judgements; his taste and techniques were formed decades before the New Criticism of the thirties, and he never practises the 'close analysis' characteristic of that school.

These are hardly arguable statements about Eliot's criticism. They go a very little way, however, towards describing what an Eliot essay is like. To do that would require a more impressionistic account, leading to statements that might prove highly debatable, since the rhetoric of his criticism is opaque enough to leave a good deal in doubt. What does seem clear is that Eliot is Arnold's successor in terms of the audience he expects for criticism: a minority audience, aware of itself as a cultural leadership,

The Use of Poetry and the Use of Criticism (1933), pp. 30-1.
'A Note on the Verse of John Milton', *Essays and Studies*, XXI (1935), reprinted in his *On Poetry and Poets* (New York, 1957), p. 157.

and peculiarly vulnerable, like Arnoldians, to the seductions of intellectual snobbery. It might be unfair to attribute to Eliot himself the stock-market approach to literary values that characterizes a good many of his followers; but certainly, in this regard, Eliot finishes what Arnold began. A price-scale of values for an intellectual *élite* among the dead poets, of a kind that would certainly have puzzled Dryden, Johnson, and Coleridge, is part of the Eliot inheritance, however little he may like it. But the object of Eliot's criticism is not just an Addisonian ambition to correct taste: more narrowly, it is the correction of taste with a view to conditioning his own future readership and audiences. The real parallel among our classic critics lies not in Addison but in Dryden, and an Eliot essay – though not openly prefatorial and self-justifying, like most of Dryden's criticism – serves a comparable purpose.

Thomas Stearns Eliot was born in 1888 in St Louis, Missouri, of New England family, and was educated at Harvard, Paris, and Oxford. At the beginning of the First World War he settled in London, and soon accepted British citizenship, renouncing (as Henry James never did) the liberal ideals of American society. The famous preface to *For Lancelot Andrewes* (1928), in which he declared himself 'a classicist in literature, an Anglo-Catholic in religion, and a royalist in politics', was evidently designed to burn all boats and set a term to boyhood and youth. His conversion to Christianity seems to date from the late twenties, after the appearance of *The Waste Land* (1922), and only *The Sacred Wood* (1920), among his critical writings, is innocent of the neo-scholastic tinge. But Eliot's rejection of liberalism, or the cult of individual man, certainly dates from the years before 1914 and from his early association with Ezra Pound and T. E. Hulme – even, perhaps, from Irving Babbitt's Harvard lectures against romanticism. The originality of his essay 'Tradition and the Individual Talent',[1] with which his critical career effectively begins, lies not in its anti-liberalism but in its application of this fashionable doctrine to the immediate critical situation. It is so evidently an unofficial manifesto of Eliot's criticism, or an account of the principles the young critic planned to bring to bear upon English poetry, that we may

---

[1] *Egoist*, October–December 1919 (in two parts), reprinted in *The Sacred Wood* (1920) and *Selected Essays* (1932).

examine its principles before looking at Eliot's career as a critic in detail.

'Tradition and the Individual Talent' is not the kind of essay that invites discussion. Its tone is dryly pontifical, and Eliot's distaste for debate and free speech is firmly suggested in the rhetorical properties of the essay. It asks not to be examined – which is a very good reason for examining it. The deliberate perversities of Eliot's use of language are part of the Arnoldian minority-appeal of the essay: we are invited from the start to enter where only a few will follow by a denial of a popular 'fallacy': 'we dwell with satisfaction upon the poet's difference from his predecessors, . . . endeavour to find something that can be isolated in order to be enjoyed.' This prepares the reader for a redefinition of key-terms – 'tradition' does not mean 'a blind or timid adherence' to the successes of a former generation, but

it involves, in the first place, the historical sense, which we may call nearly indispensable to anyone who would continue to be a poet beyond his twenty-fifth year; and the historical sense involves a perception, not only of the pastness of the past, but of its presence; the historical sense compels a man to write not merely with his own generation in his bones, but with a feeling that the whole of the literature of Europe from Homer, and within it the whole of the literature of his own country, has a simultaneous existence and composes a simultaneous order . . .

And this 'historical sense' is 'what makes a writer traditional'. But it is an odd historical sense that denies chronology and conceives of the past as both 'the timeless and the temporal'; it might have been franker, we begin to feel as the essay proceeds, to call it 'the anti-historical sense', and it is a tribute to the fading power of historical studies that Eliot, like Arnold, seeks to maintain a façade of history behind which to develop a doctrine of poetry very like Arnold's own – the poetry of the past existing as a 'simultaneous order' and inviting study not for what it was to the poet and his first readers, but for what it is to the practising poet of our own day – 'the object as in itself it really is', in Arnold's words, where 'really' aptly suggests a certain contempt for previous judgements. Contempt for historical criticism is confirmed in Eliot's argument as it develops: poets do not express themselves in poetry, but escape from themselves by 'a continual extinction of personality'; so that historical criticism, by implication, is convicted of looking for the wrong things. It looks to the poet and his historical situation, whereas the poem itself points away from both towards some ideal of impersonal truth: 'Honest criticism and sensitive appreciation is directed not upon the poet, but upon the poetry', for, ultimately, the individuality of the poet is irrelevant, his business being 'not to find new emotions, but to use the ordinary ones'. Again the Arnoldian echo, this time from the 1853 preface, where Arnold demands poems about 'those elementary feelings which subsist permanently in the race'. 'Romantic', as in Babbitt and Hulme, is here a term of abuse, and Wordsworth's formula 'emotion recollected in tranquillity' is rejected as inexact, on the grounds that 'poetry is not a turning loose of emotion, but an escape from emotion; it is not the expression of personality, but an escape from personality'. Even if we could accept so question-begging a use of terms, it would still not be clear why such a view should lead us to conclude that 'to divert interest from the poet to the poetry is a laudable aim'. It would be an odd escape-story that omitted first to describe the prison, and how the captive managed to get out of it.

What Eliot calls 'the historical sense', then, can be grouped among other attacks upon historicism in the age that followed Arnold. But Eliot's real historical sense is not to be dismissed: it is far finer than Arnold's, who seems to live and think in a strait-jacket of mid-Victorian enlightenment. There are plenty of passages in *The Sacred Wood*, and even later, notably in *The Use of Poetry and the Use of Criticism*, that make us wonder what a delicately intuitive historian of literature was lost in Eliot. In the early essays, attacks on the historical principle, and examples of acute historical judgement, coexist oddly ('the timeless and the temporal'): 'If we write about Middleton's plays we must write about Middleton's plays, and not about Middleton's personality,' he writes in the essay on Middleton (*For Lancelot Andrewes*) – but only, it becomes clear as the essay proceeds, because we do not know enough about Middleton's life to do anything else. Who, without prompting, could guess that Eliot could be as relativistic a critic as the following passage suggests? (It is from the

1936 essay on Tennyson's *In Memoriam*): 'Innovation in metric is not to be measured solely by the width of the deviation from accepted practice. It is a matter of the historical situation: at some moments a more violent change may be neccesary than at others. The problem differs at every period.' This does not make *In Memoriam* sound like part of a 'simultaneous order'. If only the tone were not so coldly judicial, it might almost be Sainte-Beuve. And yet, Eliot might plead, this is merely a technical question: on the *subject* of poetry he remains sceptical of historical proof: '*If* poetry is a form of "communication", yet that which is to be communicated is the poem itself. . . . The poem's existence is somewhere between the writer and the reader. . . . Consequently, the problem of what a poem "means" is a good deal more difficult than it at first appears'.[1] Any tastes Eliot had towards historical inquiries into poetry – and we may guess them to have been strong – were frustrated by an ideological conviction that poetry is not communication at all. The lecture 'Shakespeare and the Stoicism of Seneca', read before the Shakespeare Association in 1927, is an elaborate and outrageous joke against the historical method:

> I propose a Shakespeare under the influence of the stoicism of Seneca. But I do not believe that Shakespeare was under the influence of Seneca. I propose it largely because I believe that after the Montaigne Shakespeare . . . and after the Machiavelli Shakespeare, a stoical or Senecan Shakespeare is almost certain to be produced. I wish merely to disinfect the Senecan Shakespeare before he appears. My ambitions would be realized if I could prevent him, in so doing, from appearing at all.

Eliot's critical convictions cannot be said to evolve in any very striking sense. His alleged change of heart over Milton between 1935 and 1947 is more like a tactical withdrawal under fire; his growing scepticism, as he ages, over the utility of criticism – any criticism – certainly modifies his tone of voice, but hardly his deepest convictions about literature. Correspondences pop up oddly, decades apart, in his writings: thoughtful readers of the

---

[1] *The Use of Poetry and the Use of Criticism* (1933), p. 30.

1919 essay 'Tradition and the Individual Talent' will know just where they are in his poem 'The Dry Salvages' (1941):

It seems, as one becomes older,
That the past has another pattern, and ceases to be a mere sequence –
Or even development . . .

Eliot did not have to 'become older' to learn that the past is not 'a mere sequence'. It is all in *The Sacred Wood*. Still, preoccupations change where theologies do not, and if there are no Eliot juvenilia and no dramatic changes of front, the mass of his five hundred essays, reviews, and published lectures does fall comfortably enough into three periods, not unlike the Arnoldian dialectic of two literary periods separated by an intermediate decade of social interests. Eliot's career evolves in a broadly similar way: from the first, pre-Christian decade (1919-28) of literary preoccupation, mainly with sixteenth and seventeenth-century dramatists and poets in *The Sacred Wood* (1920), *Homage to John Dryden: Three Essays* (1924), and *For Lancelot Andrewes* (1928); through a second decade of social and religious criticism (1929-39) following on his conversion and his final break with 'modernism', in *Dante* (1929), *Thoughts after Lambeth* (1931), *After Strange Gods* (1934); to the post-war Olympian period, which marks a certain renewal of interest in critical (especially dramatic) issues, though hardly in the concentrated form of the first decade. It already seems clear – and not only for such reasons as this abrupt analysis may suggest – that any serious estimate of Eliot as a critic must depend upon the early essays. Stiff, sly, and pompous as their language sometimes is, they are none the less even-tempered, conscientious, and exploratory, and Eliot's frigid distaste for debate is less evident here, and less damaging, than in his later writings. Reshaped as *Selected Essays* in 1932, and since enlarged, the early essays are a nearly complete monument to his genius as a critic.

The appearance of *The Sacred Wood* in November 1920 seems at first to have startled hardly anybody, and the book made its way slowly in the world. Most of the seventeen essays had already appeared in a variety of journals. The reviewer in *The Times Literary Supplement* (2 December 1920) noted with approval the dry, precise manner of the young American critic so different from the flowery Edwardian mode of current literary journalism: Eliot, he wrote, 'does not try to write prose-poetry about poetry, to make his criticism the poor relation of poetry' – though he was mildly shocked by Eliot's worst contribution to the style of English criticism, the glancing insult which attacks too abruptly to admit reply: 'He tries to annoy them [admirers of Meredith] by slipping in contemptuous remarks about Meredith which cannot be refuted because they say nothing except that Mr Eliot despises Meredith and those who admire him.' Eliot's habit of killing off his literary and theological enemies in a parenthesis, like the hero of an E. M. Forster novel – '(not that Montaigne had any philosophy whatever)'[1] – was rather charitably interpreted, by the same reviewer, as 'a malice the more insidious because unconscious'. The design and unity of *The Sacred Wood* seems to have passed unnoticed, even by later idolators of Eliot – probably because everyone now reads these essays, or most of them, as they stand depleted and engulfed in later and larger collections, the attacks upon the impressionistic Edwardian school (Arthur Symons, George Wyndham, Charles Whibley, and others) in 'The Perfect Critic', and 'Imperfect Critics' being omitted from *Selected Essays* (1932) as ungracious or out of date. In his 1928 preface to *The Sacred Wood*, Eliot claimed that 'what coherence they [the essays] have, is the problem of the integrity of poetry, with the repeated assertion that when we are considering poetry we must consider it primarily as poetry and not another thing'. This claim to aesthetic detachment is not much more convincing than Arnold's – Eliot's criticism is partisan from the start, and increasingly so with the years. What unites the essay is not any doctrine of the 'integrity' of poetry, but of its availability. Eliot behaves towards the dead poets of Europe with all the casual skill of a shoplifter in a department-store. He knows what he wants and what he can use, and he seizes upon it as coolly as if no established scale of values already existed among the English poets. He arrives at his values by a process of unhurried irreverence, gently defining what he means (and, very characteristically, what he does not mean), concluding with judgements which are felt to be radical and vaguely momentous: Marlowe's verse, when he died,

[1] 'Shakespeare and the Stoicism of Seneca', op. cit.

was moving 'towards this intense and serious and indubitably great poetry which, like some great painting and sculpture, attains its effects by something not unlike caricature'; Jonson's plays represent 'a part of our literary inheritance craving further expression. . . . There is a brutality, a lack of sentiment, a polished surface, a handling of large bold designs in brilliant colours, which ought to attract about three thousand people in London and elsewhere'. This last appeal to minority-values is uncharacteristically frank – in general, only the most masterly and refined rhetorical analysis could explain how much contrives to be suggested in these essays, as against how relatively little is openly stated, and how powerful and 'insidious' (as *The Times* put it) is the youthful irreverence that inspires them. The title – presumably an afterthought – suggests a revealing metaphor. The 'wood', no doubt, is the sacred grove of Nemi, near Rome, described in rich romantic detail by Sir James Frazer[1] in the first chapter of *The Golden Bough* (1890–). Even as late as imperial times, Frazer tells us,

in the sacred grove there grew a certain tree, round which at any time of the day, and probably far into the night, a grim figure might be seen to prowl. In his hand he carried a drawn sword, and he kept peering warily about him as if at every instant he expected to be set upon by an enemy. He was a priest and a murderer; and the man for whom he looked was sooner or later to murder him and hold the priesthood in his stead. Such was the rule of the sanctuary. A candidate for the priesthood could only succeed to office by slaying the priest, and having slain him, he retained office till he was himself slain by a stronger or a craftier.

This 'rule of succession by the sword', by which a runaway slave might make his bid for a precarious liberty, provides a key to the unity of Eliot's first critical essays. A youthful poet turns critic to justify his own place in the line of succession, to stake a claim. He is priest and murderer. Perhaps the metaphor is doubly suggestive: Eliot, the new priest of the 'tradition', inherits by a kind of critical massacre, belittling the rights of dead poets to historical existence and boldly plundering their remains.

[1] In an early article Eliot names Frazer (with Henry James and F. H. Bradley) as one of the three principal intellectual influences of his life. Cf. his 'Lettre d'Angleterre', no. 3, *Nouvelle revue française*, XI (1 November 1923).

The plunder, in the essays of the twenties, is various, but mainly Elizabethan in *The Sacred Wood*, Metaphysical and Restoration in the following collections. The Renaissance emphasis is in itself a little surprising: in a literary sense Eliot is so much the child of Arnold (in theology and politics, of course, they stand almost as far apart as the distance between Right and Left) that one might have expected him to echo Arnold's youthful horror of 'those d—d Elizabethans'. But we can still guess why he did not. In the first place, though a Francophile like Arnold, he shared none of Arnold's distaste for English civilization as such. In criticism and in poetry, Eliot is a British patriot, though the England he loves is a happy self-deception of pomps and royalties, noble houses like the Wilton of Sir Philip Sidney and his sister, a Church Established:

> Elizabeth and Leicester
> Beating oars
> The stern was formed
> A gilded shell
> Red and gold . . .[1]

Only those who insist upon reading Eliot as total irony will deny the note of infatuation with an age which British nationalists are irresistibly led to glorify. James Anthony Froude, upon whose mid-Victorian historical extravaganzas this passage, according to Eliot's own note, is based, may have been a thought too Protestant for his taste, but surely not too patriotic. And secondly, Eliot sees in the Elizabethans and their successors qualities invisible to Arnold. Arnold thought them responsible for the confused and fragmentary quality of English romanticism: Eliot, very characteristically, sees them not as historical influences at all, but simply as a school where the apprentice-poet can learn his craft. And in this cause he is ready to make an alliance with the Devil himself. The more outrageously out of fashion the poet, indeed, the better Eliot seems to like the notion of finding a use for him: Tennyson and Swinburne are respectfully handled, for example, Shelley and Keats not. More characteristically, Eliot joins and leads a vogue already under way, such as the late Victorian and

---

[1] *The Waste Land* (1922), ll. 279-83.

Edwardian vogue for Donne which had culminated in Grierson's edition of 1912. Essays like 'The Metaphysical Poets' and 'Andrew Marvell' (1921) aptly explain by justification techniques Eliot was already using in verse: the 'telescoping of images and multiplied associations' which, in Donne and the dramatists of his age, is 'one of the sources of the vitality of their language'; and the famous phrase by which he sums up the peculiar essence of Marvell's Horatian Ode, 'wit, a tough reasonableness beneath a slight lyric grace', might be an account of the central style of *The Waste Land*. The celebrated hint in the first of these essays – it is hardly elaborate enough to be called a theory – of a 'dissociation of sensibility',[1] of thought from sensation, is best studied in this light: that of Eliot's own poetic ambitions in the twenties. It identifies a breach he sought to heal: 'A thought to Donne was an experience; it modified his sensibility . . . [But] in the seventeenth century a dissociation of sensibility set in, from which we have never recovered; and this dissociation, as is natural, was aggravated by the influence of the two most powerful poets of the century, Milton and Dryden.' Eliot's majestic historical sense suddenly reveals two systems of vast correspondences, a poetical tradition tragically split beyond a point where romanticism could help. But his own use of the theory seems out of touch with the theory itself. We should expect Milton and Dryden to be judged as equal offenders: but in fact Milton is ignored until 1935 and then lightly dismissed, Dryden celebrated in an early essay of 1921 as a mentor for poets of today and tomorrow: 'In the next revolution of taste it is possible

---

[1] The phrase, which has proved the most successful of all Eliot's adventures in critical jargon, is mysteriously echoic. F. W. Bateson (*Essays in Criticism*, 1 (1951)) has suggested a source in Rémy de Gourmont, who twenty years before had suggested that Laforgue died before he could '*dissocie[r] son intelligence de sa sensibilité*'. Eric Thompson, in a reply (ibid., 11 (1952)), suggests F. H. Bradley as a source. Goethe is another possible candidate, and there is no doubt that Eliot was acquainted with Goethe as a poet and critic at an early stage in his career, as his Hamburg Lecture of 1955, 'Goethe as the Sage' suggests. Cf. *Winckelmann und sein Jahrhundert* (1805), from the section 'Antikes': '*Noch fand sich das Gefühl, die Betrachtung nicht zerstückelt, noch war jene kaum heilbare Trennung in der gesunden Menschenkraft nicht vorgegangen.*' (Emotion, thought were not yet fragmented, and that scarcely remediable split in the healthy abilities of men had not yet occurred.) But 'feeling' in Eliot's language (as Mr Thompson insists) refers to sensation rather than to emotion.

that poets may turn to the study of Dryden. He remains one of those who have set standards for English verse which it is desperate to ignore.' In other words Dryden, for all his 'commonplace mind', is useful as a verbal quarry for Eliot and poets like Eliot. Milton is not.

Eliot's two lectures on Milton,[1] like his essays on poetic drama, overlap the second period of political and theological interests, and even the third, exhausted phase of critical activity. They take tone and colour from the fact that they are belated. Both are written in a convoluted style of qualification and reservation that grows more complex with the years, so that it is only by a narrow margin that the first lecture can be called an exercise in the qualified rejection of Milton, or the second one of qualified assent. By the thirties, negatives and limiting judgements settle thickly upon the prose of Eliot – 'by this I do not mean to say that . . .' 'perhaps', 'somewhat'. Argument advances crabwise: the Milton of the first lecture is called 'a very great poet indeed', but 'a bad influence'. But to be a bad influence is not necessarily 'a serious charge'. But Milton's poetry 'could *only* be an influence for the worse, upon any poet whatever', and the twentieth-century poet too must struggle against it. And then, startlingly, Eliot shows his hand: 'The kind of derogatory criticism that I have to make upon Milton is not intended for such persons who cannot understand that it is more important, in some vital respects, to be a good poet than to be a *great* poet . . .' It is Eliot's rooted assumption that criticism is an aid to his own career as a poet, rather than any intuition of a 'dissociation of sensibility', that governs his choices here. A 'good' poet is one who, like Dryden, is useful to later 'poetical practitioners'; a 'great' poet, such as Milton, may lack the merits of the salvageable. The faint retraction embodied in the second Milton lecture changes nothing in critical terms, though Eliot seems aware that such Christian Miltonists as Charles Williams and C. S. Lewis, whom he quotes, have respectabilized Milton as a theologian in the intervening decade. Milton as an ally against a godless age is a possibility which evidently takes him by surprise,

[1] Delivered in 1935 and 1947, and collected in *On Poetry and Poets* (New York, 1957) and, in part, in *Selected Prose of T. S. Eliot*, edited by John Hayward (Penguin Books, 1953).

but he is eager to accommodate himself to the new rules of the game: 'It is probably beneficial to question the assumption that Milton was a sound Free Churchman and member of the Liberal Party.' It is all rather like a game of musical chairs, played out to liturgical music.

The Sacred Wood, then, though it remains central to Eliot's achievement as a critic, offers us only elusive hints concerning his system of values, and few certainties beyond an intuition of his egoistical purpose in using criticism as 'a by-product of my private poetry-workshop'[1] in judging and rejecting the work of the past by the standards of his own immediate needs as a poet. Certainties followed, in the second decade (1929-39), but they were of a kind to alarm his disciples and darken a reputation in an age even more starkly controversial than the 1860s. It is easy now to see that the bright young people of the twenties for whom a volume of Eliot's poems, and even *The Sacred Wood*, had talismanic force, had failed to note the illiberal echoes in Eliot's first works. They are faint, but they are there: the contrast posed between a heroic past and a decadent present, the distaste for argument, the contempt for cosmopolitanism, the references easily interpreted, rightly or wrongly, as anti-Semitic. (And, in any case, the bright young people of the twenties can hardly have known that the next decade would find them Marxists.) Looking back, we can see as inevitable a schism between master and disciples which left the disciples with a sense of angry betrayal, and the master with some sense of relief. Eliot, like Arnold, preferred to walk by himself.

Eliot's second period opens with a delightfully disarming prelude, the monograph *Dante* (1929), a frankly amateurish, enthusiastic introduction to Dante for readers who possess little Italian, and the kind of book that no one could dislike. Eliot's love for Dante, infectiously suggested, looks literary rather than neo-scholastic, a poet's rather than a convert's enthusiasm. An ensuing pamphlet, *Thoughts after Lambeth* (1931), collected, like *Dante*, in the *Selected Essays* of 1932, is a sensible and moderate comment on the Anglican conference of 1930, but sets its face firmly against

---

[1] 'The Frontiers of Criticism' in his *On Poetry and Poets* (New York, 1957), p. 117.

humanism in its conclusion: 'The World is trying the experiment of attempting to form a civilized but non-Christian mentality. The experiment will fail; but we must be very patient in awaiting its collapse; meanwhile redeeming the time: so that the faith may be preserved alive through the dark ages before us . . .' The echoes of *Ash-Wednesday* (1930) are over-powering, and even the ultimate direction of *The Waste Land* (1922) seems clearer as the story of Eliot's later development unfolds. The Harvard lectures of 1932-3, reluctantly published as *The Use of Poetry and the Use of Criticism* (1933) – 'another unnecessary book', he sourly calls it in the preface – is a sketchy, occasionally suggestive survey of poets as critics from Sidney to I. A. Richards, but the shades are falling. This is the Lenten period of his career, to stretch his own metaphor. Eliot is already half bored with poetry, and more than half bored with criticism, and intensely bored with his own role as a poet-critic. 'The sad ghost of Coleridge beckons to me from shadows,' he concludes glibly, after repeating the vulgar fallacy that 'poets only talk when they cannot sing'. And there is worse to come.

After Strange Gods (1934), a collection of three lectures delivered at the University of Virginia in 1933, a few months after Hitler's accession to power, was published in 4,500 copies (now exceedingly difficult to come by), and never reprinted. It is the oddest of Eliot's books, and certainly the most difficult to justify. Perhaps it is a fulfilment of the promise made in a footnote in the *Use of Poetry* (p. 137n.), where, after quoting Maritain on 'the unconcealed and palpable influence of the devil' on many writers of the time, Eliot adds solemnly: 'With the influence of the devil on contemporary literature I shall be concerned in more detail in another book.' The promise rings ominously, especially when the eye travels to a footnote opposite: 'The Roman and Communist idea of an index of prohibited books seems to me perfectly sound in principle.' The austere subtitle to *After Strange Gods* – 'A Primer of Modern Heresy' – strikes a certain inquisitorial chill, and refusals to discuss grow explicit and insistent. 'I refuse to be drawn into any discussion . . .' is a phrase from the *Use of Poetry* (p. 35n.) often echoed by Eliot in the thirties and after. 'In our time,' he proclaimed in the preface to *After Strange Gods*, controversy seems to me, on really fundamental matters, to be futile. It can only usefully be practised where there is common understanding. It requires common assumptions. . . . The acrimony which accompanies much debate is a symptom of differences so large that there is nothing to argue about. . . . In a society like ours, worm-eaten with Liberalism, the only thing possible for a person with strong convictions is to state a point of view and leave it at that.

The lectures that follow take as their starting-point the fifteen-year-old essay 'Tradition and the Individual Talent', and we are made to understand the neo-conservative seduction of a word which, in the early essay, seems strikingly and deliberately incongruous. Eliot's poetic tradition had nothing to do with a historical sequence: his political 'tradition' has. There is praise for the tradition of the Old South and for the resurrectionist group of neo-agrarians such as John Crowe Ransom and Allen Tate, for old New England, for 'stability', 'unity of religious background' ('reasons of race and religion combine to make any large number of free-thinking Jews undesirable'), 'orthodoxy'. The two lectures that follow are a diatribe against free inquiry and the sinister effects of the modern movement whereby 'morals cease to be a matter of tradition and orthodoxy' (p. 58), and against the novels of George Eliot, Hardy, Joyce, and D. H. Lawrence – Lawrence who suffered a 'deplorable religious upbringing' which gave him 'his lust for intellectual independence' and left his vision 'spiritually sick' (pp. 63, 65). With this book, offered not as literary criticism but as an attack upon views currently fashionable, Eliot's tragic break with the dominant impulses of his age is total and permanent.

The third period of Eliot's activity as a critic, since the Second World War, is profoundly anti-climactic. There is little attempt to renew the anti-liberal controversies of the thirties, but his return to literary issues seems only half-convinced. *Notes towards the Definition of Culture* (1948) only palely reflects a pre-war concern for intellectual values in a stable society. *Poetry and Drama* (1951) and *The Three Voices of Poetry* (1953) suggest a spark of enthusiasm for a poetic drama which has its roots deep in the Elizabethan essays of *The Sacred Wood*; but the despairingly high ideal of achieving a 'musical order' in language 'without losing that contact with the ordinary everyday world with which drama must come to terms', as in Shakespeare's last plays, is, on his own telling, unattainable, and his plays are distinguished flops. The dominant tone of his last essays and lectures is sarcastic and irritable, and the target is usually the very criticism his own example created. Like a startled Frankenstein, Eliot recoils from the monster he has made, wearily disclaiming responsibility: 'I fail to see any critical movement which can be said to derive from myself,' as he told a Midwestern audience in 1956.[1] There is not much twentieth-century criticism which does not stand condemned by its chief ancestor in this late effusion of despair, for all the many polite evasions ('I do not mean that they are bad books'): the scholarly tradition of 'explanation by origins', as in J. L. Lowes's study of Coleridge, *The Road to Xanadu* (1927); excesses of subtlety provoked by Joyce's *Finnegans Wake* (1939) and Eliot's own works; biographical criticism; non-biographical criticism practised by Richards and Empson as verbal analysis, or 'the lemon-squeezer school of criticism'. Finally we arrive full-circle to the very position that Eliot, in the suppressed anti-Edwardian essays of *The Sacred Wood*, had youthfully condemned: an elderly, dilettante, 'appreciative' criticism whereby the critic may 'help his readers to *understand and enjoy*'. Anyone old enough to have observed the march of English criticism continuously for fifty years might be justified in murmuring: 'This is where we came in.'

These, then, are the three voices of T. S. Eliot the critic: first, the youthful, exploratory enthusiasm of the twenties, where an almost ideal balance between poetic and critical activity is realized; second, an abortive career of social and religious advocacy in frankly obscurantist causes; and third, a bold but exhausted attempt to recover the creative urge, followed at once by denial and desperation. The imposing sense of a vast critical intelligence that emerges, especially in the twenties, is not of a sort that can be defined and codified, and the question with which this chapter began must remain unanswered. Eliot made English criticism look different, but in no simple sense. He offered it a new range of rhetorical possibilities, confirmed it in its increasing contempt for historical processes, and yet reshaped its notion of period by a

[1] 'The Frontiers of Criticism', op. cit., p. 117.

handful of brilliant intuitions. It is not to be expected that so expert and professional an observer of poetry should allow his achievement to be more neatly classified than this.

I. A. RICHARDS

The most elementary mistake one could make about the criticism of I. A. Richards (b. 1893) – it is also one of the commonest – is to suppose that he pioneered a school of twentieth-century criticism of which Eliot is a member. The dates alone forbid such a notion: Eliot is the older man by five years, and his first, and best, critical work, *The Sacred Wood* (1920), appeared before Richards had published at all. Richards is simply the most influential theorist of the century, as Eliot is the most influential of descriptive critics; and, as so often, practice anticipates theory. Still, Richards has his own, independent achievement as an aesthetician which could have happened almost as readily if Eliot had never existed; and he is inescapably a part of this story by virtue of the techniques of analysis that he inspired.

Richards's claim to have pioneered Anglo-American New Criticism of the thirties and forties is unassailable. He provided the theoretical foundations on which the technique of verbal analysis was built. The fact, on the whole, has proved an embarrassment to the New Critics: Richards's theories are appallingly vulnerable, and have been under expert fire from philosophers and psychologists for many years; and further, his own books since the twenties have been increasingly eccentric. He is one of those unfortunate thinkers whose later works tend to discredit not only themselves and their author, but earlier books as well. But only his influence on descriptive criticism is in question here, it must be insisted, and not the whole range of his aesthetic.

After reading Moral Sciences at Cambridge, Richards was abruptly invited, in the summer of 1919, to lecture on critical theory in the infant Cambridge School of English. The decision was momentous: Richards's major books, which all appeared in the twenties, were based upon his experience of Cambridge audiences, and his own influence upon the teaching of English there was massive and lasting. His interest in psychology was already wide-ranging and eclectic, if unprofound, and it is through

his agency that the new science first impinged directly and powerfully on English criticism. Its relevance to literary studies emerges
clearly enough in his first book, *The Foundation of Aesthetics* (1922),
a collaboration with two friends of undergraduate days, C. K.
Ogden and James Wood – a characteristic attempt to define
'beauty' by studying its effects on the audience of art. In *The
Meaning of Meaning* (1923), Ogden and Richards created a new
jargon in semantics with a distinction between the 'symbolic' use
of language in science and its 'emotive' use in poetry, and in his
first work of strictly literary aesthetics, *The Principles of Literary
Criticism* (1924), Richards continued to explore alone the 'emotive' language of poetry, culminating in *Practical Criticism* (1929),
which disclosed the results of lecture-room experiments conducted in Cambridge by means of analysis of texts stripped of all
evidence of authorship and period. With this book, which is very
far from being his last, Richards's period of major influence ends;
he spent less and less time in Cambridge, lectured in China, ex-
perimented in Basic English with Ogden, and in 1939 settled in
the United States.

Richards, like Ogden, is extravagantly polymath, and his work
straddles such distinctions between kinds of criticism as I have
tried to maintain here, besides scores of other interests. Primarily,
it is clear, he is a theoretical critic, like Coleridge; and, like Coleridge, he indulged in literary analysis only as illustration of a
method. The analogy does not carry us far. Coleridge was a
literary man to the tips of his fingers who sacrificed every interest
out of an obsessive love of poetry: Richards, on the evidence of his
books alone – for his reputation as a teacher is strangely opposite –
is of all the major English critics the one most difficult to visual-
ize with a book of verse in his hands. His interest in poets seems
abstracted to the point where all English poetry is an illustration
of an aesthetic principle or a mass of data to provide experiments
towards a theory of communication. And his criticism is not only
more abstract than Coleridge's: it is also violently opposed in tone.
Both men write as amateurs, and both (in their intensely English
way) are naïvely proud of their amateur status, as if the run of
a gentleman's library and a few bright ideas were bound to
be more fruitful than the soul-destroying concentration of the

specialist. But Coleridge's amateurishness is fervent and affectionate: Richards's is callowly iconoclastic, and his language seems designed to trade upon the fashionable anti-romanticism of Cambridge between the wars. He dismisses the past even more cavalierly than Eliot. The first chapter of the *Principles*, 'The Chaos of Critical Theories', is an all-but-total dismissal of the 'almost empty garner' of all European criticism before Richards: 'a few conjectures, a supply of admonitions, many acute isolated observations, some brilliant guesses . . .' The stage is set for the insinuation of an assumption implicit everywhere in Richards's criticism: that the findings of experimental science are intellectually impressive as the findings of no other kind of inquiry can be, and that literary criticism must equip itself with experimental weapons. Criticism, for Richards, is pre-Baconian, and the object of his own aesthetic is to hurry it forward, with the help of the new psychology, towards the happy condition where the critic can use laboratory techniques and make falsifiable assertions.

The oddity of this programme is obvious enough, but it is no odder than its application in detail. We should expect such a programme to insist upon poetry as a communication between poet and reader ('the arts are the supreme form of the communicative activity'). Any attempt to harness psychology to the service of criticism is bound to insist upon poetry as a strictly analysable *human* activity, like Wordsworth's 'man speaking to men', since the realities of psychology are exclusively human. But, by a baffling contradiction, Richards does just the reverse. He shrugs off the formidable prospect of a psychological school of criticism in direct descent from the biographical criticism of the Victorians. Perhaps, in the twenties, the mantle already looked too threadbare to be worth picking up, and Richards is certainly a pundit acutely aware of the power of intellectual fashion. The almost total absence of psychological criticism – there are, of course, isolated examples such as *A Psychoanalytic Study of Hamlet* (1922) by Freud's disciple Ernest Jones – is the most astonishing negative fact of all English criticism in the twentieth century. The escape must have been a very narrow one: even at this distance, it looks like an impossible paradox. At the very moment when psychology was respectabilizing itself as a science, and at the very moment when the most influential of English critics – himself a man of some psychological training – was seeking to respectabilize criticism in a similar sense, criticism abandoned its traditional interest in poets in favour of an elaborate pretence that poems are autonomous, self-sufficient artefacts. Richards dismisses the prospect so airily that we are hardly given time to take breath and start an argument. In the fourth chapter of the *Principles*, at the very point in the book where the doctrine that 'communication is . . . [the artist's] principal object' is proclaimed, Richards adds unequivocally:

Whatever psycho-analysts may aver, the mental processes of the poet are not a very profitable field for investigation. They offer far too happy a hunting-ground for incontrollable conjecture . . . Even if we knew far more than we do about how the mind works, the attempt to display the inner working of the artist's mind by the evidence of his work alone must be subject to the gravest dangers. And to judge by the published work of Freud upon Leonardo da Vinci or of Jung upon Goethe, . . . psycho-analysts tend to be peculiarly inept as critics.

This is highly unconvincing. To generalize from two instances is an obvious absurdity, and to object that psycho-analytical conjecture must in any special sense be 'uncontrollable' is false, since such criticism could be as subject as any other descriptive kind to the demand for evidence ('Show me *that* in the poem'). In any case, why should the critic limit himself to 'the evidence of the work alone'? There is also biographical evidence, after all. Of course Richards's disinclination, so soon after his announcement of the communication-theory, to view the communication from the poet's end may have its practical justification. He is passionately drawn to the world of the experimental sciences: 'only the simplest human activities', he exclaims regretfully in the first chapter of the *Principles*, 'are at present amenable to laboratory methods'; and there is no doubt that readers of poetry are easier to dragoon into laboratories than poets are. Most poets, after all, are dead, and those who are alive are notoriously difficult to pin down. But any lecture-room will offer a ready supply of readers, and you may mount experiments on their ability to read, and classify the results, with careless impunity. There is only one practical difficulty: some readers are better informed than others, and Richards shared the modish prejudice of the years between the wars against historical information. It is at this point that the experiment called 'practical criticism' was conceived.

Richards proposes three objectives in *Practical Criticism* (1929): to document 'the contemporary state of culture', to create a new kind of reading-habit 'for those who wish to discover for themselves what they think and feel about poetry' (apparently by mounting similar experiments upon themselves), and to reform the teaching of literature. With these objects he distributed to his Cambridge audiences largely modernized texts of unfamiliar poems, with invitations to comment freely. A selection of these comments, which he calls 'protocols', forms the substance of the book, followed by an analysis of characteristic errors and suggestions for educational reform.

Richards's own conclusion from his experiment is that the state of literacy is outrageously low. His guinea-pigs were well above average – 'I see no reason whatever to think that a higher standard of critical discernment can easily be found under our present cultural conditions' (p. 5) than at Cambridge University. And yet, according to his own analysis, ten kinds of failure crippled the responses of his protocol-authors, ranging from failure to understand the plain sense to sentimentality, inhibition, and doctrinal adhesions. The failure of Richards's pupils might be thought implicit in the test he offers them, for there is no reason to think that any poetry was ever written for the purpose to which Richards applies it here, as he comes near to admitting, with damaging force, in his introduction: 'The precise conditions of this test are not duplicated in our everyday commerce with literature' (p. 5). This is a sizeable understatement. It seems more natural to suppose that all but the simplest poems exist in traditions which dictate in some sense the significance of the poem, and that poems torn from their historical context tend to mean some other thing, or to descend into the merely meaningless. If this is so, then *Practical Criticism* and its record of failures in response is not an indictment of English education – justly indictable as that may be – but an impressive body of evidence to suggest that unhistorical reading is bad reading.

Such unhistorical reading, however, encouraged by Richards as an 'experiment' though never recommended as an ideal, is promoted to the ultimate ideal of analysis in the 'New Criticism' which arose in England in the late twenties, spread to the United States in the years before the Second World War, and showed signs of dominating academic criticism, especially in America, after 1945. John Crowe Ransom's *The New Criticism* appeared in 1941, two years after Richards settled in the United States, and fixed upon anti-historical criticism the sad epithet of 'new' which has inevitably grown less appropriate with every passing year. By the late thirties it already looked characteristically American – so much so that it is easy to forget its largely British origins. The conflict in the United States, indeed, over the historical element in criticism has always been more dramatic than in England: partly because in America the scholarly conservatives were more conservative; and partly because the special needs of American universities genuinely call for an emphasis on techniques of analysis and explanation of texts – a need which the historical critics had tended to overlook, and which the New Critics seemed eager to supply.

None the less, there can be no doubt that the neo-critical tradition takes its rise in the England of the twenties. Eliot stands rather loosely to the movement, part pioneer, part sceptic; Richards provides a ramshackle aesthetic to build upon, and the example of a criticism that is 'practical' rather than pedantically historical; and the first neo-critical analysis occurs in a 'word-by-word collaboration' between Robert Graves and the American poetess Laura Riding, *A Survey of Modernist Poetry*, a reasoned defence of some post-1918 poetry published in London in 1927. The account of Shakespeare's 129th sonnet there was, according to Richards's account,[1] William Empson's model in his *Seven Types of Ambiguity* (1930).

WILLIAM EMPSON

The Graves-Riding analysis of 'Th' expense of Spirit in a waste of shame' illustrates most of the assumptions and tactics of

[1] *Furioso* (New Haven, Spring 1940), quoted in Stanley E. Hyman, *The Armed Vision* (New York, 1948), p. 294.

Empson's later analyses in *Seven Types*. In their view, many modern poems, notably those of e. e. cummings, are only spuriously difficult in their eccentric spelling and punctuation: 'They are too clear, once the plain reader puts himself to work on them. Braced as they are, they do not present the eternal difficulties that make poems immortal . . .' (p. 75). A Shakespeare sonnet is genuinely difficult, and a line like

Mad in pursuit and in possession so

represents 'a number of interwoven meanings' (Graves-Riding make no special play with the term 'ambiguity'). The analysis is only partly vitiated by a naïve faith in the absolute authority of spelling and punctuation in the pirated 1609 text of the Sonnets, and it is still in principle historical enough to claim that 'Shakespeare's punctuation allows the variety of meanings he actually intends'. What counts for more is the richly seminal doctrine that 'difficulty' is chief among the poetic virtues: 'If we choose any one meaning, then we owe it to Shakespeare to choose at least one he intended and one embracing as many meanings as possible, that is, the most difficult meaning. It is always the most difficult meaning that is the most final (p. 74).' And the account that follows notes both properties of structure ('the very delicate interrelation of the words of the first two lines') and verbal ambiguities too ('the double meaning of *waste* as both 'expense' and 'wilderness').

The authority for naming the Graves-Riding *Survey* as Empson's inspiration is Richards himself. Born in 1906, William Empson came to Magdalene College, Cambridge (Richards's own college) in 1925 to read mathematics, a year after the appearance of Richards's *Principles of Literary Criticism*. In 1927, the year when the *Survey* appeared, he

switched over for his last year to English. As he was at Magdalene, this made me his Director of Studies. He seemed to have read more English Literature than I had, and to have read it more recently and better, so our roles were soon in some danger of becoming reversed. At about his third visit he brought up the games of interpretation which Laura Riding and Robert Graves had been playing with the unpunctuated form of 'The expense of spirit in a waste of shame'. Taking the sonnet as a conjuror takes his hat, he produced an endless swarm of lively rabbits from it and ended by 'You could do that with any poetry, couldn't you?' This was a Godsend to a Director of Studies, so I said, 'You'd better go off and do it, hadn't you?' A week later he said he was still slapping away at it on his typewriter. Would I mind if he just went on with that? Not a bit. The following week there he was with a thick wad of very illegible typescript under his arm – the central 30,000 words or so of the book.[1]

Empson's first and most influential book, in fact, *Seven Types of Ambiguity*, was first drafted in two weeks by a twenty-one-year-old undergraduate. It appeared in 1930 and again, heavily revised and with some brutally concessive notes, in a second edition of 1947. There have been only three books of criticism since, and two very slim volumes of neo-Metaphysical verse largely written in the thirties. The early critical books represent a sort of ebb-and-flow between the two chief preoccupations of the New Criticism: verbal and structural (or 'organic') analysis. *Seven Types* divides the 'difficulty', provocatively rechristened 'ambiguity', of Graves and Laura Riding (or 'any verbal nuance, however slight, which gives room for alternative reactions') into seven types representing 'stages of advancing logical disorder'. The 'tensions' in question here are essentially those between words. With the second critical book, *Some Versions of Pastoral* (1935), his interest shifts to the total meaning of whole works, with many evidences of powerful Marxist and Freudian influence. Empson has later insisted that his Marxism in the thirties and after – at least until the Communist revolution in China in 1949, which he witnessed – was more serious than his writings reveal, and *Some Versions* assumed the class-analysis of society and the ideal status of the 'proletariat'; though he frankly admits, in his first chapter, that the book is 'not a solid piece of sociology'. Pastoral, for Empson, is one of the conventions out of which 'ambiguity' may arise, since it consists in 'simple people expressing strong feelings in learned and fashionable language' by 'putting the complex into the simple'. Again, he divides into the magical number of seven: first, proletarian literature as it may evolve, the modern proletarian standing in for the traditional shephered – a manifesto for a Socialist literature, this, and Empson's unique excursion into

[1] *Furioso*, op. cit.

legislative criticism – followed by the sub-plots of drama, a Shake-spearean sonnet, Marvell's 'Garden', the Adam of *Paradise Lost*, Gay's *Beggar's Opera* (an urban pastoral), and *Alice in Wonderland* ('The Child as Swain'). Marxism and criticism meet (though in a paradoxical and self-defeating sense) in Empson's theory that irony may be a device for reconciling ruler and ruled – in which case, one should have supposed, it ought to be condemned as a popular opium. Marxism is more consistently, though not much more plausibly, employed in the analysis of Shakespeare's 73rd sonnet, where the 'bare ruined choirs' are held to suggest the decay of the feudal, monastic order in the face of Elizabethan capitalism. The Freudian influence is prominent mainly in the last chapter, in the analysis of *Alice*, where Empson (in defiance of Richards's sanction) boldly sets out to 'use psycho-analysis where it seems relevant', and proceeds to interpret the book, through a wealth of unconscious sexual symbolism, as a neurotic form of the pastoral in which 'child-becomes-judge': 'The symbolic completeness of Alice's experience is I think important. She runs the whole gamut [of sexual experience]; she is a father in getting down the hole, a foetus at the bottom, and can only be born by becoming a mother . . .' (pp. 272-3). It is full circle. Empson, at first a disciple of Richards in his rejection of biographical criticism, seems poised here on the edge of a species of biographical exegesis more intim-ate than anything practised by the Victorians. He pauses, indeed, to praise Ernest Jones's analysis of *Hamlet*.

With his third book, *The Structure of Complex Words* (1951), largely a collection of revised articles published in the thirties and forties, Empson returns to verbal analysis of an even more rig-orous kind than that of *Seven Types*. Key-words are now dis-tinguished and tested. We seem further from Richards than ever, though the dedication courteously calls him 'the source of all ideas in this book, even the minor ones arrived at by disagreeing with him'. But there is nothing 'minor' about Empson's attack on 'the simple Emotive theory' of the language of poetry which, as Empson notices, 'would make most literary criticism irrelevant, let alone the sort of verbal analysis that most interested me' by appearing to dismiss all poetry as not strictly significant. Empson now approaches history for the second time, but from a different, linguistic angle: he invents a set of symbols to apply to senses of key-words listed in the *Oxford English Dictionary* – a linguistic form of historical criticism to which the nineteenth century, if only for lack of tools, never submitted. And finally, since his return to England from China and his appointment as Professor of English at Sheffield (1953), Empson has produced *Milton's God* (1961), a magnificently vituperative attack upon Christianity in terms of a defence of *Paradise Lost*, and a stream of articles, mainly on Shakespeare, Milton, and the novel, in which his powerful, if amateur, biographical and psychological interests re-emerge. 'I think a critic should have an insight into the mind of his author,' he wrote in brave disregard of fashion in 1955, 'and I don't approve of the attack on "The Fallacy of Intentionalism".'[1]

Empson did not invent the technique of verbal analysis which dominated critical fashion in the forties and fifties; but he was the first to systematize it, and he popularized much of its characteristic jargon ('ambiguity', 'irony', 'tension'). And the technique cannot reasonably be dismissed as a passing phase, as Eliot tried to do in his sneer about 'the lemon-squeezer school of criticism'.[2] Verbal nuance, or 'ambiguity', is a characteristic poetic fact, and it is arguable that the property of poetry to suggest more than it states is what makes it what it is – the final distinction between poetry and mere 'verse' which both Wordsworth and Coleridge had pursued, and which the Victorians abandoned as a hopeless quest. That English criticism should have had to wait some three hundred years, until the 1920s, for such a crucial discovery suggests how laborious and fumbling our early aesthetics were, and how immature the study still is: by mid twentieth century, English criticism is still barely adolescent. But to say all this is not to deny the absurdity of some of Empson's examples, or the dangers and limitations of his method in the hands of others. For verbal analysis has one great limitation: it is appropriate only to brief examples, usually short poems, and Empson's *Complex Words*, where he proceeds by a rigorous selection of key-words, only doubtfully adapts the technique to longer works such as epics and novels. Preciosity, too, remains a constant menace, though it is

[1] From a letter to *Mandrake* (autumn 1955); cf. p. 155n., above.
[2] 'The Frontiers of Criticism'; cf. p. 195, above.

not unavoidable, and the analyses of some of Empson's followers in England and America point to a new and terrifyingly uncritical kind of Alexandrianism. Empson himself is only occasionally prone. The quality of his mind is too animated to drown itself in a mass of gratuitous detail. Of all the English critics, he is the most variously ingenious, and the readiest to make a fool of himself in public. His mind sparks off original ideas with frightening rapidity – we are not really surprised to learn that *Seven Types* was drafted in two weeks. Lavishly self-indulgent to his own theories, he treads a borderline between brilliance and absurdity. He cares almost as little as Coleridge about accurate quotation, overstates by force of habit, and exultantly reveals his own past howlers in errata-lists and footnotes to later editions. The ironic element in his criticism – Empson's own ambiguity – ultimately defies analysis, Empsonian or other, but only the most unwary of his reviewers has ever been foolish enough to doubt his fervent dedication to poetry. 'When it was done,' Empson wrote of his *Complex Words*, 'I felt *Nunc dimittis*; I was free, I was ready to die.'[1] This is, at first sight, oddly dedicated language. But if we look again at Empson's critical achievement, it is clear in retrospect that passion as well as ingenuity has played its part, and that the mind that produces the 'endless swarm of lively rabbits' would have tired long ago if it had no better motive than to show off.

F. R. LEAVIS

The most influential British-born critic of the twentieth century, however, has been the less original and more predictable F. R. Leavis (b. 1895) – the only native critic of our age, perhaps, to penetrate in his influence (as Arnold once did) below the intellectual *élite* who actually read criticism, and to enter by indirections into British school-room teaching. His influence on the teaching of English has been profound in schools; in the universities he remains a major controversial figure, and there are probably few Departments of English in the Commonwealth which do not boast, or conceal, at least one disciple. And yet the nature of his achievement seems to have escaped serious analysis, perhaps because, in the hurly-burly of charge and counter-charge as to

[1] *Mandrake*, op cit.

whether Leavis's criticism is good or bad, it has not occurred to anyone to ask very seriously what it is.

The classic view of Leavis is that his criticism belongs to the school of verbal analysis, and that, in consequence, it is an eccentric British counterpart to the American New Criticism. This is the conclusion of Stanley E. Hyman, in his *The Armed Vision* (1948), who finds that Leavis's quarterly *Scrutiny* (1932-53) contains 'some of the sharpest close reading of our time', and that his own criticism is 'at its best when technical and exegetical' (p. 273). And Laurence Lerner, in a valedictory article on *Scrutiny* published soon after its demise,[1] has labelled Leavis a child of I. A. Richards, a 'practical critic' employing the analytic techniques of *Practical Criticism*: 'The achievement of *Scrutiny* is, in a way, peculiar to the twentieth century: it is the building up of a body of practical criticisms, of substantiated literary judgements, that has surely no equal in extent and quality.' *Scrutiny*, he continues, set out from the beginning 'to apply their methods [i.e. those of Eliot, Graves, Richards, Middleton Murry, and the American New Critics] not sporadically but systematically, over the whole field of English Literature', and the Scrutineers proceeded by 'a minute and brilliant examination – by a scrutiny – of actual passages'.

There is remarkably little evidence, it must be said at once, either in Leavis's books or in the files of *Scrutiny* itself, for this very substantial legend that Leavis was a verbal analyst. I know of only one example of anything like an extended analysis on seemingly neo-critical lines in Leavis's own books – that of Matthew Arnold's sonnet on Shakespeare in *Education and the University* (1943); and even there Leavis's purposes lie well outside those we would normally attribute to Richards and Empson. The analysis is offered as an example, merely, of how spurious much familiar anthology-poetry is, and in no sense as analysis for its own sake. But there are interesting reasons why the commentators have been so easily misled. In the first place, Leavis's criticism had an undeniable air of contemporaneity: the New Criticism is presumably new, Leavis is undoubtedly new, therefore Leavis is a New Critic – so the unconscious argument may once have run. Again, he

[1] 'The Life and Death of *Scrutiny*', *London Magazine* (January 1955).

chose, when he founded his review in 1932, to entitle it *Scrutiny*, and it is easy to assume that the Leavis school scrutinized 'actual passages' – the more so because they always encouraged liberal quotation.[1] Again, Leavis himself occasionally talked as if he believed in verbal analysis – however much a comparison with the criticism of Empson, or of American New Critics such as Cleanth Brooks and John Crowe Ransom, would show that he does not practise it; he seems, in principle at least, a critic eager not to stray from texts. 'No treatment of poetry', he writes in the introduction to *Revaluation* (1936), 'is worth much that does not keep very close to the concrete: there lies the problem of method. . . . In dealing with individual poets the rule of the critics is, or should (I think) be, to work as much as possible in terms of particular analysis – analysis of poems or passages – and to say nothing that cannot be related immediately to judgements about producible texts.' That sounds very like the Richards-Empson tradition in criticism, and no doubt that tradition genuinely influenced Leavis to the extent that he always felt a compulsion to appear to play the game according to the new rules. But Leavis instantly makes it clear that he does not consider mere analysis is the real object of the critic: the critic's discipline of confining himself to 'producible texts', he goes on, 'while not preventing his saying anything that he should in the end find himself needing to say, enables him to say it with a force of relevance and an edged economy not otherwise attainable'.

Leavis's concern with verbal analysis, then, is relatively superficial – perhaps a strategy to placate a school whose method, being only a method, may have seemed to him too trivial to argue with and too fashionable to attack. His real concern lies with what he calls the thing he 'finds himself needing to say', and this characteristic object defines the difference between *Scrutiny* and the New Criticism well enough. The run of New Critics, ultimately, feel no compulsion to assert anything as critics; their business lies in

---

[1] The title was more probably suggested by a series of articles 'Scrutinies' in Rickword's monthly (later quarterly) *The Calendar of Modern Letters* (1925-7), which gave rise to two collections under similar titles edited by Rickword, and to an admiring selection, *Towards Standards of Criticism* (1933), edited by Leavis.

discrediting one method (the historical and biographical) and in instituting another, a form of analysis from which, relatively speaking, history and biography have been self-consciously excluded. Their convictions are often shadowy and (one suspects) probably uninteresting. Leavis is all passionate conviction.

Leavis's career as a critic begins in discipleship to Eliot. One might even say that its progress can be traced in terms of his alienation from this influence; but it might be fairer to argue that it is Eliot that has moved, and Leavis who has stood four-square by the critical attitudes which his master represented in the 1920s. He bought a copy of *The Sacred Wood*, he tells us in a late essay, at the moment when it appeared, when he was twenty-five, and 'for the next few years I read it through several times a year, pencil in hand'.[1] But like most disciples, he is embarrassed to describe the nature of Eliot's influence as a critic: 'it was a matter of having had incisively demonstrated, for pattern and incitement, what the disinterested and effective application of intelligence to literature looks like, what is the nature of purity of interest . . .' The last phrase, as I have suggested, points to a radical misunderstanding of Eliot's early criticism and its close relationship to Eliot's career as a poet. But, for Leavis, the misunderstanding was fruitful.

Leavis's first independent book of literary criticism, *New Bearings in English Poetry* (1932), opens frankly with an acknowledgement of the same debt: 'How little I suppose these considerations to be original, the book will make plain: it is largely an acknowledgement, vicarious as well as personal, of indebtedness to a certain critic and poet.' In *New Bearings* Eliot's poems, up to and including *Ash-Wednesday*, are explained (but hardly 'verbally analysed') and justified, with Pound and Hopkins sharing pride of place as moving spirits of poetic modernism; other late Victorians, W. B. Yeats, and the Georgians are summarized and dismissed in language which Leavis never again equalled in ironic potency. The next book, *Revaluation* (1936), a collection of *Scrutiny* essays predetermined for book form, follows closely upon *New Bearings* as part of a single plan: 'the planning of the one book was involved in the planning of the other. An account of the present of poetry,

---

[1] *The Common Pursuit* (1952), p. 280.

to be worth anything, must be from a clearly realized point of view . . . [which] must have been determined and defined as much in relation to the past as to the present.' *Revaluation*, in fact, is a backward exploration into literary history to rediscover those poetic qualities already extolled in Eliot, Pound, and Hopkins. They are identified in the Metaphysicals and Pope and missed, on the whole, in the poetry of the romantics.

In the early forties Leavis's concern shifted realistically towards the novel, a form which, in its substantial moral preoccupations, has suited the implacably moralistic quality of his mind better than any but a few poets; and in 1948 he collected a group of essays under the title of *The Great Tradition: George Eliot, Henry James, Joseph Conrad*. The great tradition in English fiction, in this account, has been the tradition of serious moral concern – Leavis calls such novelists 'significant in terms of the human awareness they promote; awareness of the possibilities of life' (p. 2). It begins in Jane Austen – a novelist whom his wife, Q. D. Leavis, had already treated in a careful and brilliant group of articles in *Scrutiny* (1941-4), unfortunately never realized as a book – and passes through George Eliot, James, and Conrad to D. H. Lawrence, whom Leavis reserved for a separate study in 1955. After *The Great Tradition*, the quality of his interests regrettably shifted from literary criticism to literary politics. His attacks upon the 'cultural establishment' of the British Council and the BBC, and indeed upon anyone who appeared to qualify his achievement, however mildly, took on an air of strident self-justification, and the study of Lawrence, though it contains passages of the old perception, shows a falling off in power to organize material. The later career of Leavis, indeed, suggests a corruption of an unusual kind. Unlike Eliot, he never retreated. But he remained in the same positions so obstinately that one suspected he was there at all only out of force of habit, and his vehemence often seemed out of all proportion to the contradictions under attack, while his absolute refusal to admit honest errors of judgement sapped the confidence of some of his most serious admirers. The tailpiece entitled 'Retrospect 1950', appended to a new edition of *New Bearings* (1950), suggests how a reasoned confidence in the real excellence of parts of *Scrutiny* could harden into a cultish worship of revealed truth:

I may say that this placing of Auden [as 'adolescent'] has been en-
forced in *Scrutiny* by detailed criticism in more than half a dozen
reviews, coming from half a dozen different hands. The dismissal of
Spender (once in conventional esteem the Shelley of the Poetic Renaissance), Day Lewis, MacNiece, George Barker, Dylan Thomas, has also
been done critically in *Scrutiny*. My brief placing reference to Empson
and Bottrall has also its due backing there in a number of reviews by
different hands.

This is quite peculiarly self-deceived, and we are entitled to object
that support of a *Scrutiny* view by a *Scrutiny* reviewer is, in itself,
no evidence for anything. Such in-group complacency looks all
the more dangerous when we turn to the files of *Scrutiny* itself and
observe the gross inferiority of disciples to master, and the alarming glibness of most reviews of modern poetry that appear there.
And his self-deception seems still more serious when we turn up,
in the Epilogue to *New Bearings*, the passage so evasively defended
in the Postscript of 1950. The 1932 'placing' of Ronald Bottrall
reads: 'There is another young poet [besides Empson] whose
achieved work leaves no room for doubt about his future. Mr
Ronald Bottrall's development has been remarkably rapid and
sure – it is convincing – and his published volume, *The Loosening
and Other Poems*, establishes him as a very considerable poet
indeed . . .' Is it conceivable that any review, whether in *Scrutiny* or
anywhere else, could provide 'due backing' to such a judgement?
The high quality of *New Bearings* is hardly affected by such bad
prophecies, and prophecy, in any case, is not the business of criticism. But Leavis believed so passionately in the defence of 'values'
by the correct 'placing' of individual poets in a hierarchy of excellence – it is part of his inheritance from *The Sacred Wood*, fiercely
formalized – and was so convinced that these values were embattled and in imminent danger of extinction, that a simple *peccavi*
became a tactical impossibility for him. To give way on one point
would have seemed like surrendering along an entire front.

Leavis fought his war for 'values' heroically. But the cause itself
remains something of a mystery, since he always refused to commit himself to general positions. It is the central paradox of his
achievement that, while it challenges the reader with its apparent
severity and fierce discrimination, it refuses to discuss the criteria

by which it proceeds. And we know exactly why Leavis always declined to talk of ultimate principles: his refusal is not a diplomatic evasion, but arises out of a firm conviction that the critic must remain available to readers of all doctrinal persuasions, that he has a duty not to show his hand. The title of a late collection of essays, *The Common Pursuit* (1952), derives from Eliot's 'The Function of Criticism', 'one of those essays of Mr Eliot which I most admire', as Leavis confesses in the preface: 'The critic . . . should endeavour to discipline his personal prejudices and cranks – tares to which we are all subject – and compose his differences with as many of his fellows as possible in the common pursuit of true judgement.' Once again, Leavis is a more Eliotian critic than Eliot himself, and the discipline must have cost him something in personal reticence, as well as in terms of whatever causes he privately supported. The independence of pre-war *Scrutiny* of the fashionable – almost compulsory – Marxism of the day is striking evidence for Leavis's determination that the critical pursuit should remain common to all intelligent men. A 1937 article by one of his followers on the directors of the Left Book Club dared to chide them for their failure to achieve 'a stricter maintenance of the standards they profess' – an article later defended, in an editorial note, as representing 'the considered point of view held by *Scrutiny*';[1] and another anonymous note defines the nature of Leavis's outward political independence: 'If *Scrutiny* could make it more difficult for intelligent persons to invoke the Webbs on Russia as Mr [Boris] Ford does, we should feel that a useful function had been performed.'[2] Independence is not a virtue in itself; but this kind of actively critical independence looks better, in retrospect, than the aberrations of most critics and poets in the days when German and Russian collectivist ideas were fashionable.

We are left to guess, then, from his evident affection for J. S. Mill, George Eliot, Henry James, Conrad, and D. H. Lawrence, at the exact nature of Leavis's radical agnosticism, as we are left to wonder whether the critical pursuit can be carried as far as he

[1] H. A. Mason, 'Education by Book Club?', *Scrutiny* (December 1937); note (March 1938), p. 428.
[2] *Scrutiny* (March 1938), p. 428.

supposes before doctrinal splits threaten its coherence. Doctrinal reticence, indeed, involved Leavis in controversies all the more personal and vindictive for the failure of either side to identify points of principle in the *Scrutiny* attitude. Even the technical and linguistic pre-suppositions of his criticism, such as his repeated insistence upon the need for 'concreteness' and 'specificity', or for the 'realization' of feeling in poetic language, do not cease to be vague and uncertain because they are passionately held, and we may despair of a lucid account of central doctrine from a critic who has always shown himself indifferent to the study of linguistics and, indeed, too sensitive to the charge of academic pedantry to pursue any informational inquiry for long. The most serious charge to be made against his criticism is twofold: he has hurried towards value-judgements, especially in his later work, without respect for the essential delicacy and complexity of literary values; and he has not known enough about anything – or cared much about finding out. In scholarly terms, he remains a British provincial, moved by no perceptible foreign influence except the usual twentyish fixation with France. But his career provides an apt and adventurous conclusion to this history. It shows the analytical revolution begun in England by Dryden triumphant and complete. And it could only have happened at all in a society in which the claims of literary analysis are so widely accepted that criticism, far from having to assert or defend its right to exist, is in some danger of being mistaken for a way of life.

Chapter 10

THE MID-CENTURY SCENE

THIS book is a history, not a manifesto, and the historian who discourses about the present inevitably describes less accurately than he should wish, approving and condemning more boldly. To describe the scene in English criticism since Eliot's shift of interest away from literature in the 1930s is open to every historian's peril. The terrain is unmapped, and must for the time being remain so. The subject, at the best, is an untidy one, and every attempt to make it look tidy must suffer from some distortion and suppression of evidence. And, of course, it is vast, for no other literary tradition – not even the French – attributes so much importance to the role of the critic as the English today, and certainly no linguistic area can rival the English-speaking world in the wealth of its critical activity or in the intensity of its critical debates.

The story is complicated further by the emergence of the United States in the thirties as a vastly productive centre of literary criticism, and especially of academic criticism. The experience has been a unique one. No other European literature has ever been subject to such a sudden access of energy as the English at the hands of the American. One is abruptly reminded that less than one-quarter of all native speakers of English now live in the British Isles, and that a large majority live in North America. And yet the American influence on British criticism since the thirties – like the less noticed, but not less remarkable, influence in the opposite direction – has not been all of a piece. Happily enough, there is no characteristically British critical tradition in the mid twentieth century, and no American tradition either. Those who think otherwise are generalizing on evidence which is either partial or out of date. Americans who complain of a special British tone in London literary periodicals are usually found, on interrogation, to be talking about 'Bloomsbury' – and Bloomsbury is all but dead, and was never the whole story; and Englishmen who think that the quality of American criticism can be identified with the last plump Ph.D. thesis they have glanced at are wildly underestimating the variety of literary scholarship in the United States. There are no national traditions in English criticism today, on either side of the Atlantic. There does, however, exist a variety of critical schools, and they are largely Anglo-American schools. We might group them under three headings – the Moralists, the New Critics, and the Historians – remembering always that criticism since the Second World War has tended to stir these elements together and to defy category; and we shall often find it useful, in discussing all three in turn, to forget that the Atlantic Ocean exists at all.

THE MORALISTS

Most English critics before Arnold and Ruskin assumed that all good poetry is morally edifying, and that (as Johnson had insisted in his preface to Shakespeare) 'it is always a writer's duty to make the world better'. But there is a tradition in twentieth-century criticism stemming from Arnold which is distinct from all previous moral theories of literature. The difference may be simply stated: Johnson, like other Renaissance and eighteenth-century critics, took it for granted that everyone is more or less agreed about the difference between right and wrong, and that the moral duty of the poet lies simply in observing a recognized code: 'justice', he goes on confidently, as if he were speaking for all Christendom, 'is a virtue independant on time or place.' Modern moralism, by contrast, is more often agnostic, exploratory, and self-consciously élitist. Its tone is not that of the common preacher anticipating assent: it is more often embittered and embattled. Its very dogmatism is based upon the uncertainty of its dogma and the difficulty of finding an audience. Johnson does not have to raise his voice: the modern moralist tends to shout, as D. H. Lawrence (1885-1930) seems to do in the last decade of his life, indicting the sanctions of White Protestant societies, whether British or American, in his *Studies in Classic American Literature* (1923) or in the essays posthumously collected as *Phoenix* (1936). So does Lawrence's disciple John Middleton Murry (1889-1957), who in a spate of books, and in his periodical *The Adelphi*, always proclaimed that criticism 'depended on values – a delineation of what is good for man.'[1] George Orwell (1903-50), too, used such authors as Dickens and Kipling to flay the infantilism of the British literary Left; and F. R. Leavis, whose criticism has been discussed at length in the previous chapter, offers an unusually pure example of critical moralism. The vast school of Shakespearean criticism inspired since 1930 by G. Wilson Knight has ambitiously interpreted dramatic characters as if they were philosophical ideas. And there is a brilliant and eccentric American example in the dissident figure of Yvor Winters (b. 1900), a critic with a strikingly home-grown air about him whose work, uniquely among critics of this kind, looks independent of Arnoldian influence, bluntly and unfashionably insisting through the thirties and forties that the critic's business is to assert what the 'best poems' are, and that any poem, being 'a statement in words in which special pains are taken with the expression of feeling',[2] ought to make simple sense, even if written by Hopkins or T. S. Eliot.

The moralists are the prophetic figures in modern criticism. They most readily excite discipleship. Their influence may even extend to matters of conduct; in some cases, indeed (as in Lawrence and Orwell) the critical interest is a late extension of some wider moral purpose. They are self-righteously non-professional. They tend (however scholarly in themselves) to despise scholarship, they are prone to conspiratorial theories of 'Establishments' and, however well established themselves, they insist upon being regarded as outcasts. George Orwell, aggressively pouring his tea into his saucer in the BBC canteen, may be taken as the eternal model of the modern English moralist. The influence of such men stands highest in an age which, like the thirties and forties, is avid for moral certainties of a novel kind. In the fifties, in an atmosphere notably less assertive and more studious, it tended to dilute itself with uncertainties and, even in the act of spreading, to lose confidence and force. It seeks intermixture with

---

[1] J. Middleton Murry, *Selected Criticism 1916-57*, edited by Richard Rees (Oxford, 1960), p. viii (quoted from Murry's journal).

[2] *In Defence of Reason* (New York, 1947), p. 363. This collection represents most of Winters's critical work over more than fifteen years.

history, with sociology, and with politics, as in such latter-day moralists as Richard Hoggart (b. 1918) and Raymond Williams (b. 1921); and such studies of 'the cultural situation' and its antecedents as Hoggart's *The Uses of Literacy* (1957) or Williams's *Culture and Society, 1780–1950* (1958) and its sequel *The Long Revolution* (1961), seem scholarly rather than prophetic in their quiet, hesitant insistence that the truth is an object of study rather than a preserve of the right-minded: 'Issues much more difficult than those I have directly treated were being approached' in *The Uses of Literacy*, as Hoggart gently assures us in his conclusion. ' . . . These are issues I am not qualified to pursue. In order to be able to till my own part of the field I felt I could reasonably take for granted a general agreement on certain assumptions, an agreement sufficient to allow me to use, without closer definition than emerges from the detailed illustrations, words such as "decent", "healthy", "serious" . . .' The concern for culture as a cause to be defended, and the assumption that such a concern is proper to an educated minority, place Hoggart in the tradition of Arnold. But the very explicitness of his language, his readiness to name and even to question 'certain assumptions', suggest a loss of confidence, a new open-mindedness, a prospect of growth. Moralism is as common today as ever it was in English criticism. But it lacks its former certainty, and its influence, though widespread, is now less sharp than once it was.

THE NEW CRITICS

The origins of the so-called New Criticism have already been described in the first work of Robert Graves and William Empson where, even before 1930, both verbal and structural analysis was practised, and the characteristic search for what Graves had called 'the most difficult meaning' was accepted as the ultimate object of good reading. But neither Graves nor Empson is noticeably antihistorical; and neither is the most distinguished and original of American Empsonian critics, Kenneth Burke (b. 1897). Their successors among the American New Critics decidedly are, and the final character of the New Criticism is hardly defined until its translation to the United States in the late thirties. In its American form, indeed, the New Criticism had something like the character of a school. Its pioneer, John Crowe Ransom (b. 1888), who taught English at Vanderbilt University in Tennessee from 1924 to 1937, and later at Kenyon College in Ohio, bequeathed to such pupils as Allen Tate (b. 1899) and Robert Penn Warren (b. 1905) a neo-conservative respect for the Old South and its coherent social values which may owe something to the Eliot of *After Strange Gods*. In the American New Critics, contempt for late nineteenth-century values is general: not only for historical criticism and its accompanying pedantries, but for agnostic enlightenment, democratic optimism, industrialism, and such international ideals as Marxism. It is a frankly reactionary movement, and the word 'New' must always have held for it an air of pleasing paradox.

The Aesthetic Movement of Pater and Wilde had tended to belittle the study of the origins of poetry, and Eliot's famous remark that a 'poem's existence is somewhere between the writer and the reader'[1] is clearly intended to foster a similar scepticism. But it is hardly until the thirties that any general attack is mounted upon the whole concept of historical criticism; and hardly until the forties, when New Critics began to fill major posts in universities in the United States, that anti-historical manifestoes become fashionable. The influential college anthology *Understanding Poetry*, edited by Cleanth Brooks and Robert Penn Warren, which appeared in New York in 1938, condemned in its preface the use of poetry for any purpose beyond itself, whether historical or moralistic, and declared itself 'conceived on the assumption that if poetry is worth teaching at all, it is worth teaching as poetry'. The same anti-cognitive enthusiasm reveals itself sharply in other documents, even in the scholarly handbook that synthesizes so much of the school, René Wellek and Austin Warren's *Theory of Literature* (1949). 'I should like to think that criticism has been written, and may be again, from a mere point of view,' wrote Allen Tate in 1955, in the preface to his collection *The Man of Letters in the Modern World*, and neo-critical studies such as Warren's account of 'The Ancient Mariner'[2] or Brooks's assemblage of analyses entitled *The Well Wrought Urn* (1947) are strik-

---

[1] *The Use of Poetry and the Use of Criticism* (1933), p. 30.
[2] Reprinted in his *Selected Essays* (New York, 1958).

ingly indifferent to historical probability. 'If literary history has not been emphasized,' wrote Brooks in his preface, 'it is not because I discount its importance, or because I have failed to take it into account. It is rather that I have been anxious to see what residuum, if any, is left after we have referred the poem to its cultural matrix.' On a similar principle, Peer Gynt sought a kernel to his onion, and found that when he had peeled and peeled away he was left with nothing but his tears. For all poetic meaning may, if we choose, be reasonably referred to its historical setting, and to argue as if the value of poetry lies in what is 'left' after historical interpretation has done its work is to argue away the very existence of what we seek.

The fullest accounts of the doctrines of the New Criticism appeared as late as 1946-9 in two articles in the *Sewanee Review* by W. K. Wimsatt Jr and Monroe C. Beardsley, 'The Intentional Fallacy' and 'The Affective Fallacy', both collected in Wimsatt's *The Verbal Icon* (1954). Two of the assumptions of romantic criticism are held up to the light and pronounced fallacious.'The design or intention of the author is neither available nor desirable as a standard for judging the success of a work of literary art,' as Wimsatt and Beardsley protest in the first; and as for the second, 'the Affective Fallacy is a confusion between a poem and its results. . . . It begins by trying to derive the standard of criticism from the psychological effects of the poem, and ends in impressionism and relativism.' But these manifestoes, though richly symptomatic of the New Criticism, are late to appear, and suffer from the over-confidence of a movement already victorious. The real merits of the school are not to be studied in its attempts to theorize. It is rootedly pragmatic and particular, a way of teaching rather than a formal doctrine, and based upon an urgent impatience with academicism rather than upon any coherent principle. In American universities in the thirties and forties it must have felt like a clean wind. But a reaction was already forming under the leadership of Ronald S. Crane in the late thirties in the Chicago School of neo-Aristotelians which, employing a more formidable scholarship and a less popular style, insisted upon a return to questions of design and structure by whatever method and upon whatever assumption seemed appropriate to the particular case.

The Chicago view, according to Crane himself, was 'pluralistic and instrumentalist', insisting that 'we must accord to critics the right of free choice as between different basic methods'. This programme makes the Chicago critics look more eclectic than in fact they were. They represent a heresy of the New Criticism – still neo-critical, after all, in their interest in structural analysis, as in Crane's exemplary account of the plot of *Tom Jones*, and diverging from the orthodoxy of the New Criticism only in two minor respects: in their slightly more tolerant attitude to historical data; and in their attacks upon what Crane called the neo-critical 'impoverishment of poetic theory' through an incessant search for irony, tension, and paradox. But these are family quarrels. For Crane, too, accepts such neo-critical slogans as 'poetry as poetry and not another thing'.[1] The Chicago School may, in its day, have shaken a little of the confidence of the New Criticism. But only in a radically anti-historical atmosphere in English studies could it ever have achieved a reputation for historical criticism.

THE HISTORIANS

There is no such thing as a historical school of criticism in twentieth-century English, if by 'school' we mean anything coherent or reasonably homogeneous. Literary history, since its birth in eighteenth-century England in the works of the Wartons and of Johnson, has never had such a shamefaced air as in the half-century since the First World War. The confident Victorian tradition of literary history, embodied in such a figure as Leslie Stephen and in such an enterprise as his *Dictionary of National Biography* (1885-1909), had already passed its zenith by the time chairs of English were founded in Oxford and Cambridge, around the turn of the century, though in the United States and in Scotland literary history survived longer and, in America at least, provoked a more extreme reaction. Even as historical a critic as George Saintsbury, as I have shown, could not think of any principled defence of an art he practised voluminously for half a century, and vast, composite

[1] Quoted approvingly from Eliot in *Critics and Criticism* (Chicago, 1952), p. 83. Four of Crane's major essays, including 'The Concept of Plot and the Plot of *Tom Jones*' and 'The Critical Monism of Cleanth Brooks' appear in this symposium.

enterprises like the *Cambridge History of English Literature* (1907-1916) or the *Oxford History of English Literature* (1945-) have, on the whole, an exhausted air, while the Pelican *Guide to English Literature* (1954-61), edited by Boris Ford and belonging rather to the anti-historical reaction, can hardly be said to attempt a narrative scheme at all. The old, free narrative tradition of Thomas Warton, Hazlitt, Saintsbury, and Oliver Elton is simply defunct in England, though a few Americans like Hardin Craig, and David Daiches, a Scot, still practise an art which, in its unpretentious way, must always have had a broadly educative function and which once aspired to something more.

And yet, if we peer closer, two strands seem visible in the complex pattern of largely academic historiography as it has been practised on both sides of the Atlantic. The one is largely Christian, the other largely Marxist and ex-Marxist. The Christian tradition is essentially British – Anglican, indeed – and has powerful medieval affinities, emerging from the ruck of late Victorian editing of medieval texts into an astonishingly clear light with such good academic critics as W. P. Ker (1855-1923) in his *Epic and Romance* (1896) and *The Dark Ages* (1904); or his pupil R. W. Chambers (1874-1942), who succeeded him to the Chair at University College, London, in 1922. A devoted Anglican, he sought to establish a sense of continuity between modern England and its medieval, catholic past; and the novelist-critic Charles Williams (1886-1945) and his friends Dorothy Sayers (1893-1957) and C. S. Lewis (b. 1898) have continued in that task. Lewis's *The Allegory of Love* (1936), largely written in his early, agnostic days, and his volume on the sixteenth century published as part of the Oxford History of English Literature in 1954, may stand as models of unexpected vigour in the decaying tradition of literary history, for they successfully unite a polemical energy hardly inferior to Orwell's with an unfashionable respect for such virtues as formal excellence and decorum, and for such defunct forms as the Christian epics of Spenser and Milton. The Ker-Chambers-Lewis tradition in historical criticism, though it never came near to holding the centre of the stage in its own day, and though it attracted little disinterested enthusiasm, still contrived to define itself in a hostile atmosphere and to make itself known.

The Marxist tradition in modern English, on the other hand, has been overwhelmingly American, for the flirtation of the British intelligentsia with Marxism in the era of the Spanish Civil War was too transient, and too stubbornly English and moralistic, to create a genuine Marxist school of letters. The American outcome, though no doubt heretical too by strict political standards, bears the evidence of Marxist influence more deeply etched upon its character. Much of it, paradoxically, is ex-Marxist and even anti-Marxist; but we feel the weight and seriousness of social concern even in the later writing of such critics as Edmund Wilson (b. 1895) and Lionel Trilling (b. 1905), whereas the post-war criticism of British ex-Marxists like W. H. Auden and Stephen Spender bears little or no scar of past political wars.

All Marxist criticism is inevitably historicist, and in a special sense, since it judges all contemporary literature in relation to its political effect, and all past literature in relation to its social setting. It is, like much nineteenth-century criticism, rootedly relativistic. No Marxist critic could write an essay called 'The Intentional Fallacy'; no Marxist critic could reasonably belong to the Aesthetic Movement or to the New Criticism, and none holds views individualistic enough to qualify (in the special sense in which I have been using the term in this chapter) as a Moralist. And yet, of course, all good critics have an intensely individual quality, including Wilson and Trilling, and the description of Marxist only fits them in a loose sense. It was from his Princeton professor Christian Gauss, so Edmund Wilson tells us in the dedication to *Axel's Castle* (1931), that he learned that 'literary criticism ought to be a history of man's ideas and imaginings in the setting of the conditions which have shaped them'. This is a programme any Victorian would have approved, and Wilson's study, in this first book, of Yeats, Valéry, Eliot, Proust, Joyce, and others must have provided thousands with an eminently serviceable introduction to the modern movement, remarkable for its unambitious clarity and for its tolerance (especially in its opening chapter defining Symbolism) of some unexpectedly bourgeois values: 'Each [Symbolist] poet has his unique personality; each of his moments has its special tone. . . . And it is the poet's task to find, to invent, the special language which will alone be capable of expressing his personality˜and feelings.' Wilson's talents as a critic are, in the noblest sense, journalistic, and have been expanded in a mass of reviewing of an unusually weighty and reflective kind: talents for summarizing invitingly and intelligently, and for quick, simple definition of complex historical movements. Exceptionally, he is not an academic, and his style lacks the deadening pressure of qualification which even so committed a critic as Lionel Trilling feels bound, at times, to admit. Trilling's passionate sense of history – a symptom, perhaps, of his political interests in the thirties and forties – raises itself again and again to the level of a moral concern, and his name belongs almost as readily to the category of Moralists as it does here. His first book, aptly, was a study of Matthew Arnold (1939), and is full of an intense concern for questions of society and of class, while his essay of 1942, 'The Sense of the Past', later collected in *The Liberal Imagination* (1950), is the most effective of all historian's answers to the New Critics. As Trilling insists, the New Critics 'forget that the literary work is ineluctably a historical fact, and . . . that its historicity is a fact in our aesthetic experience'. This quality of the 'pastness' of poems, as Trilling calls it, dignifying a term used a generation before by Eliot in 'Tradition and the Individual Talent', is offered now as a prime object of critical study, for 'it is only if we are aware of the reality of the past as past that we can feel it as alive and present'.

Such intelligent compromise offers to reconcile the functions of critic and historian, so oddly divorced in the years between the two world wars. The revival of respect by critics for the historical process, and by literary historians for critical discrimination, is a marked symptom of English criticism both in Britain and in the United States since 1945. And a wise eclecticism is the best thing that could happen to our critical tradition, reminding us that it was only by an historical accident that literary critic and literary historian were ever set at odds with each other. Anyone, indeed, who supposes that there is one critical method which is apt to every critical adventure must be gravely under-estimating the immense variety of the thousands of documents we call English literature. There is no one way, and the search for theological certainties by critics between the wars was bound to end in failure.

And yet their failure has proved more significant than success could ever have been. For poetry, by its uniquely ambiguous status, resists interpretation by any single criterion, and the good critic is one who recognizes that it is only because he knows as much as he does that he is able to discriminate at all.

Chapter 11

THEORY AND PRACTICE SINCE 1960

SINCE 1960, criticism has been more under attack from within than without. The attack from within has been conducted under the name of critical theory.

Critical theory was moved by a variety of impulses. One was the quick fading of intellectual Marxism with the collapse of the New Left after the student riots of Paris in May 1968. Eight years later the death of Mao Tse-Tung, once the living hero of the movement, and his subsequent official disgrace, deprived Marxism of all but its most dogged or abstract enthusiasts. The Communist Party had failed; now, with even greater abruptness, independent Marxism had failed too. 'Marx is dead.' That was the moment for theory; and *La Nouvelle Critique*, the literary successor to intellectual Marxism, was waiting and ready.

Its birthplace was Paris. Manifestos had appeared as early as 1966, the year of Jacques Lacan's collected *Ecrits*, the first volume of Gérard Genette's *Figures*, and *Les mots et les choses* by Michel Foucault. The *Mythologies* of Roland Barthes, academic leader of the school, had appeared nine years earlier, in 1957, and Barthes was to write voluminously down to his sudden, accidental death in 1980. By the early 1970s, French theories had acquired a noisy and subversive minority-influence both in Britain and the United States, their influence fading more slowly in America than in Europe. That was because the vast scale of higher education in the United States had given theory more perches to sit on; and in an increasingly conservative age like the 1970s, it may have been an advantage that in United States formalistic theories like the American New Criticism and its successor, *La Nouvelle Critique*, were often frankly conservative and élitist in inspiration. (The contrasting French assumption that such theories were somehow radical was always a paradox, and at times a self-conscious one.) In England the fashion came and went more rapidly: much English criticism since 1960, like Helen Gardner's *In Defence of the Imagination* (1982), was openly hostile to the Parisian school and its imitators. But it was none the less highly conscious that 1966–style theory had become unignorable as a force, whether for good or ill.

Such theorizing briefly enjoyed a dazzling multiplicity of labels. Structuralism, or the hypothesis that the beliefs and habits of tribes and communities reveal patterns of symmetry like binary opposition, was anthropological in origin and literary only by late analogy. Semiology (or semiotics) means the study of the signs of a community considered as a system of such patterns, and represents one large aspect of structuralism – so much so that they came near to swallowing each other in post-war France. Together, they were held to prove that a work of literature is only part of a wider social pattern; that the intentions of an author were of less moment than the total pattern of which he was a part, and perhaps of no moment at all; and that individual critical judgement, being unverifiably personal, lacked and had always lacked any serious intellectual standing. Hermeneutics shared many of these larger assumptions; though the term originally signified critical interpretation, usually of Scripture, it had come to signify to a secular age the study of multiplicities of interpretation, commonly with the implication that no correct interpretation of a literary work is there to be found.

As these views grew increasingly and competitively subjectivist in the 1960s, structuralism led rapidly into post-structuralism and deconstruction, where literature looked less like an object of study in itself than an occasion to examine the reader-reactions it provoked. Linguistics was held to have proved that language cannot imitate reality. The realistic novel, then – and indeed all the mimetic claims that literature has ever made – were judged to have been crudely erroneous.

For my present purpose these views have more in common

than not, and a history of descriptive criticism like this is more concerned with what they have in common than with what distinguishes them. All denied the possibility of objective judgement in literature; all, in slogans like the Death of the Author, denied any intelligent interest in authorial intention in particular or in historical enquiry in general, unless as an anthropological curiosity. Many denied rationality itself. They were *ludique* – playful.

Modern critical theory of that school, or *La Nouvelle Critique*, was based at once on a paradox and a contradiction. The paradox lay in its very title. Though called *nouvelle*, it was never even in its heyday very new, being born of that Victorian passion for the sociology of thought that flourished between the early writings of Marx in the 1840s, Durkheim's writings towards the end of the century, and Saussure's Geneva lectures on linguistics of 1906–11, first published posthumously in 1916 as *Cours de linguistique générale*. Even its full literary awareness can only with difficulty be stretched beyond the 1930s, when its cult-novelist, James Joyce, ceased to write. Its philosophical assumptions, too, were strikingly Victorian, and it took no observable account of Wittgenstein or Karl Popper. It none the less dubbed its opponents in historical and descriptive criticism 'traditionalist', unaware that literary history as we know it today is a great deal newer than critical theory in general, which is at least as old as Aristotle, and largely newer than Marx or Durkheim. But then an *avant-garde* of the 1960s that had accepted Marxism as the latest political idea was unlikely to be troubled by the antiquity of its assumptions. It was content to hail such theories as *La Nouvelle Critique*.

That was its paradox. Its contradiction involved two of its principal doctrines, which were in evident conflict. First, it held that descriptive criticism had slight claims to 'scienticity', or reliable procedures and conclusions, since it had not yet learned to advance by means of agreed verbal definitions or stated criteria; never doubting that to know what something is on the one hand, and to be able to offer a sufficient and agreed account on the other, are always and necessarily the same. And second, it insisted that since Saussure had demonstrated language to be based on arbitrary signs, no language can be said to imitate the real. But if language is incapable of doing that, then it is hard to see why criticism should be asked to provide definitions or stated criteria – such definitions being necessarily expressed in language. The dilemma was absolute, the *impasse* unpassable. On that view, a critical account must fail at the outset in the very task that the theorist had insisted it must perform in order to count at all.

The contradiction was always based, in any case, on a weak sense of linguistic history. The view that most words are arbitrary signs was not new: it had been voiced by Aristotle, Aquinas, Rabelais, Locke and Johnson.[1] It was equally based on an ignorance of Saussure, whose *Cours* had openly acknowledged that the arbitrariness of the sign had long been an uncontested principle in the very nineteenth-century tradition of linguistics that had trained him. And, above all, the view was inconsistent with its own practice. The great theorists of the 1970s, like Barthes and Derrida, were famous for lecturing at length on why nothing can certainly be known or said in the disabling instrument or prison-house of language. But such scepticism cannot survive its own example. It is a contradiction to say that nothing can be said, and a multiple contradiction to say it at length.

It was, however, one that was eagerly shared by English and American disciples. In 1982, for example, *Modern Literary Theory*, a collection of essays edited by Ann Jefferson and David Robey of Oxford appeared in London. In its introduction, the editors attacked academic criticism of a 'traditional-ist' sort, or the critical analysis of texts, for being based on nothing more persuasive than a consensus, since it lacked 'a truly adequate definition of its subject-matter'; adding crushingly that 'almost every other academic discipline can say in exact terms what its subject-matter is' (p. 4). The editors did not say what those disciplines are, however, or quote

[1] See Hans Aarsleff, *From Locke to Saussure* (London, 1982), especially pp. 63ff.

instances of such agreed definitions. In the second chapter, David Robey attributed to Saussure the discovery of the arbitrary sign, unaware that it was a commonplace by his time; and argued that it had led to an understanding of that 'essential disjunction between language and reality that became the foundation of the structuralist movement', where all meanings consist of 'closed systems wholly independent of the material world' (p. 43). In that case, one is left wondering why literary studies should be urged to seek exact terms, or indeed terms of any kind. If language in its nature cannot accurately describe anything at all, then it is not much of a charge against academic critics to say that they are failing to describe either literature or literary criticism.

English criticism reacted in a variety of ways to the literary structuralism and post-structuralism of the 1960s. On the one hand, there were those who believed that since *La Nouvelle Critique* was called new, there must be something new about it, and who laboured to discover what it was. In *The Modes of Modern Writing* (1977), David Lodge hailed Saussure's arbitrary sign as 'an idea of the greatest importance' (p. 61), unaware that Saussure had accurately called it a commonplace, and insisted that it had devastating implications for literature, and above all for the realistic novel: 'It will be obvious how this view of language militates against any mimetic theory of literature' (p. 63) – adding, perhaps with a touch of glee, that the whole notion was bound to be 'disconcerting' to Anglo-American critics, cast here in their traditional role of men cosily convinced of an inherited faith in mimesis and realism, and hopelessly conservative in consequence.

Such arguments were better calculated to inflame than to persuade, and the strident theoretical debate that filled the 1970s could be as lively and as personal as the mid-Victorian quarrel over God. The French, who had first offered the world this confection of ideas, had by 1980 largely lost interest in the matter, so that by the late 1970s the debate had moved to their admirers in Cambridge, Yale and beyond. But theory, even there, never took total possession of the field. The opaque, mandarin style of the French sages had not recommended them universally in the more sceptical atmosphere of British and American universities, for one thing; and for another, their casual and inaccurate attitude to cultural history told against them.

The first step was to expose the misunderstanding of Saussure: an exposure that was to lead to a new and more accurate English version of the *Cours* by Roy Harris (1983), executed to satisfy a cultural curiosity about pre-1914 linguistics highly surprising to professional linguists themselves. The arbitrary sign was shown to be no objection to literary realism in particular, or to the mimetic value of language in general; *dog* being no less an accurate description of a well-known species because, like *chien* in French or *Hund* in German, it could as well have been something else. Signs can be at once arbitrary and accurate, as every motorist needs to know when he reads a road-sign. He would not survive if he did not. There is no evidence, in any case, that the great realistic novelists of the nineteenth century denied the arbitrary principle or even doubted it; so that the sense in which it militates against mimesis, whatever it is, cannot be exactly obvious. The realist George Eliot, as long ago as 1856, publicly attacked the notion that to know a word is to understand what it stands for, or even to be certain that it stands for anything at all.[1]

The structuralist fashion, in any case, was built on an historical misunderstanding. David Lodge puzzled in *The Modes of Modern Writing* over the thought that Continental structuralism 'took so long to make itself felt in the Atlantic cultural hemisphere' (p. 58), unaware that one pioneer of modern semiology was C. S. Peirce, an American who died before the First World War. The doctrine was Atlantic, then, before it was French at all: a fact cleverly concealed by the *nouveaux critiques* of the 1960s, perhaps on the celebrated principle that originality is the suppression of sources. Saussure, too, who died at much the same time as Peirce, was

---

[1] 'The natural history of German life: Riehl', *Westminster Review* (1856); reprinted in *Essays and Leaves from a Note-book by George Eliot* (Edinburgh, 1884), pp. 229f.

not a Frenchman, though he wrote in French. Lodge was surprised that the doctrine had no impact in Anglo-America till the 1960s. But it had. The American linguist Leonard Bloomfield reviewed it coolly in the *Modern Language Journal* of 1923, welcoming its 'clear and rigorous demonstration of fundamental principles', and adding that most of it had long been 'in the air'; he also deplored Saussure's ignorance of psychology and phonetics, and regretted his emphasis on single words rather than entire sentences. In the same year, C. K. Ogden and I. A. Richards dismissed the *Cours* in *The Meaning of Meaning* (1923) as 'neglecting entirely the things for which signs stand' (p. 8). Whatever that remark suggests about an understanding of Saussure, it does not suggest simple neglect; and a decade later Richards was to praise Coleridge, in his *Coleridge on Imagination* (1934), as an early pioneer of semasiology or the theory of signs.

The Anglo-Saxons found Saussure over-familiar, in fact. As early as 1951, J. R. Firth, by then the doyen of British linguists, was calling his concept of the sign 'over-valued', preferring a remark by the great Victorian philologist Henry Sweet, who in 1877 had urged more attention to 'the phenomena of living languages' and less to their history. Synchrony, or the study of a language at a given stage of its development, was, after all, Victorian. 'Language is essentially based on the dualism of form and meaning,' as Sweet had put it, restating the arbitrary sign in other terms.[1] By the 1960s, when the chief writings of the French new critics were becoming available, Saussure's views already looked both stale and vulnerable to students of language in Britain and America, who by then had moved to Chomsky and beyond.

Critics in the English-speaking world did not reject the French New Criticism, when they did, because it was new and radical, but because they saw it was neither. It was old and conservative. Any claim that language cannot describe the real is likely to favour a conservative interest, if only because

---

[1] J. R. Firth, 'General linguistics and descriptive grammar' (1951), in his *Papers in Linguistics 1934–51* (Oxford, 1957), p. 217n.; Henry Sweet, 'On English philology and phonology' (1877), in his *Collected Papers* (London, 1913), p. 85.

proposals for change are necessarily couched in language; an anti-mimetic theory of language, then, favours the cause of doing nothing. Saussure's distinction between *langue* and *parole* – or the totality of a given language, on the one hand, and an individual use of it on the other – would not have surprised or instructed any Victorian grammarian, since grammar is commonly a study of *langue* exemplified by *paroles*; and the arbitrary sign, similarly, had long been a commonplace among instructed readers of English, who could have read of it in Locke's *Essay* (1690) or the preface to Johnson's *Dictionary* (1755), as well as in Henry Sweet or J. R. Firth. Johnson's formulation is perhaps the most memorable of all: 'Words are the daughters of the earth, and things are the sons of heaven.'

The Anglo-American tradition of criticism since the 1960s, for all that, still labours under the occasional charge of having been obstinately inhospitable to the French New Criticism; and it is sometimes challengingly asked what influence those critical theories have had on critical practice in England and America. But that is a classic instance of asking the wrong question. It is hardly possible to be merely 'influenced' by *La Nouvelle Critique*. If, as Lacan, Barthes and Derrida insisted, language were indeed incapable of representing the real, then it is hard to see how descriptive criticism could exist at all. *La Nouvelle Critique* was the literary equivalent of National Socialism. You could accept and submit, or arm and oppose. There was never a middle ground. Johnson could not have written the 'Life of Pope' at all if he had believed in the doctrine of *différence* – the indefinite postponement of meaning – or Coleridge his account of Wordsworth, or Arnold his *Essays in Criticism*. All that, admittedly, is to make the large assumption that such doctrines are sincerely held and consistently applied; and in that sense it is a serious question whether the *nouveaux critiques* themselves ever believed in their own doctrines. They wrote and lectured, after all, using language much as anyone else.

By the 1980s, at all events, after an acrimonious interlude, criticism in English had repelled a challenge which, if successful, would have defeated any intelligent project of describing any work of literature whatever, since it denied the power of language to describe anything at all. A point had been gained, a liberty won.

The sudden rise and fall of critical theory between 1960 and 1980 had its deeper causes.

One was a widespread loss of faith in the Arnoldian tradition of literature as a moral teacher. Lionel Trilling, Matthew Arnold's American biographer, died in New York in 1975 – his last and finest book, *Sincerity and Authenticity* (1972), offering a revived interest in the moral effects of a literary education that some of his earlier writings had brought into doubt. The vigour of that tradition in the hands of a great New York critic, for whom Hegel and Freud counted for as much as Arnold, demonstrates that the cause of moral analysis was never insular, and that it is in no way open to the charge of cultural parochialism. That charge, however, was common by the 1970s. The death in 1978 of two latter-day Arnoldians, F. R. Leavis of Cambridge and F. W. Bateson of Oxford, had followed a long period of waning influence for literary humanism. Leavis's *Scrutiny* ended as early as 1953, and his writings after that date tend to be damagingly repetitious; and though Bateson's *Essays in Criticism* still continues as an Oxford quarterly under its deliberately Arnoldian title, it has long since ceased to make any exclusive claim to a moral tradition.

It is not easy to identify the causes of that loss of faith in the moral effects of literature, marking as it does the slow decay of a long, fertile and highly English tradition. A cynical answer, often heard and perhaps at least partly true, would be that Arnoldians had not behaved well enough in themselves to justify the claims they had once made for literary education as a moral instructor. Another cause was the sudden confusion made by theoretical demands for verbal definitions: demands which, however unreasonable, took their usual and easy effect of confounding debate and creating intellectual despondency.

A third and more tangible cause lay in the sudden end in the

1970s of an educational boom that had lasted continuously in Britain and the United States since 1945. Anglo-American criticism after 1945 had been to a unique degree academic. It was the first critical school in history to be dominated by academe: the first where most critics had felt themselves shaped by an experience of university life, and the first where many of them were themselves university teachers. After so long a boom, the bust was felt to be awful. A career in teaching ceased to look available; the professional student of literature on both sides of the Atlantic was suddenly made to feel useless. He could react, at times, in sullen defiance, calling necessity a virtue and insisting vengefully on a lack of significance in all human discourse. That was the theoretical moment of the 1970s. Even at the height of that enthusiasm, after all, nobody ever claimed theory to be useful. You could teach it, no doubt; you could not teach by it. In undergraduate classes from Cambridge to California it had to be ignored – to be all the more earnestly discussed in graduate seminars and international conferences where academic speaks to academic. In its very nature it could not be applied, only expounded. Dedicated post-Saussurian partisans of non-mimetic theories of language continued to mark scripts in much the usual way, never doubting that a student's essay still needed to be accurate of fact and correctly phrased and spelt. Theory was a gesture rather than a conviction, and nobody ever dreamed of going to the stake for it.

But to boast a remoteness from everyday concerns, as theory helped one to do, could be a convenient escape-hatch from the wreck of political conviction in the years after 1968. It could be consoling to make a point of being pointless. The point of such critical theory, after all, is that there is no point. We only imagine we know anything; great novels and poems do not instruct us about timeless moral truths, as the Arnoldians had once supposed, or about the life of dead ages; and our confident estimates of poets and dramatists are founded on considerations merely habitual or personal, so the theorists claimed, which we can neither justify nor even define.

It was a dilemma to know whether one should confront

such a dogma or ignore it. The one certain truth was that theory in that familiar style must, in the long run, prove fatal to literary education and to the public subventions by which it survived. If objectivity is unobtainable, then there is no evident reason why exchequers should subsidize anyone to attain it. In its essential obscurity, in any case, veiling lofty abstractions under foamy layers of polysyllables, such a view was self-consciously inaccessible to the ordinary reader and to the young. Theory was always proudly *élitist*; it seldom offered its wares to schoolchildren or to freshmen. It was a game for grown-ups, and a minority of grown-ups at that. To succeed, for such a doctrine, would have been to fail, since coteries rejoice in their privileged isolation. A dandy wishes to influence taste; but he would be deeply alarmed if everyone dressed exactly like himself.

The critics reacted in more ways than one. The most rewarding reaction, perhaps, was to invest literary journalism with a new and untraditional significance. If academic criticism was determined to look remote and trivial, ordinary readers still asked advice on what to buy or borrow. They wanted – even needed – reviews. In 1963, the *New York Review of Books* was founded as the outcome of a printing strike, to be followed in 1979 for similar reasons by the *London Review of Books*; it quickly became the energizing fortnightly competitor to the weekly *Times Literary Supplement*, which had been founded as long ago as 1902. By 1980, English was enjoying a golden age of literary journalism, rather like the years that followed the founding of the *Edinburgh Review* in 1802. The long, even very long article returned unexpectedly into currency. Theories could be briskly discussed there; so could the novels, largely realistic or mimetic, that continued to pour unashamedly from publishers on both sides of the Atlantic, much as if deconstructionists had never spoken; so could the largely realistic or mimetic plays that continued to be written unabashed for the theatres of London and New York. It was refreshing to see how little theory could invade or damage the life of literature.

No one in that lively age who engaged in journalism could afford to see his activity as a relaxation from the more demanding requirements of academic criticism. Rather the reverse. No requirements could be more demanding than those laid upon the literary journalist in the tug-of-wars fought out daily and weekly – sometimes fortnightly or monthly – in the great literary journals of London and New York. That art is as difficult as any literary art that there is. Academics and professional journalists compete here on even terms – a peculiarly Anglo-Saxon formula, this, for critical debate – and in a forum that had never existed on such a scale before. By the 1970s, criticism had ceased to be mainly a matter of treatises, and the historian of the future will have to take as much notice of the journals as of the book-shelves. It will be an untidy and enlivening history he will have to tell.

The critical book, which flourished almost to excess in the publishing boom of the 1960s, has found it more difficult since the 1970s to survive on either side of the Atlantic. Not all the pressures are economic: some are severely intellectual. How long does a critique have to be, before padding begins? It is arguable that the natural unit of descriptive criticism ever since Dryden has been the essay or article, a book hundreds of pages long being an unnatural phenomenon at best. Johnson and Arnold worked largely through forms as brief as essays or prefatorial lives; and a good deal of inter-war criticism, in the days when modern literature was being pioneered as an academic subject, was first executed as lectures, articles or essays, to be collected only later into volumes. That sensible tradition lasted into the 1950s and beyond, as with William Empson's *Structure of Complex Words* (1951), Mark Schorer's *The World We Imagine* (1969), and Graham Hough's *Selected Essays* (1978). Such books were composed piecemeal; they were not written seriatim, and do not ask to be read in that way. Critical books often dispense with the mandatory beginning and the mandatory end.

And yet, critical books composed as books still happen, and need to happen. Empson's *Milton's God* (1961) had to be as long as it is; and a much briefer book by his admirer

Christopher Ricks, *Milton's Grand Style* (1963), short as it is, could not easily be shorter. The descriptive book ceases to be routine before the 1970s; but by the same token it becomes something of a triumph. Walter Jackson Bate of Harvard has enlarged the tradition of the Johnsonian literary life with *John Keats* (1963), *Coleridge* (1968) and *Samuel Johnson* (1977), where the very titles read like a roll-call of humanism; and his study of Keats suggests in its preface that the interest of that life was 'deeply human and moral', exemplifying 'the steady growth of qualities of both mind and character that are equally appropriate to other forms of achievement'. That was a bold claim to make for literary humanism, at its date, and the ensuing years were to make it look bolder still. All three lives excel at perceiving how richly and intimately life and creation meet, extending even to a patient and unfashionable attention to formal properties of metre and syntax. In an age where criticism sometimes looks like heartless dissection, these are learned celebrations by an academic American and in a humane tradition of three great Englishmen.

The largest new conquest of territory by criticism since 1960 was its revived interest in narrative, which was itself triggered by the renaissance of English fiction and theatre in the mid–1950s. Since much of the debate was made by novelists, many of whom were themselves academic teachers, it is perhaps pointless to speculate whether the novels provoked the criticism or vice versa.

The new debate began with a flurry of articles by Iris Murdoch, some of them emerging out of her lectures as an Oxford philosopher in the 1950s on 'The Ethics of Liberalism'. Her prolific career as a novelist began at much the same time, with *Under the Net* (1954); and her critical views were promptly extended by her husband John Bayley in *The Characters of Love* (1960), a book subtitled 'A Study in the Literature of Personality'. The fictional argument had begun in philosophy, then, and primarily in a sense of dissatisfaction with two traditions of moral philosophy then fashionable, French existentialism and British empiricism: neither of them, as Iris Murdoch argued in a notable article, offering any sufficient concerns with life outside the self.[1] That 'dryness', as she called it, was literary as well as philosophical, arising out of an exaggerated modern reaction against the liberal tradition of fiction exemplified by Dickens, George Eliot and Tolstoy, who had memorably achieved a 'plurality of real persons' based on a profound tolerance of other minds. The article amounts to a full-blooded confrontation with the 'dry' modernism of T. S. Eliot and his school, and it included a whimsical attack upon Eliot himself, who was still living: 'I am unable to be confident from Mr Eliot's writings that he has ever enjoyed and admired any novel.' The revived social realism of the new British fiction of the 1950s was based, then, on a deliberate and even defiant rejection of a dominant literary vogue. Realism was the creation of literary and political radicals, even iconoclasts, and no mere habitual activity. That has not prevented it from being mistaken for traditionalism by those who confuse a deference to French formalism with independence of mind.

The Anglo-American tradition, in any case, already had its native theorists of narrative, such as the Chicago critic Wayne C. Booth in his *Rhetoric of Fiction* (1961). Four years earlier, Ian Watt, a British critic living in California, had produced a study of Defoe, Richardson and Fielding entitled *The Rise of the Novel* which, like many Marxist and post-Marxist interpretations of fiction, had the merit of perceiving that one can only offer to change society if confident of being able to describe it. That is why radical scepticism always strikes harder at the Left than at the Right, even when it is proposed by the Left.

By the early 1960s, fictional criticism in the English-speaking world was launched on a double track, and one where formal and realistic interests were to run parallel courses. That double view was conveniently summarized in the first volume of an American learned journal, *Novel*, in 1967, where Booth, Watt and others were usefully invited to

[1] Iris Murdoch, 'The sublime and the beautiful revisited', *Yale Review*, 49 (1960). See also her 'Against dryness', *Encounter* (January 1961), reprinted in *The Novel Today*, edited by Malcolm Bradbury (London, 1977).

justify or reconsider what they had recently written. A distaste for anything that smacks of an exclusive over-emphasis guides that debate. 'Art has got to have form, whereas life need not,' as Iris Murdoch had remarked at the end of her 1960 essay – warning against the rigidities and self-sufficiencies of form in some modern fiction, with its loss of respect for the sheer contingency and happenstance of individual life: 'A novel must be a house fit for free characters to live in; and to combine form with a respect for reality with all its odd contingent ways is the highest art of prose.'

That eloquent close exemplified a mood in which the argument over fiction was enjoyed by a generation. A tradition of realism can respect the demands of form, as Henry James had once done, without allowing form to take control; and that mood has helped to create plays and novels which, in original and in translation, have become world-wide the most favoured mode of social realism that there is. Those who complain that the English obsession with realism has locked their traditions away, and damagingly, from advanced modern thought have the whole modern world to argue with. The world wants English realism, in novels, plays and films. Literary realism is in any case not a phenomenon that is chemically pure: it admits of mixture, even welcomes it. The critical debate among novelists and academics about narrative since 1960 has demonstrated how to take an intelligent interest in literary form without submitting to an exclusive formalism, still less to a heartless scepticism that leaves no place for moral concern.

The rejection of formalism had some larger consequences. Realism in fiction is the natural successor to Renaissance humanism by way of Enlightenment, and of still earlier doctrines about literature as an imitative act. Extreme versions of formalism, like *La Nouvelle Critique*, rejected far more than a tradition of fiction that began with Defoe or Sir Walter Scott. Iris Murdoch's invocation of Shakespeare as the first great master of free character in fiction is illuminating here. Without Shakespeare, no realistic novel: it is probably no accident that the nation that produced the greatest of all humanistic playwrights has, since the eighteenth century, led the way in social fiction. To deny the descriptive powers of modern fiction, then, is to lose contact with something more than realism: it is to sever a tradition that leads back to Shakespeare and beyond.

That loss of contact, or threatened loss, was to lead by a natural reaction to a demand for a new and revived humanism.

Humanism here means that doctrine of literature classically expounded in Aristotle's *Poetics* and in Sidney's *Apology for Poetry*. It sees fiction as an imitation, or mimesis, of the real. It can be boldly confident about its capacity to account for mimesis, like Aristotle and his Renaissance followers; or, like more modern critics, it can be content to appeal to ordinary experience, denying any obligation to offer a theoretical account of what literary description so often and so manifestly does.

That last view is not as unphilosophical as amateur philosophers sometimes suppose. It is not obvious that being able to do something – whether describing art or life, on the one hand, or performing some everyday skill like riding a bike on the other – is the same as being able to give a sufficient account of what one is doing. A high-wire acrobat serves as an extreme illustration of that difference: if he began to wonder what kept him balanced high above the crowd, he would be all the more likely to fall off. That style of defence for modern descriptive criticism has sometimes been seen as obscurantist. But then we have never been told why a *theory* of criticism, parasitic as (in its very nature) it is upon such individual critical acts as reading novels or seeing plays, should be seen as in any way fundamental to what the critic does. The search for a theoretical 'basis' was always a search for the Philosopher's Stone. It is experience itself that validates the humanistic truth that literature is about life: the countless occasions when we imitate literature in our lives, or imitate life when we write.

The new humanism has left its chief mark, and fittingly, on

the criticism of Shakespeare himself. Strictly speaking, that tradition had never been snapped. F. P. Wilson's papers were collected six years after his death as *Shakespearian and Other Studies* (1969): much of it composed in the 1940s and even earlier, and perhaps the finest book to appear on the English Renaissance since the Second World War, and by a scholar who had published only sparingly in his lifetime. Revised and expanded from his earlier writings, such essays as 'Shakespeare and the Diction of Common Life' were perfected before and after first publication through a gradual process of accumulated scholarship, in the cause (as Wilson put it) of making modern men 'good Elizabethans, if possible intelligent Elizabethans' (p. 100). In a similar tradition, J. I. M. Stewart, himself a realistic novelist under the pseudonym of Michael Innes, demolished in his *Character and Motive in Shakespeare* (1949) the dry formalistic view that Renaissance dramatic character was a mere effect of convention, 'arbitrary devices for starting a yarn'. In fact, as Stewart convincingly argued, such conventions as 'the Calumniator Believed' bear witness rather to 'some central human predisposition' by which works like *Much Ado* and *Othello* are prompted and sustained:

A convention, like a superstition, may represent a significant perception gone fossilized or inert. And to reanimate a convention, to strip it of sophistication so that its essence is again near the surface and working, is perhaps part of the instinct of the original artist (pp. 100–1).

Sixteenth-century humanism soon found a still more comprehensive defender. In *Scenic Form in Shakespeare* (1971) and *The Origins of Shakespeare* (1977), Emrys Jones defended the intellectual tradition of Erasmus against the strictures of his late teacher, C. S. Lewis; proposing rather a Shakespeare who was a master of classic form, a Tudor genius whose mind and learning are still massively underestimated. Jones quotes a remark by a Shakespearian older than himself, Frank Kermode, that Shakespeare was 'a person of enormously superior intelligence', and mockingly adds that there must be something the matter with a critical tradition that encourages anyone to find that remark other than commonplace.[1]

Humanism has had its calumniators ever since the sixteenth century. They have not always been believed. They hardly deserve to be believed; nor do their claims to radicalism need to be taken seriously. C. S. Lewis, a complete conservative, was an anti-humanist long before that cause in the 1960s was given its implausible air of radical chic. It has been the resounding achievement of English critics since the mid-century to have perceived the radicalism of social realism in our fiction and in our theatre, and to have reasserted a truth about literature that Erasmus and Shakespeare would have understood.

[1] Frank Kermode, 'Shakespeare's learning', in his *Shakespeare, Spenser, Donne* (London, 1971), p. 183; Emrys Jones, *The Origins of Shakespeare* (Oxford, 1977), pp. 3f.

SELECT BIBLIOGRAPHY
OF MODERN EDITIONS AND STUDIES

The place of publication is noted, unless it is London,
following the short title

1. FIRST PRINCIPLES

HISTORIES

FOUR comprehensive histories of (or including) English criticism have
already appeared, though one was never completed. George Saintsbury's *A History of English Criticism* (Edinburgh, 1911), extracted from
his earlier *History of Criticism and Literary Taste in Europe*, 3 vols. (Edinburgh, 1900-4), is a genial Victorian survey that takes us as far as Arnold
and Pater. The second, J. W. H. Atkins's unfinished *English Literary
Criticism*, 3 vols. (Cambridge, later London, 1943-51), is a more detailed and less readable history based upon principles similar to Saintsbury's, and completed to about 1800. The third book, René Wellek's
History of Modern Criticism, 4 vols. (New Haven, 1955-), is an encyclopedic account by a Czech-American scholar of all Western literary
criticism, including Russian and American, since about 1750, and the
fourth, *Literary Criticism: a Short History* (New York, 1957), is a 755-
page 'argumentative history' by two American New Critics, W. K.
Wimsatt Jr and Cleanth Brooks, both of classical criticism and of
English criticism since the sixteenth century. A fifth book of considerable but patchy distinction, T. S. Eliot's Harvard lectures of 1932-3,
The Use of Poetry and the Use of Criticism (1933), mainly on 'the criticism
provided by the poets themselves' (p. 32), may also be cited here, as
well as David Daiches's *Critical Approaches to Literature* (1956), which
describes itself as being concerned, not with 'the history of criticism as
such', but with 'methodology', or 'the varying ways' in which literature
can be discussed.

ANTHOLOGIES

Among the most useful anthologies of criticism are *Loci Critici*, edited
by George Saintsbury (Boston, 1903); *English Critical Essays (Sixteenth,
Seventeenth, and Eighteenth Centuries)*, edited by Edmund D. Jones
(Oxford, 1922) (World's Classics); *The Great Critics*, edited by J. H. Smith

and E. W. Parks (New York, 1932, enlarged 1939); *A Calendar of British Taste from 1600 to 1800*, edited by E. F. Carritt (1949); *Criticism: the Major Texts*, edited by W. J. Bate (New York, 1952); and the twin volumes *Literary Criticism: Plato to Dryden*, edited by Allan H. Gilbert (New York, 1940), and *Pope to Croce*, edited by G. W. Allen and H. H. Clark (New York, 1941). Hugh Sykes Davies's Pelican *The Poets and their Critics* (1943), enlarged as 2 vols. (1960-2) marshals critiques of the major English poets, and R. W. Stallman's *The Critic's Notebook* (Minneapolis, 1950) provides extracts from theoretical and controversial criticism, mainly of the twentieth century, under abstract headings.

STUDIES

On the 'access of doubt' in English criticism in the 1950s, T. S. Eliot's *On Poetry and Poets* (1957), including the 1956 lecture 'The Frontiers of Criticism', is primary evidence, as well as Helen Gardner's *The Business of Criticism* (Oxford, 1959), which includes the earlier *Limits of Literary Criticism* (Oxford, 1956), and John Holloway's collection *The Charted Mirror* (1960), which includes the 1956 broadcast 'The New "Establishment" in Criticism'.

THE THREE KINDS OF CRITICISM

LEGISLATIVE CRITICISM

Most Elizabethan criticism was collected by G. Gregory Smith in his edition *Elizabethan Critical Essays*, 2 vols. (Oxford, 1904), to which must now be added new editions of Puttenham's *The Arte of English Poesie*, edited by Gladys D. Willcock and Alice Walker (Cambridge, 1936); Abraham Fraunce's *The Arcadian Rhetorike* of 1588, edited by Ethel Seaton (Oxford, 1950); and Richard Wills's *De re poetica* of 1573, edited by A. D. S. Fowler (Oxford, 1958), the last two for the Luttrell Society. There is a *History of Literary Criticism in the Renaissance* (New York, 1899), by J. E. Spingarn.

THEORETICAL CRITICISM

Much of seventeenth-century criticism was collected by J. E. Spingarn in his edition *Seventeenth-Century Critical Essays*, 3 vols. (Oxford, 1908-9), and further extracts, mainly theoretical, will be found in *Critical Essays of the Eighteenth Century, 1700-25*, edited by W. H. Durham (New Haven, 1915) and *Eighteenth-Century Critical Essays*, edited by Scott Elledge, 2 vols. (Ithaca, N.Y., 1961). There is no comprehensive history of English literary aesthetics; cf. E. F. Carritt's

Philosophies of Beauty from Socrates to Robert Bridges (Oxford, 1931), Samuel H. Monk, *The Sublime: a Study of Critical Theories in Eighteenth-Century England* (New York, 1935), and, for a study of Locke's influence, Ernest L. Tuveson, *The Imagination as a Means of Grace* (Berkeley, Cal., 1960). For a list of writings of the great age of English aesthetics, see J. W. Draper, *Eighteenth-Century Aesthetics: a Bibliography* (Heidelberg, 1931).

DESCRIPTIVE CRITICISM

René Wellek's *The Rise of English Literary History* (Chapel Hill, N.C., 1941), traces the art of historical description from the Middle Ages to Thomas Warton. For the groundwork of the literary antiquaries, see David C. Douglas, *English Scholars, 1660-1730* (1939, revised 1951); and for an account of the Battle of the Books, R. F. Jones, *Ancients and Moderns* (St Louis, 1936). Augustus Ralli, in his *History of Shakespearean Criticism*, 2 vols. (Oxford, 1932), has traced one aspect of the story.

For editions and studies of individual descriptive critics since Dryden, see below.

2. JOHN DRYDEN

Dryden's prose was first collected by Edmond Malone as *Prose Works*, 4 vols. (1800), and much of the criticism was re-edited by W. P. Ker as *Essays*, 2 vols. (Oxford, 1900). The first complete edition of the criticism is by George Watson, *Of Dramatic Poesy and Other Critical Essays*, 2 vols. (1962, Everyman's Library). For a compilation of quotations, see *The Critical Opinions of Dryden: a Dictionary*, edited by John M. Aden (Nashville, 1963). The complete works were edited by Sir Walter Scott in 18 vols. (1808) and revised by George Saintsbury (1882-93); there is a Californian edition in progress, edited by E. N. Hooker and H. T. Swedenberg (Berkeley, Cal., 1956-).

The best general studies of Dryden are Johnson's Life in his *Lives of the English Poets* (1779-81), George Saintsbury's *Dryden* (1881), and D. Nichol Smith's Clark lectures, *Dryden* (Cambridge, 1950). For biography, Malone's life in his edition of Dryden's prose, above, has been supplemented by J. M. Osborn's *Dryden: some Biographical Facts and Problems* (New York, 1940) and Charles E. Ward, *The Life of Dryden* (Chapel Hill, N.C., 1961). Studies of Dryden as a critic include W. P. Ker's introduction to his edition of the *Essays*, above; Louis I. Bredvold's *The Intellectual Milieu of Dryden* (Ann Arbor, 1934); Frank L. Huntley's *The Unity of Dryden's Dramatic Criticism* (Chicago, 1944) and *On Dryden's Essay of Dramatic Poesy* (Ann Arbor, 1951); and H. T.

Swedenberg's *The Theory of the Epic in England, 1650-1800* (Berkeley, Cal., 1944).

RYMER AND DENNIS

Rymer's *Critical Works* have been edited by Curt A. Zimansky (New Haven, 1956), and Dennis's by E. N. Hooker, 2 vols. (Baltimore, 1939-43).

3. THE AUGUSTANS

For a brief general study, see R. S. Crane, 'English Neoclassical Criticism: an Outline Sketch' in *Critics and Criticism Ancient and Modern*, edited by Crane (Chicago, 1952).

POPE

The volume in the Twickenham edition of the poems of Pope (General Editor, John Butt) containing the *Essay on Criticism* has been among the last to appear (1961); but meanwhile George Sherburn's edition of the *Correspondence*, 5 vols. (Oxford, 1956), has brought new material to light concerning Pope's literary relationships. The best general account of Pope is in Johnson's *Lives* (1779-81); Edith Sitwell's *Alexander Pope* (1930), George Sherburn's *The Early Career of Pope* (Oxford, 1934), and R. K. Root's *The Poetical Career of Pope* (Princeton, 1938) should also be consulted, as well as William Empson's essay ' "Wit" in the *Essay on Criticism*' in his *The Structure of Complex Words* (1951).

ADDISON

The Milton papers of 1712 were revised and collected in the year of Addison's death as *Notes upon the Twelve Books of Paradise Lost* (1719), and have since been edited by Edward Arber (1868) and by Albert S. Cook (Boston, 1892). The whole of the *Spectator* has been edited by G. Gregory Smith, 8 vols. (1897-8), reprinted in 4 vols. in Everyman's Library (1907, 1958). Addison's *Letters* were edited by Walter Graham (Oxford, 1941). There are studies of Addison in Johnson's *Lives* (1779-1781) and in Macaulay's *Essays* (1843); the standard life is now Peter Smithers's *The Life of Addison* (Oxford, 1954). The best critical essays are by C. S. Lewis in *Essays on the Eighteenth Century Presented to David Nichol Smith* (Oxford, 1945), and C. D. Thorpe's 'Addison's Contribution to Criticism' in *The Seventeenth Century: Studies by R. F. Jones and others* (Palo Alto, 1951).

FIELDING

The standard lives of Fielding are by Wilbur L. Cross, *The History of Henry Fielding*, 3 vols. (New Haven, 1918), and by F. Homes Dudden, *Fielding: his Life, Works, and Times*, 2 vols. (Oxford, 1952); and there is an independent study of the criticism by F. O. Bissell, *Fielding's Theory of the Novel* (Ithaca, 1933). See also W. L. Renwick, 'Comic Epic in Prose', in *Essays and Studies*, XXXII (1946); Ronald S. Crane, 'The Concept of Plot and the Plot of *Tom Jones*', in *Critics and Criticism*, edited by Crane (Chicago, 1952); and the section on Fielding in Ian Watt's *The Rise of the Novel* (1957), especially pp. 241ff.

4. SAMUEL JOHNSON

The complete works of Johnson are being edited by Allen T. Hazen and others (New Haven, 1958-), and there are one-volume selections by Mona Wilson (1950, in the Reynard Library) and by R. W. Chapman (Oxford, 1955). The 1765 preface to Shakespeare, together with the *Proposals* of 1756 and a selection of the Shakespearean notes, were collected by Walter Raleigh as *Johnson on Shakespeare* (Oxford, 1908, revised 1925). The best edition of the *Lives of the English Poets* is still G. Birkbeck Hill's, 3 vols. (Oxford, 1905). The *Letters* were magnificently edited by R. W. Chapman, 3 vols. (Oxford, 1952).

Apart from the early lives of Johnson by Mrs Thrale (1786), John Hawkins (1787), and James Boswell (1791) – the last of which should be consulted in the edition of G. Birkbeck Hill revised by L. F. Powell, 6 vols. (Oxford, 1934-50) – there are modern studies by Joseph W. Krutch (New York, 1944) and Walter J. Bate (New York, 1955). W. K. Wimsatt has written two studies of Johnson's language, *The Prose Style of Johnson* (New Haven, 1941) and *Philosophic Words* (New Haven, 1948), as well as a lecture on the *Dictionary* collected in *New Light on Dr Johnson*, edited by F. W. Hilles (New Haven, 1959), which also contains an article by Hilles on the Life of Pope. There are critical essays by F. R. Leavis (*Scrutiny*, 1944), reprinted in *The Importance of Scrutiny*, edited by Eric Bentley (New York, 1948), and by T. S. Eliot in his *On Poetry and Poets* (1957); and specialist studies include Jean H. Hagstrum's *Johnson's Literary Criticism* (Minneapolis, 1952), G. J. Kolb's *Dr Johnson's Dictionary* (Chicago, 1952), and Arthur Sherbo's *Johnson, Editor of Shakespeare* (Urbana, Ill., 1956).

For the rise of literary-historical studies, see under 1, above. Early Shakespeare criticism, including Morgann on Falstaff, is collected by

D. Nichol Smith in *Eighteenth-Century Essays on Shakespeare* (Glasgow, 1903, revised Oxford, 1963); and there is a rich mine of information in the edition of Bishop Percy's *Letters* now in progress (Baton Rouge, 1944-) by D. Nichol Smith, Cleanth Brooks, and others. Whiter is fully discussed by F. P. Wilson in his lecture 'Shakespeare and the Diction of Common life', *Proceedings of Br. Academy*, XXVII (1941).

5. WORDSWORTH AND COLERIDGE

Wordsworth's 1800 preface, with other essays and with much of Coleridge's *Biographia*, was edited by George Sampson (Cambridge, 1920), and the preface with its subsequent revisions and additions has been meticulously edited by W. J. B. Owen in *Anglistica* (Copenhagen), IX (1957). Coleridge's works are now being collected for the first time (General Editor, Kathleen Coburn), 23 vols. (1964-), and there is a useful one-volume selection edited by Stephen Potter in the Nonesuch Library, *Select Poetry and Prose* (1933, enlarged 1950). The *Shakespearean Criticism* (mainly lectures of 1811-12) was edited by T. M. Raysor, 2 vols. (Cambridge, Mass., 1930, revised for Everyman's Library, 1960); and the *Miscellaneous Criticism* (mainly the lectures of 1818), also edited by Raysor, followed in 1936. *Coleridge on the Seventeenth Century*, edited by R. F. Brinkley (Durham, N.C., 1955), assembles critical comments under author-headings. The *Biographia Literaria* was edited by J. Shawcross, 2 vols. (Oxford, 1907), and by George Watson in Everyman's Library (1956, revised 1960). The *Notebooks* are being edited for the first time by Kathleen Coburn, 11 vols. (New York, 1957-), and the *Collected Letters* by E. L. Griggs, 6 vols. (Oxford, 1956-).

The standard life of Coleridge is E. K. Chambers's *Coleridge: a Biographical Study* (Oxford, 1938, revised 1950), while Humphry House's Clark lectures, *Coleridge* (1953), reconsider his personality and his poetry. J. L. Lowes's *The Road to Xanadu* (Boston, 1927, revised 1930) studies the relation between his poetry and his reading, and I. A. Richards's *Coleridge on Imagination* (1934; with comments by Kathleen Coburn, Bloomington, Ind., 1960), M. H. Abrams's *The Mirror and the Lamp: Romantic Theory and the Critical Tradition* (New York, 1953), and Herbert Read's *The True Voice of Feeling* (1953) discuss his critical ideas. There is an essay on Coleridge as a critic by F. R. Leavis (*Scrutiny*, 1941), reprinted in *The Importance of Scrutiny*, edited by Eric Bentley (New York, 1948).

6. LAMB, HAZLITT, DE QUINCEY

For general studies of romantic criticism, see under 5, above; and for an anthology, *English Critical Essays* (*Nineteenth Century*), edited by Edmund D. Jones (Oxford, 1916) (World's Classics).

LAMB

The works of Lamb have been edited by E. V. Lucas, 7 vols. (1903-5, revised in 6 vols. 1912), as well as the *Letters*, 3 vols. (1935); and the *Criticism* has been collected in one volume by E. M. W. Tillyard (Cambridge, 1923). *The Specimens of English Dramatic Poets* were edited by Israel Gollancz, 2 vols. (1893). The best general studies are by E. V. Lucas, *Life of Lamb* (1905, revised 1921), and Edmund Blunden, *Lamb and his Contemporaries* (Cambridge, 1933). See also R. C. Bald, 'Lamb and the Elizabethans', in *Studies in Honor of A. H. R. Fairchild* (Columbia, Missouri, 1946).

HAZLITT

The *Complete Works* were exhaustively edited by P. P. Howe in 21 vols. (1930-4). There is no good one-volume selection of the criticism, but the *Characters of Shakespear's Plays*, the *Lectures on the English Poets*, the *Lectures on the English Comic Writers*, *Table Talk*, and *The Spirit of the Age* have all appeared in World's Classics (1901-24). The standard lives are by P. P. Howe, *The Life of Hazlitt* (1922, revised 1928), and Herschel Baker, *William Hazlitt* (Cambridge, Mass., 1962), and there is a respectful analysis of Hazlitt's critical theory by Elisabeth Schneider in *The Aesthetics of Hazlitt* (Philadelphia, 1933, revised 1952), as well as two candid Victorian portraits by Leslie Stephen in the second series of his *Hours in a Library* (1876), and by George Saintsbury in his *Essays in English Literature*, *1780-1860* (1890).

DE QUINCEY

The works were edited incomplete by David Masson in 14 vols. (Edinburgh, 1889-90), and the *Literary Criticism* by Helen Darbishire (Oxford, 1909). The *Recollections of the Late Poets* have been edited by Edward Sackville-West (1948), who has also written a critical biography, *A Flame in Sunlight* (1936). As with Hazlitt, there are Victorian studies by Leslie Stephen in the first series of his *Hours in a Library* (1874), and by George Saintsbury in his *Essays in English Literature*, *1780-1860* (1890).

7. MATTHEW ARNOLD

The complete prose works are being edited for the first time by R. H. Super (Ann Arbor, 1960-), and there is a one-volume selection of *Poetry and Prose* edited by John Bryson in the Reynard Library (1954), as well as a collection of *Essays, Including Essays in Criticism 1865, On Translating Homer*, etc. (Oxford, 1914). Some of the letters were edited by G. W. E. Russell, 2 vols. (1895), and the *Letters to A. H. Clough* (Oxford, 1932) and the *Note Books* (Oxford, 1952) have both been edited by H. F. Lowry. *Culture and Anarchy* has been edited by J. Dover Wilson (Cambridge, 1932), and *Five Uncollected Essays* by Kenneth Allott (Liverpool, 1953).

There is a critical biography by Lionel Trilling, *Matthew Arnold* (New York, 1939, revised 1955), and a study of both poetry and criticism by E. K. Brown, *Arnold: a Study in Conflict* (Chicago, 1948). T. S. Eliot's view can be consulted in the 1930 essay 'Arnold and Pater' in his *Selected Essays* (1932), and in his *The Use of Poetry and the Use of Criticism* (1933). John Holloway's *The Victorian Sage* (1953) includes a study of Arnold's language of persuasion, and his *The Charted Mirror* (1960) a general assessment. There is a study of Arnold's criteria of criticism by John S. Eells, *The Touchstones of Arnold* (New York, 1955), and of his controversial phase in William Robbins's *The Ethical Idealism of Arnold* (1959).

8. HENRY JAMES

There are studies of the aesthetic movement in Graham Hough's *The Last Romantics* (1949) and in Frank Kermode's *Romantic Image* (1957). James's prefaces have been collected as *The Art of the Novel*, edited by R. P. Blackmur (New York, 1934), the *Notebooks* were edited by F. O. Matthiessen and Kenneth B. Murdock (New York, 1947), and some of the letters by Percy Lubbock in 2 vols. (1920). There are numerous overlapping editions of James's critical essays, including *The Art of Fiction*, edited by Morris Roberts (New York, 1948), and *The House of Fiction*, edited by Leon Edel (1957). Three of his literary exchanges have been collected: *Letters to A. C. Benson and Auguste Monod*, edited by E. F. Benson (1930); *James and R. L. Stevenson*, edited by Janet A. Smith (1948); and *James and H. G. Wells*, edited by Leon Edel and G. N. Ray (1958). There is a study of the criticism by Morris Roberts, *James's Criticism* (Cambridge, Mass., 1929), and of the prefaces by Leon Edel, *The Prefaces of James* (Paris, 1931).

9. THE EARLY TWENTIETH CENTURY

There is a survey of twentieth-century criticism, British and American, in Stanley E. Hyman's *The Armed Vision* (New York, 1948, abridged and revised 1955), and of the theoretical aspects of the New Criticism, especially in Eliot and Richards, in Murray Krieger's *The New Apologists for Poetry* (Minneapolis, 1956). John Crowe Ransom's *The New Criticism* (Norfolk, Conn., 1941) is an important historical source, especially on Richards, Empson, Eliot, and Winters. A symposium by the Chicago Critics, *Critics and Criticism Ancient and Modern*, edited by R. S. Crane (Chicago, 1952), contains articles on Richards, Empson, and the American New Critics by Crane, Elder Olson, and others; and Crane's *The Language of Criticism and the Structure of Poetry* (Toronto, 1953) returns to the attack. For an anthology, see *English Critical Essays: Twentieth Century*, edited by Phyllis M. Jones and Derek Hudson, 2 vols. (Oxford, 1933-58) (World's Classics).

ELIOT

The Pelican *Selected Prose of Eliot*, edited by John Hayward (1953), offers a wide selection from Eliot's criticism in all periods. Edmund Wilson, an early admirer of Eliot's first essays, acknowledged them sympathetically in his *Axel's Castle* (New York, 1931), while the contradictions in his aesthetic were attacked by Yvor Winters in 'Eliot or the Illusion of Reaction' – collected first in his *The Anatomy of Nonsense* (Norfolk, Conn., 1943), and later in his *In Defence of Reason* (New York, 1947) and *On Modern Poets* (New York, 1959) – and defended by Seán Lucy in his *Eliot and the Idea of Tradition* (1960). Cf. Donald Gallup, *Eliot: a Bibliography* (1952), and the files of *Criterion*, which Eliot edited from 1922 till 1939.

LEAVIS

Articles and reviews from the first fifteen years of *Scrutiny* (1932-47) have been selected by Eric Bentley in his anthology *The Importance of Scrutiny* (New York, 1948) (1932-53), while the whole periodical has been reprinted with an index, 20 vols. (Cambridge, 1963). There is a comment on Leavis by Lionel Trilling in his *A Gathering of Fugitives* (Boston, 1956), and a longer and more enthusiastic study by Vincent Buckley in his *Poetry and Morality: Studies in the Criticism of Arnold, Eliot, and Leavis* (1959).

10;11 THE MID-CENTURY SCENE; THEORY AND PRACTICE SINCE 1960

A history of post-war criticism is still to be written, and the last volume of René Wellek's *History of Modern Criticism* (1986) ends around 1950. Meanwhile, a number of accounts have been provided on the mid-century theoretical debate, to be distinguished only with difficulty from the debate itself. These include Jonathan Culler, *Structuralist Poetics* (1975) and its sequel *On Deconstruction* (1983); George Watson, *Modern Literary Thought* (Heidelberg, 1978); Frank Lentricchia, *After the New Criticism* (Chicago, 1980), on critical theories in North America since the 1950s; David Lodge, *Working with Structuralism* (1981); Christopher Norris, *Deconstruction: Theory and Practice* (1982), a sequel to his earlier study of William Empson (1978); and Vincent B. Leitch, *Deconstructive Criticism* (1983). Other titles are cited within these two chapters.

INDEX

Numerals in bold type indicate the principal entries

THE HOGARTH PRESS

This is a paperback list for today's readers – but it holds to a tradition of adventurous and original publishing set by Leonard and Virginia Woolf when they founded The Hogarth Press in 1917 and started their first paperback series in 1924.

Some of the books are light-hearted, some serious, and include Fiction, Lives and Letters, Travel, Critics, Poetry, History and Hogarth Crime and Gaslight Crime.

A list of our books already published, together with some of our forthcoming titles, follows. If you would like more information about Hogarth Press books, write to us for a catalogue:

40 William IV Street, London WC2N 4DF

Please send a large stamped addressed envelope

HOGARTH FICTION

The Colonel's Daughter by Richard Aldington
New Introduction by Anthony Burgess
Death of a Hero by Richard Aldington
New Introduction by Christopher Ridgway

All in a Lifetime by Walter Allen
New Introduction by Alan Sillitoe

Epitaph of a Small Winner by Machado de Assis
Translated and Introduced by William L. Grossman

Mrs Ames by E.F. Benson
Paying Guests by E.F. Benson
New Introductions by Stephen Pile

A Day in Summer by J.L. Carr
New Introduction by D.J. Taylor

Beat the Devil by Claud Cockburn
New Introduction by Alexander Cockburn

Chance by Joseph Conrad
New Introduction by Jane Miller

Lady Into Fox & A Man in the Zoo by David Garnett
New Introduction by Neil Jordan

Born in Exile by George Gissing
New Introduction by Gillian Tindall
Will Warburton by George Gissing
New Introduction by John Halperin

Saturday Night at the Greyhound by John Hampson
New Introduction by Christopher Hawtree

All Day Saturday by Colin MacInnes
June in Her Spring by Colin MacInnes
New Introductions by Tony Gould

HOGARTH LIVES AND LETTERS

The Smith of Smiths by Hesketh Pearson
New Introduction by Richard Ingrams

Flannelled Fool by T.C. Worsley
New Introduction by Alan Ross

HOGARTH CRITICS

Tradition and Dream: The English and American Novel from the Twenties to Our Time by Walter Allen
New Afterword by the Author

The Condemned Playground: Essays 1927-1944 by
Cyril Connolly
New Introduction by Philip Larkin

Seven Types of Ambiguity by William Empson
Some Versions of Pastoral by William Empson
The Structure of Complex Words by William Empson

Music Ho!: A Study of Music in Decline by Constant Lambert
New Introduction by Angus Morrison

The Common Pursuit by F.R. Leavis

England, Half English by Colin MacInnes
New Foreword by Paul Weller

By Way of Sainte-Beuve by Marcel Proust
Translated by Sylvia Townsend Warner
New Introduction by Terence Kilmartin

The Country and the City by Raymond Williams
The English Novel from Dickens to Lawrence by
Raymond Williams

The Common Reader 1 by Virginia Woolf
The Common Reader 2 by Virginia Woolf
Edited and Introduced by Andrew McNeillie
Three Guineas by Virginia Woolf
New Introduction by Hermione Lee

HOGARTH POETRY

Cyril Connolly

The Condemned Playground

Essays 1927-1944

New Introduction by Philip Larkin

The playground is the literary scene of the Thirties, with its ebullience, mediocrity, frivolity and talent. It is the leafy streets of Chelsea in which Connolly worked and wandered, and it is the world of art itself where men try to make 'mudpies that endure'. It has room for Joyce and Swift, Horace and Housman, for anarchists from Barcelona and revolutionary students from Greece, for conversations in Berlin and meditations in the Midi. With its wicked parodies, elegant criticism and elegiac autobiography this is a book to linger over – Connolly at his inimitable best.

William Empson
Seven Types of Ambiguity

Chaucer, Milton, Marvell, Pope, Hopkins and T. S. Eliot are among the poets cited in this brilliant analysis of the effects which ambiguity, deliberate or unconscious, creates in English verse. Hailed as a masterpiece on its first publication in 1930, when Empson was twenty-four, *Seven Types of Ambiguity* is now acknowledged as a great work of modern criticism – theoretically daring and scholarly, yet witty, controversial and immensely readable.

Raymond Williams
The Country and the City

When this book was first published it was immediately hailed as a masterpiece. By concentrating on changing attitudes to the country and the city as they are portrayed in English literature from the sixteenth to the twentieth centuries, Raymond Williams shows the fascinating, shifting associations of these two traditional poles of life, and closely relates them to social developments. The range of the analysis is as impressive as its depth: this is a work which not only makes us look at the world afresh – in fact and in literature – but also helps us to understand why we see it as we do.

Walter Allen

Tradition and Dream

The English and American Novel from the Twenties to
Our Time

New Afterword by the Author

This new edition of Walter Allen's invaluable critical
survey of British and American fiction throughout the
twentieth century continues where his classic study *The
English Novel* left off. As well as discussing the most
famous novelists of this century, it is notable for its early
recognition of authors – such as Willa Cather and Patrick
Hamilton – whose works are generally praised, and of
those who have yet to achieve the fame they deserve.
Entertaining and comprehensive, *Tradition and Dream*
will long remain indispensable both to the student and to
the general reader.

Virginia Woolf
The Common Reader 2

Edited and Introduced by Andrew McNeillie

The Common Reader, Second Series, is, like the first, an informal, informative and witty celebration of our literary and social heritage. In it Virginia Woolf turns her brilliant eye upon the novels of George Gissing; the poems of John Donne; the diary of Parson Woodforde. We meet Dr Burney and Beau Brummell, Christina Rossetti, Mary Wollstonecraft, and many others, in the company of a writer of genuis.